Construction Businesses ~~RES UNIVER~~ Development
Meeting New Challenges, Seeking Opportunity

Construction Business Development
Meeting New Challenges, Seeking Opportunity

Christopher N Preece
BSc (Hons), PhD, FCIOB, MCIM, ILTM
School of Civil Engineering,
University of Leeds

Krisen Moodley
BSc (Hons), MSc
School of Civil Engineering,
University of Leeds

Paul Smith
MBA

ELSEVIER
BUTTERWORTH
HEINEMANN

OXFORD AMSTERDAM BOSTON HEIDELBERG LONDON NEW YORK PARIS
SAN DIEGO SAN FRANCISCO SINGAPORE SYDNEY TOKYO

Butterworth-Heinemann
An imprint of Elsevier
Linacre House, Jordan Hill, Oxford OX2 8DP
200 Wheeler Road, Burlington, MA 01803

First published 2003

British Library Cataloguing in Publication Data
Preece, Christopher N.
    Construction business development: meeting new challenges, seeking opportunity
    1. Construction industry – Customer services   2. Customer relations   3. Construction industry – Marketing
    I. Title   II. Moodley, Krisen   III. Smith, Paul
624′.0688

Library of Congress Cataloging in Publication Data
A catalog record for this book is available from the Library of Congress

ISBN 0 7506 5109 1

For information on all Butterworth-Heinemann publications visit our website at
www.bh.com

Typeset by Charon Tec Pvt. Ltd, Chennai, India
Printed and bound in Great Britain

Contents

Preface   vii
Acknowledgements   ix
Notes on Contributors   xi

1   Introduction   1

PART 1: PLANNING TO TAKE THE LONG-TERM VIEW

2   **Strategic business development**   7
    Krisen Moodley and Christopher Preece

3   **Marketing planning – planning the way ahead**   17
    Philip Collard

4   **Case study of marketing in an SME in construction**   31
    Evelyn Vernea

5   **Marketing of civil engineering consultancies in the
United Kingdom**   39
    Paul Macnamara

PART 2: TOOLS AND TECHNIQUES

6   **Customer relationship management**   71
    John Pratt

7   **Customer care**   81
    Christopher Preece and Krisen Moodley

8   **Bidding and winning strategies**   90
    Simon White

9   **Public relations: business development's vital ingredient**   105
    Alan Smith

10   **Change in context**   119
    Paul B. Smith

PART 3: CHALLENGES OF A NEW AGE

11   **e-Business development**   139
    David Bentley and John Butler

12   **Knowledge management**   **154**
     Christopher Preece and Krisen Moodley

13   **Business development and collaborative working**   **167**
     Paul Wilkinson

14   **The business development manager as hero!**   **180**
     Mark Lench

Index   195

Preface

What are the business development skills required in the construction industry of the early twenty-first century? This book examines the opportunities and distinct challenges of doing business in this highly competitive and market-driven environment. Construction has changed. It requires new and innovative approaches from its business leaders and managers.

Each chapter represents the insights of construction business development practitioners, consultants and researchers. The text uses illustrations and cases to describe the approaches and strategies required.

Acknowledgements

The authors and contributors would like to thank their respective families, friends and colleagues for supporting them throughout the lengthy process of writing this book.

Notes on Contributors

Christopher Preece PhD, BSc (Hons), FCIOB, MCIM, ILTM – Leading research within the School of Civil Engineering, at the University of Leeds, in the fields of business and marketing management in the construction industry. In collaboration with a number of leading edge civil engineering and building companies and consultancies, the focus of these studies is on increasing client satisfaction and improving the business culture of the construction industry through more effective and competitive strategies. His interests include procurement and the prequalification process, corporate communications, human resource management and construction education. He has published widely, delivered keynote addresses, chaired and organized conferences, nationally and internationally. His professional involvement includes national committee work for the Chartered Institute of Building. He is also a Member of the Chartered Institute of Marketing.

Krisen Moodley BSc, MSc, AIArb – Programme leader for MSc. Taught courses in Construction Management, in the School of Civil Engineering, University of Leeds. After graduating from the University of Natal, his initial employment was as a quantity surveyor with Farrow Laing in Southern Africa, before his first academic appointment at Heriot-Watt University. He spent four years at Heriot-Watt before joining Leeds in 1994. His research interests are concerned with the strategic business relationships between organizations and their projects. Other specialist research interests include: procurement, project management and corporate responsibility. Krisen has published and presented papers both nationally and internationally. His recent books include Corporate Communications in Construction and contributions to Construction Reports 1944–1998 and Engineering Project Management.

Paul Smith – Chartered surveyor by training, Paul Smith spent the early part of his career working on the client side of the industry as a property developer and client project manager. He then moved from project-specific into corporate work. This coincided with obtaining his MBA from the City University Business School.

During the depths of the recession of the early 1990s he combined his industry-specific background and business training by establishing 'Project Leadership' as a consultancy vehicle to undertake project and corporate restructuring work for both client and contracting organizations. As the recession cleared, his interest moved from 'firefighting' to long-term 'corporate change' in order to avoid the boom and bust syndrome.

As a consultant and line manager at director level, he has undertaken a number of long-term assignments with the objective of moving traditional corporate structures from their traditional adversarial inward looking focus, to an external customer focused organization capable of working in the new environment of partnering and collaborative working. This quest to move from an adversarial, to a customer-focused organization, is also the subject of his doctoral thesis, which he is currently in the final stages of completion at the University of Leeds.

David Bentley BSc, CEng, MICE – Managing Director NetConstruct, Leeds. In 1970 David Bentley found computing for the construction industry was in its infancy. Punch cards, Fortran programming and data-centres were at their height, and the latest office technology was the massive trolley-mounted valve calculator which had to be booked days ahead! Progressively however, computing worked its way into every discipline, with design and cost–control applications leading the way. Twenty more years in construction, including a Business Development Director appointment with one of the UK's leading contractors, created an ideal base for starting his own business. NetConstruct was founded in the early 1990s, to exploit the convergence of IT and marketing, and later the Web. Now, NetConstruct has over 150 e-business clients, many in construction, ranging from small specialists to multi-national plcs and the public sector.

John Butler BSc, MBA, FBCS, CEng, MILT – Division of Informatics at Edinburgh University. John Butler wrote his first program in 1969 and after graduating worked on early communications networks from 1974 to 1983. At that time networks were beginning to coalesce into what is now the Internet. He was later involved on one of the first Local Area Networks in the UK which he later oversaw becoming a major computing service for computer scientists. More recently he has worked with learning technology and library automation projects and is currently affiliated to the Centre for the Study of e-business at Edinburgh University, a consortium of Departments of Informatics, Business Studies and Law.

Philip Collard BSc (Hons), MBA, MCIM – Over the last 15 years Philip has worked as a marketing consultant for a large variety of primarily professional services and contracting firms in the construction industry. He provides strategic and marketing planning advice on direction and new business development. This includes advice on implementation, setting up marketing systems, marketing databases, key client relationship management plans, satisfaction research and general consultancy, covering a wide range of essential marketing support activity. He is Managing Director of MarketingWorks Training and Consultancy Ltd which specializes in providing research-based workshops and consultancy solutions, which will help firms reorganize their business development activities to focus on winning new business.

Philip is also Chairman of Construction Marketer Ltd which runs the Construction Marketing Conference, the Construction Marketing Question Time and a business developers' network and is consultant editor and columnist of the new monthly journal *Construction Marketer*. He undertakes consultancy assignments and marketing training workshops all over the UK and is a principal speaker at national conferences.

Mark Lench – Managing Director of Mark Lench Marketing, a specialist provider of marketing and business development support to companies operating in engineering and construction markets. He has over twenty years of engineering, marketing and business development experience with global engineering and construction companies serving the petroleum, chemical, power and civil infrastructure industries.

Prior to establishing his own company, Mark held senior management positions with AMEC, Bechtel and NG Bailey. During his time as marketing director at NG Bailey, the company achieved record levels of turnover and profitability, and won several prestigious industry awards in recognition of its performance. At AMEC, Mark was responsible for the development of business strategy for the Caspian region covering Azerbaijan, Iran, Kazakhstan and Russia. He was instrumental in setting up AMEC's regional office in Baku, Azerbaijan, and the granting of AMEC's licence for performing work offshore Russia, notably Sakhalin Island.

Prior to joining AMEC, Mark spent seven years with Bechtel and was a member of the company's strategy team for Europe, Africa, the Middle East and South-West Asia. He travelled extensively throughout Europe, Africa and Central Asia leading marketing and business development initiatives.

Mr Lench holds a BSc (Hons) in Chemical Engineering from Loughborough University and a Diploma in Industrial Studies (DIS). He is a member of the Institute of Directors, the Institute of Petroleum and an associate member of the Chartered Institute of Marketing.

Paul Macnamara – Paul has a background in civil engineering, principally highways, drainage and services for consultants and local authorities, on regeneration and infrastructure projects, and retail, industrial and commercial developments throughout England and Wales.

Paul works for Halcrow as Senior Project Manager responsible for client contact, overseeing land development projects throughout the whole process from inception to the completion of the construction works. The principal focus is on the initial, planning stages, considering and addressing the constraints backed by the Halcrow expertise in fields such as transportation, water, energy and the environment. This role also includes business development on the Halcrow Land Development service in the south-west of England, involvement in business planning and marketing strategy through to client contact and sales.

Paul recently completed an MSc in Construction Management through the University of Bath. His dissertation considered the marketing of civil engineering consultancies in the United Kingdom, and was supervised by Dr C Preece.

John Pratt MSc, FCIM, MICE, MIMC, CEng, CMC Chartered Marketer – Chairman and Chief Executive Officer of Leading Edge Management Consultancy and a Chartered Marketer. He is a past International Chairman of the Chartered Institute of Marketing and also a past Chairman of its Construction Industry Group. He is a non-executive director of The Marketing Council and the CAM Foundation and was a member of the Latham Working Group Number 7 on the image of the construction industry. He has had exposure to the construction environment, having trained as a civil engineer, when working on projects in the early part of his career with Costain Civil Engineering and Halcrows. More recently, he was Sales and Marketing Director of Steetley Brick and Tile for four years, before being appointed a main board director of the privately owned David Webster Group. He has held senior marketing posts and subsidiary board directorships of Whitecroft plc, Rentokil plc and Steetley plc. He has also had experience as a management consultant with P-E Consulting Group working for blue chip companies and government.

Alan M Smith BA (Hons), FIPR – Director, Public Relations, HBG Construction Ltd. Has been working within the European construction group HBG, Hollandsche Beton Groep nv, since 1989 when he joined UK civil engineering contractor Edmund Nuttall Ltd as Head of Public Relations. After nine years with Nuttall, he became Director, Communications, for the Institution of Civil Engineers (ICE), responsible for the Local Associations, Regional Liaison Officers and the public relations/public affairs operations of the institution. Following a year in this post, Alan returned to the HBG group in 2000 as Director, Public Relations with HBG Construction Ltd, the £700m turnover construction, properties, PFI and FM services group in the UK.

Alan is a Fellow of the Institute of Public Relations (IPR) and, in that capacity, is Chairman of CAPSIG, the Construction and Property Special Interest Group of the IPR. This is a neutral forum where members work together to promote the image of and enhance the reputation of the construction and property industry through encouraging professional best practice.

A graduate from the University of Leeds, Alan regularly lectures at both the School of Civil Engineering at that university, and at the Leeds Metropolitan University Business School's degree course in public relations, on the topic of communications in the construction industry. He is also co-author of the book *Corporate Communications in Construction – Public Relations Strategies for Successful Business and Projects* with Dr Chris Preece and Mr Krisen Moodley.

For ten years before moving into public relations, Alan was a journalist, reporting mainly from the Far East, North America and the Middle East. He can also claim fame for having worked in his youth as a chainman to the Structures Agent for John Laing Construction on the M5 motorway project and as a labourer and ganger for George Wimpey on several housing development sites in Leeds!

Evelyn Vernea – Principal RED Creative Marketing Solutions, a Glasgow-based consultancy specializing in providing a range of marketing services, advice and support to small- and medium-sized companies and public sector organizations.

Prior to setting up RED in 1994, Evelyn worked for twelve years in the Housing Association sector in Scotland, setting up housing associations and co-operations and developing housing projects, commissioning the design teams, letting the building contacts and acting as client's representative throughout the building programme.

This involvement in the construction industry has allowed Evelyn to maintain a niche in supplying marketing consultancy and assistance to SMEs within this sector. Currently, she also works with the School of the Built and Natural Environment at Glasgow Caledonian University and jointly manages, along with this body and the University of Strathclyde, a DTI-funded research project, looking at the impact of the Egan report on SMEs in construction.

Simon White Arup – A bidding specialist, working to encourage the firm into bidding more effectively, through focusing on the client and the project needs. He joined Arup in 1979, and has held a number of roles within the firm founded on information management, including company and market-related research. Presently he draws on experience of working on a number of the firm's bids, tenders and submissions to offer a specialist service in the planning, management, and effective delivery of bids and proposals. This encompasses specialist bid/proposal management, CV management and the leadership of an 'Improving bidding' workshop. His responsibilities also include advice on the interpretation and application of the European Procurement regime directives.

He is also deeply involved with the development of tools to assist in the process of value management. Using the software industry model of Requirements Engineering, this focuses on gathering, managing and communicating client objectives at the project outset, so that subsequent decisions may be more fully informed. Simon has expertise in information management systems, and has written and presented many papers at various industry conferences on this and related subjects.

Paul Wilkinson PhD, BA, MIPR, DipPR(CAM) – Paul is head of corporate communications of BIW Technologies (BIW), Europe's leading provider of web-based collaboration technologies to the construction and property sectors. After working in the charity sector, Paul joined the marketing department of consulting engineer Halcrow in 1987, completing a PhD in criminology at the London School of Economics in 1991. After seven years at Halcrow, he spent four years in senior in-house marketing and PR positions at Tarmac Professional Services (now part of Carillion), before setting up an independent communications consultancy whose clients included HBG Construction, construction consultant PCM, the Construction Best Practice Programme, the Building Centre Trust, the CAM Foundation, Greenwich Enterprise Board, and BIW – who he eventually joined in July 2000.

The authors and publishers would like to thank those who have kindly permitted the use of images in this book. Attempts have been made to locate all the sources to obtain full reproduction rights. However, if there are any instances where this process has failed to find the copyright holder, apologies are offered. In the case of error, correction would be welcomed.

1

Introduction

Why is business development important?

The construction industry has undergone considerable change in the last decade. Ever more demanding clients and fierce competition have resulted in many organizations having to look for ways of:

- differentiating themselves from their competition
- focusing on customer service
- getting to know their clients intimately
- building lasting and trusting relationships with their supply chain
- doing their marketing before trying to sell anything.

The imperative is for managers and organizations to improve their business development strategies and techniques.

The contributors to this book identify the particular issues and problems connected with developing more effective approaches in this industry. An industry with a record of poor performance in most of the areas outlined above.

How is the book structured?

Each chapter provides some practical approaches to the development and implementation of business development in construction organizations.

Chapter 2 looks at strategic business issues. The construction industry has not escaped the new more dynamic and faster changing environment. The business models of the past are being replaced by faster, flexible and more dynamic versions. The buyers of construction services, both public and private, have changed their attitudes to the performance of construction. They want fast, efficient, high-quality and reliable construction with better value for money. Construction is expected to be more collaborative and responsive with a long-term customer service driven approach. On the other hand, investors in construction organizations expect better returns on their investments. There are many alternative options for investors and construction is expected to provide similar returns to other investments. It is not longer an option to operate in the boom and bust cycles of the past. Such pressures mean that construction organizations need to look at their underlying short-term profitability and as well as their long-term strategic positions and business models.

Chapter 3 stresses the importance of a planned and strategic approach to marketing. This entails understanding the organization's wider goals and how they are going to be achieved; setting marketing objectives in relation to those corporate goals and corresponding marketing strategies to deliver on those stated marketing objectives. It is argued that it is only by adopting such a logical and reasoned approach can marketing rationalize its right to be at the heart of the management decision-making process, a cross-functional discipline that '… *is too important to leave to the marketing department*'. By being both logical and strategic in nature, it will help to dispel its current image held by many in the construction industry of it being about advertising, public relations (PR) and general promotional activities.

Chapter 4 presents a marketing/business development case study of a small/medium-sized enterprise in construction. The writer conducted research into how the firm could improve its approach to enable it to move away from a heavy reliance on public sector housing and to break into new markets, raise turnover and profit margins, and overcome an image problem. The research adopted a 'classical' marketing methodology employing an internal and external audit of the firms, market research, SWOT analysis and establishment of marketing objectives. Finally, the preparation of a marketing strategy and plan. The chapter also looks at issues concerning implementation.

Chapter 5 identifies the application of marketing and business development to engineering consultancies. Consultant practices have had to become more market oriented due to the lifting of codes of practice to allow competition, the increasing involvement of overseas based consultants and the increasing use of non-traditional forms of procurement. Previously, when there was enough work for each company to share, long-term, steady and stable relationships between client and contractor were developed. Companies then focused on product and technological excellence, but now that is not enough. The attitude and understanding towards marketing appears to be changing.

Chapter 6 looks at Customer Relationship Management (CRM). The key to successful CRM implementation depends on two things. Firstly, recognizing that apparently similar customers may behave in different ways according to their culture – so, segmenting them is necessary, but not easy. It requires data on soft, behavioural issues as well as the regular classifications of size, sector, SIC code, etc. Secondly, with such a high failure rate and high cost, you need to go into this with a well thought through plan and a high level of preparation, before even thinking about potential consultants and vendors of CRM systems. The headlong rush into new CRM systems was driven initially as a by-product of IT departments facing up to Y2K compliance problems. But with the ensuing lack of success, it is clear that marketers need to be driving the process, to ensure that customers are put at the focal point. There will be many vested interests from field sales, call centres, IT and finance departments, each with its own way of working and own systems. This means that you have to take a holistic approach – it is not a bolt-on situation or a quick fix.

Chapter 7 asserts that companies in construction have been slow to develop customer- or client-care programmes, which may provide a number of important benefits. It may help to differentiate them from the competition in highly competitive markets, improve perceptions of their clients and their professional advisors, increase client satisfaction with the services provided, encourage loyalty, and create a reputation for being a caring and client-orientated organization. Internally, the construction company may benefit from improved staff morale, increased employee participation and foster internal customer/supplier relationships. By introducing a client-care programme, a construction organization may bring about continuous improvements to the operations of the organization.

Chapter 8 looks at bidding strategy. Understanding where bidding fits into the bidder's business and growth strategy is important in preparing to bid for work. Bidding is an investment in a specific opportunity, and brings a need to bring diverse skills and aptitudes together. In responding to the invitation, the bidder needs to recognize the complex nature of the procurement, and how this has changed over the recent years, and be prepared to devote focused effort and resource to their response. Managing the process becomes critical as increasing pressure is put on both clients and bidders in order to deal with increasingly complex procurements. The need to understand the client and his objectives are key issues in bidding for and winning work. There is some conflict and tension in that bidders would wish to avoid bidding, yet clients seek benefits from competition.

Chapter 9 examines the range of key PR activities that are now an integral part of the construction industry's business development. It will cover the conventional PR functions in passing, briefly referring to press relations, internal communications, corporate affairs, customer liaison, supply chain liaison, communicating health and safety. However, it is not intended to review the whole plethora of the public relations remit or to even list what should or should not be part of the function in the construction industry. What is important is to examine the most influential roles of the PR practitioner in support of the business development function in the construction industry today and how recent developments have radically altered priorities in this interface. Thus, we will look in some detail at the impact of PFI/PPP upon the function as well as examining community relations and its vital role in the business development context.

Chapter 10 looks at the management of change. The advent of specific change programmes such as TQM, BPR and Culture change with their own specific programmes and philosophies marked a significant departure in the treatment of change. It gave managers specific products to address specific operational issues and moved the focus from the macro(strategic) to the micro(operational) level. The risk inherent in this development was the separation of action from strategy. Schaffer and Thomson (1992) term the preoccupation of actions without clear goals, particularly in the area of performance improvement, as a modern form of the 'rain dance'. They argue that there is a fundamental flaw that confuses ends with means and processes with outcomes. To counter this preoccupation with mindless actions they advocate that 'successful change programmes begin with results'. With results driven improvements a company only introduces innovations in management methods and business processes that help achieve specific goals. The review of change in its many forms highlights that there are no universal change models or formulas. Consequently, a key consideration is not about endorsing a particular methodology than at helping people 'do' change effectively while in the middle of the change process. They postulate that the more they have studied change 'the more humble we have become about dictating the "best" way to do it.'

Chapter 11 considers the impact of the Internet and e-business on construction. E-business applications designed to increase competitiveness are numerous and continually evolving, but they do not come with an 'increase competitiveness' label on them. Instead, the Internet has taken every discipline within an organization – be it client handling, design, planning, estimating, buying, recruitment, project management, cost control, construction, maintenance or support services – into a period of turbulent change which is set to last for a decade or more. Once the people in a particular discipline have accepted the possibility of a new e-business way of working, and are prepared to listen to possible solutions, they will have entered a period of constant evaluation and implementation. This radically changes the role of the construction business development manager too.

Chapter 12 looks at the importance of knowledge. As information becomes more important, the role of knowledge takes on a more important role. Convergence in broad strategic goals and production capability means that new ways of gaining strategic advantage must be found. Knowledge and its management has become the new arena for competitive advantage and differentiation. Businesses of all types can no longer escape the importance of knowledge in their development. Commentators commonly refer to a new era of business activity based in a knowledge economy. It is clear that knowledge has a role to play in business development.

Chapter 13 looks at the challenges and opportunities in collaborative working. It briefly reviews the background to the concept of 'collaborative working' and its gradual adoption by some within the industry. Progress has been hampered by both cultural and technological barriers. If organizations are to adopt more collaborative approaches (some, of course, may not wish to, but they risk a desperate race to catch up if collaboration becomes the norm rather than the exception), they will need to change their internal culture and develop new ways of working with other organizations. This will prompt changes to business development activities to reflect the growing importance of long-term relationships, both up and down the supply chain (could 'alliance competence' become a new area of market differentiation?). As collaborative working is built on a combination of people, processes and technology, the lack of an infrastructure to support new approaches has also hampered progress, though the advent of new collaboration technology could hasten the necessary supply chain integration – and provide further potential for businesses to develop competitive advantages.

Chapter 14 asserts that construction business development is all about market and customer knowledge, strategy and tactics, relationships, teamwork, marketing, proposal preparation, commercial acumen, contract terms and conditions, risk assessment and analysis, technical know-how, time management, project experience, networking, listening … and more. It is a demanding, but ultimately rewarding role. This chapter explores the role and responsibilities of the business development manager. More accurately, it paints a picture of the possibility for the role and highlights the opportunities for the business development manager to excel. The business development manager has the opportunity to be a strategist, an account executive, a champion of change, a winner, a leader – and, ultimately, a hero.

PART 1

Planning to take the long-term view

2

Strategic business development

Krisen Moodley* and Christopher Preece*

Introduction

The long-term development and operation of a business is complex and risky. The factors that ensure a business achieves growth and profitability are difficult to determine. Many of the worlds leading business leaders and writers have offered prescriptions to sustainable business development. What we have however watched over the past few decades is the rise and fall of many organizations. Some of these companies were excellent while others were poor yet they all suffered similar fates. The construction industry has not been immune from the changes that have taken place with many longstanding companies disappearing from both the British (European) and world stages. The dynamics of business are no longer restricted to local, regional or national boundaries but take on a more global dimension.

The construction industry has not escaped the new more dynamic and faster changing environment. The business models of the past are being replaced by faster, flexible and more dynamic versions. The buyers of construction services, both public and private, have changed their attitudes to the performance of construction. They want fast, efficient, high-quality and reliable construction with better value for money. Construction is expected to be more collaborative and responsive with a long-term customer service driven approach. On the other hand, investors in construction organizations expect better returns on their investments. There are many alternative options for investors and construction is expected to provide similar returns to other investments. It is no longer an option to operate in the boom and bust cycles of the past. Such pressures mean that construction organizations need to look at their underlying short-term profitability and as well as their long-term strategic positions.

Construction and its markets

Construction is not a homogenous industry and is better characterized as a number of market segments coming together to form a representation of an industry. The traditional

* School of Civil Engineering, University of Leeds

classification is that construction comprises of civil engineering, building, repair and maintenance, and materials sectors. Such simplicity would be easy but even within this framework other classifications such as housing commercial, public and industrial construction also exists. There are also variations in project size, complexity and location. Modern procurement approaches have also created crossovers between design, execute and operational activities. This definition does not include sectors such as petrochemicals, offshore construction, power, facilities management, etc. A large modern construction services organization can operate in a complex business environment. There will be competition within market sectors as well as across sectors. The process of developing a business has to be carefully thought through.

Industrial analysis clearly indicates that construction is a fragmented industry in which no single company has a dominant position able to influence the outcomes of the industry. This is essentially true for most of the European Union and North America. There are however countries where the development and protection of large construction organizations have increased the power of these companies. The general absence of monopoly generally means that levels of competition are greater. Once the analysis of the segments and sectors start it is possible to identify dominant organizations and they are particularly prominent in the specialist sectors. Construction has generally been considered a diverse project-led industry with associated fluctuations in demand. Further fragmentation has taken place as more construction firms try to create continuous income streams and move away from the uncertainty of project-driven industries. Business development within construction is a complex activity.

Business strategy and business development

The business environment is complex and the quest for development is to succeed in chosen markets. The markets that construction firms operate within will influence their long-term business development as each sector can have unique characteristics. Managers need to consider how they are going to take decisions in the short, medium and long term, and need to think strategically. Many definitions exist for strategy in business but ultimately strategy is about survival and development of the business in the long term. These goals are dependent on the economic and financial performance of the firm over this period. Strategy is therefore what the company does to achieve its desired economic and financial performance. This does not necessarily mean what it is planning to do but rather what it actually does.

The idea of strategy suggests that all companies have them. Companies may not follow a set of procedures to have a strategy but all their actions commit the organization to strategy that leads to certain choices. Strategies may be explicit or implicit whether they are effective or ineffective, planned or emergent, and managed or non-managed. In the more formal context, strategic management is supposed to be a predetermined course of action a firm follows to achieve its economic, financial and social goals. However, this process is not static and strategy is often reactive to market moves and actions taken by others. A well-planned strategy has to have elements of flexibility in order to cope with the dynamics of the business environment.

The process of strategic business planning is already well documented and forms a blueprint for all strategic decisions and the objectives of the organization. The process of strategic management has three interlocking parts:

1 Strategic analysis
2 Strategic choice
3 Strategic implementation

(1)   Strategic analysis is concerned with the analysis of the organizations capability both internally and its external environment to match the opportunities and threats in the environments in which it operates. This process is about examining the competitive position of the firm within the industries, markets, sectors and segments that forms its operational environment. This analysis will determine the opportunities and threats to the firm and the standing of the firm within its industry. The internal assessment of the firm is about determining its competencies, and its strengths and weaknesses. This provides an assessment of its resources, skills and capability to undertake the challenges it faces. The process of analysis will determine if the company has any competitive advantages over its competitors, its relationships to its suppliers and customers, its resource strengths and its standing in its industry. These issues and many others form a view of the company and its operating environment and allows for a strategy to be developed.

(2)   Strategic choice is about making decisions that will determine the long-term strategic position of the firm. Based around a range of options open to the firm these decisions will put in place a plan that will determine how the firm chooses to position itself in the market. The decisions that are taken take cognisance of the strategic analysis of the organization that constrains the options available to decision-makers. A number of options are open to the firm such as growth, retrenchment or stability strategies that can be achieved either through internal measures or through external activity. Michael Porter also popularized the notion that to be competitive, the firm had to follow a strategy of either cost leadership, or differentiation or focus. These strategic decisions are governed by the degree of fit between the proposed strategy and the strategic analysis, and the practicality of adopting the proposed strategy.

(3)   Strategic implementation is the last phase of the strategic management process. It is about putting the decisions taken in identifying the strategy into practice. Implementation involves the creation of business plans, setting up control and feedback systems, resourcing, budgeting, training and revising organizational structure to ensure the strategy is achieved. The implementation phase is about carrying out the strategy through action. From a business development perspective much of the most important work goes on during this phase. The actions taken in business development are critical to the strategic outcomes of the firm. Business development is a key weapon in achieving strategic success. Developing the business is therefore intertwined with the strategy that the organization is pursuing.

Business development and stakeholders

Business development is not done in isolation and for a firm to succeed it has to consider the environment it operates in. Increasingly a stakeholder view is taken. Who are stakeholders? According to Freeman (1995) a 'stakeholder in an organization is (by definition) any group or individual who can affect, or is affected by achievement of the organization's objectives.' The idea that stakeholders can influence or are influenced by the goals of the organization indicates that we need to develop tools and techniques to ensure their inclusion in our strategic decision-making process and business development activity. There are a number of issues we must understand.

- Who are our stakeholders in the organization and what is their perceived stake?
- The processes and units the organization will use to engage stakeholders and develop relationships. How do these fit into the organization's business strategy and business development?
- What 'transactions' do we have with the stakeholders and the extent of the influence of these 'transactions'?

These have an impact on how we address future negotiation with stakeholders. The stakeholder management capability can be understood by the manner in which the organization integrates these three layers of understanding. Any organization may be able to identify respective stakeholders but if it does not have an awareness of how they are to be engaged such that they form part of the business strategy and business development process they are failing in their stakeholder management.

Igor Ansoff (1965) suggested that firms take the approach of splitting stakeholders into primary and secondary stakeholders. The positioning of these stakeholders was indicated by their proximity and relationship to the core business of the firm. Ansoff went on further to describe the primary stakeholders as those having a direct and necessary economic impact on the firm. These are identified as the:

- Owners
- Suppliers
- Competitors
- Employees
- Customers

These stakeholders are critical to the very existence of the firm, the exception being the competitors. These are the traditional stakeholders of the firm. Each of these stakeholders has a role to play in the development of the firm. In all cases, competitors excepted, contribute to the functioning of the firm. Competitors on the other hand seek to gain advantage. This is not only in a technological or service context but also in social and political arenas. From a business development context the primary stakeholders have an important role to play in the organizations development.

The secondary group of stakeholders are those individuals, groups and organizations that are not directly related to the core business of the firm. They do fall within Freeman's definition of stakeholders. Early theorists such as Ansoff did not regard this group as having a major influence on the firm. Secondary stakeholders include groups such as government, local authority, unions, local communities, political parties, consumer groups, etc. The diversity and potential influence of these groups suggest that secondary stakeholders can exercise the same level of influence on the development of the firm (Wood, 1990). The power of the secondary stakeholders could have a greater influence on the firm, particularly through the use of legislation. In the construction industry secondary stakeholders exercise a great deal of influence particularly regulatory authorities. Powerful lobbies such as the environmentalists can also influence business development. Traditional approaches to stakeholder engagement suggested that secondary stakeholders were less important. In the dynamic environments that exist engagement of secondary stakeholders as part of business development are essential. Our analysis of stakeholders has to go further than just categorization.

There has to be an understanding of the potential influence of the particular stakeholders over time on the organization. The adoption of stakeholder assessment that only operates in the present will inevitably suffer from the impact of a dynamic and changing environment.

Business concept innovation

Industrial maturity leads to a convergence of strategic actions by the similar firms within an industry. Firms of a similar size, scope and standing will tend to exhibit similar strategic group behaviour. The consequence of this is a convergence of the competitive environment as more firms behave in a similar manner. A demonstration of this behaviour is the move among some UK construction companies to access the facilities and services sectors to create new income streams. Initially, these moves provided increased margins but over time the competitive environment becomes tougher. Business development is about differentiating to create more value for the business.

Gary Hamel (2000) suggests that in a dynamic economy the basis of innovation is not technology or a product but the business concept. The business concept and the business model are deemed to be the same with the business model simply being the manner in which the concept is put into practice. Business concept innovation according to Hamel is to imagine dramatically different business concepts to create differentiation and wealth. The idea of business concept innovation is to introduce more strategic variety into an industry or competitive domain. If this tends to happen then the value creating potential within the domain will shift dramatically in favour of the innovator. Many companies may be happy to operate with similar strategies but an innovator can radically change this situation with a new business model and provide an increase in profits to itself. For example, the insistence of adoption of partnering and other alliances by some major construction procurers have changed the relationship with their suppliers. Longer contracts, smaller margins, more flexibility means that the clients have had the value migrate towards themselves away from the suppliers. Construction clients who have adopted these new models of innovation are in a position to leverage greater value creation for their own businesses.

Business concept innovation according to Hamel starts on the premise that the only way to escape traditional forms of competition is to build business models that are unlike those that have come before that the competition is left struggling. These new models challenge existing models and move core businesses away from their fixed positions. The rules change and the company is almost operating in a new market it has invented. Business concept innovation is not just about competitive strategy and strategic positioning, but what can be achieved across all areas of the business. Concept innovation is about finding what is different across all the areas of the business. Therefore, the starting point of business concept innovation is to understand the business model of the firm. In a construction scenario it is possible to win certain types of work continually but yet still struggle to achieve better returns. This is a situation where there is a lack of understanding of the business model is taking place.

The business model

What is a business model? People in organizations tend to talk about business models a great deal but trying to get a constant definition is difficult. Business models can mean everything from how an organization structures itself to how it earns its revenues. More often than not the definitions given to business models are no more than components of the system. There is a lack of explicit models and one of the few clear definitions that are available is offered by KMLab, Inc.

'A Business model is a description of how a company intends to create value in the marketplace. It includes that unique combination of products, services, image and distribution that drives the company forward. It also includes the underlying organization of people and the operational infrastructure that they use to accomplish their work.'

Adding to this definition the ideas of Linder and Cantrell (2001) suggest that the real business model is the organizations core logic for creating value. The business model is a set of value propositions an organization offers its stakeholders, along with the operating processes to deliver on these in a coherent system that both relies on and builds assets, capabilities and relationships, in order to create value.

Chesborough and Rosenbloom (2002) articulate these definitions further by suggesting what the functions of a business model are:

- To articulate the value proposition, that is, the value created for clients or users based on the service, product or technology offered
- Identification of the market segment that the would be suitable for the product or service
- Define the structure of the value chain within the firm required to create and distribute the offering
- Estimate the cost structure and profit potential of the product or service, given the value proposition and value chain chosen
- Describe the position of the firm within the value network linking suppliers and customers, including the identification of potential complementors and competitors
- Formulation of a competitive strategy by which the innovating firm will gain and hold advantage.

These attributes serve to justify the capital needed to realize the model and define the path of the business. Understanding of the business model is essential for business development.

Components of the business model

At the heart of the business model is the core strategy of the business. These are the overall objective of the business. It is from this that value statements and goals are developed and a sense of direction is created. The core strategy of the business will set a series of constraints for the business model and changes to strategy may influence the business model. The value proposition of the firm is derived from the core strategy. This is where the business is attempting to identify how value is created for clients through the use of its products, services and technologies. Business innovation may also be needed if a firm changes its strategy.

Identification of the market segment is attempting to capture where the firm competes. It is attempting to identify its customers, location, product, service and technological segments. By inference it also identifies those areas that it does not compete in. The market segment identification also leads to definition of the scope of the market. The scope of the market is also influenced by the life cycle of the product or service that ultimately influence the level of profits the firm attains. In developing the business model, questions could be raised over scope definition to possibly find new areas for the product or service. There is the possibility of expanding and migrating existing skills to new areas. An example of this would be the construction project managers who have exported their project management skills to non-construction-related areas. This is an example of taking existing skills and using them for customers that are not normally thought about. In setting up the business model, potential for business concept innovation is always possible.

The resources of the organization are an integral part of the business model. The resources relate to the unique skills and competencies of the firm. These unique characteristics help differentiate the firm from its competitors and help the firms business model become more unique. These core competencies are the potential creators of value and are the benefits that customers want to receive. These core competencies also offer the opportunity of their application in markets outside that normally identified within the firm. Assessment of core competencies will also determine what skills the organization does not have to achieve its goals. The competencies of the firm will impact the business model as well as its ability to be aggressive, defensive or to change.

The more traditional inputs into a business model are the assets that a firm possesses. These normally relate to infrastructure, plant, equipment, brands, patents, finance, etc. Resources are not just entries on a balance sheet, but rather are assets that are exploited for the benefit of the firm. Those resources that cannot contribute to value creating are not of use and are wasted assets. The functioning of the organization and the success of the business model is dependent on these resources as they are often the key elements in the operational side of the firm. Associated with the resources are the processes of the firm. Processes are the routines and procedures that transform the firms outputs. The processes translate the skills and resources into value for the customer. An examination of the key processes of the organization is important as they have a key role in the transformation of resources and the creation of value. Processes are also the key elements in the actual delivery of the product or service. The relationships between assets, knowledge and processes are important to the way in which a business model will function. The way in which these resources are linked and configured will offer the opportunity for value creation and advantage.

The pricing, cost and revenue structure of the firm are important. At the centre of every business model are the financial models for the organization. Every business is ultimately judged on its financial performance. At heart of the business model will be the revenue model and the pricing model that are inextricably linked together. There is a plethora of financial models and financial performance indicators available for analysis. These financial models often form the cornerstone of any decisions that are made over the business. As part of our financial models we also need to consider what value customers derive from our products or services. An understanding of the costs associated with producing this value is also essential. Financial models are only as good as the information that is put into them. A good example is the case of the Millenium Dome in London. In the initial financial model it was assumed that twelve million visitors would visit the attraction. This figure formed the basis of all revenue and other financial calculations. No single attraction in the UK had more than three million visitors and the rather optimistic figures meant that the Millenium Dome was always going to be in a financially difficult position. The financial model within the overall business model is critical as it is the catalyst for most decisions.

The value network of the firm is another component of the business model. This is the value that is created by elements that lie outside the firm, and seek to complement and expand the firms' own resources. The value network will include suppliers, partner and alliances. As business focuses more and more on core competencies, the role of external partners is critical to success. In the construction industry the role of external contractors is critical for the success of the organization. The trend towards ever-greater outsourcing and use of works contractors make the management of these groups more critical to business success. An important question to ask is how do these contractors fit into our business model let alone contribute to it? Is there competitive advantage from the way in which we manage works contractors? A large part of value creation in construction business is in the hands of works contractors yet they are often not part of the business models that construction companies consider.

The nature of the way in which we do business has changed. Rather than simply adopting a competitive approach increasingly there is the use of collaboration to achieve business goals. The influence of partners and alliances on our business model has also to be considered as part of our value network. Partners allow the firm to expand their scope by providing additional resources and competencies to the relationship. The increase in the number of concession contracts for large-scale construction infrastructure projects highlights the role of partners. Most construction service companies do not have the necessary skills to design, build operate and finance these schemes. Almost all concession contracts will be some form of alliance and the success will be dependent on the coalition partners. The role of partners has also to be considered as part of the business model as they can influence the outcome of value creation.

The customer should not be forgotten as part of the business model as they are central to value creation. The relationship between the customer and the firm is important. What patterns exist in the relationship and to what extent is there loyalty in the created in the relationship. The relationship with a customer is transactional but in an industry such as construction the relationship can be emotional as well. The customer is also looking at how there relationship with the service provider is differentiated from other companies. The model of the relationship goes beyond just loyalty and brand building, it should also consider how the firm makes its services available to the customer, how efficient is delivery and what is the quality of the product or service. Customer support and service also add value and help differentiate the business. The business model should efficient in the sense that value the customer places on the benefits exceeds the cost of purchasing or producing those benefits. Relationship marketing plays an important role in developing these areas particularly in the longer term.

Many clients, particularly those operating in a short-term perspective, are influenced by the pricing structure. Low cost often means more customers and vice versa. This situation is still prevalent in the construction sector. There is no sense relationship building if the product or service is not competitively priced, the financial models that clients are using will find the price of products unacceptable. More sophisticated customers will look beyond the price but it is still a very dominant issue. On the whole, the product or service being offered to customers must provide a bundle of benefits; competitive price, good quality, efficient, reliable and good after-sales care. This is the manner in which the customer model evolves and seeks to create value for the customer.

The final part of the business model is to look at what gives the firm its competitive edge and profit potential. Strategic convergence is more and more apparent; therefore the firm has to try to have a unique service or product. Differentiation captures the essence of how the firm competes and in particular how it is different from its competitors. This unique approach must also appeal to consumers and create value or it will fail to produce the necessary profits. Profitability also needs to be considered in the model. Ideally all businesses would like to be in a monopolistic position. The business model should try to create a situation where monopolistic-type profits can be achieved at least in the short term. Business models should seek to build a level of monopoly into their businesses.

The impact of learning and knowledge should also be considered in the business model as a mean of creating a unique position. More businesses are becoming knowledge intensive. Knowledge and its ability to accelerate learning have the capability to create advantage. In sectors characterized by knowledge intensive activities a knowledge management strategy can provide faster learning capability and hence learn faster than rivals. As technology and production advantages converge the only area to gain advantage is through knowledge and learning.

The preceding paragraphs have highlighted the role of the business model in achieving organization success. Our need to understand the business model revolves around the need of the business development manager to understand how their development activity is going to influence the business model and be influenced by it.

Joan Magretta (2002) suggests that in the overheated days of dot-com mania, the term 'business model' was thrown around with abandon and with little meaning. While there is no truly correct definition, some usages make more sense than others. Margretta argues that we should not over-react and ignore business models. Instead we need to define the term and understand how it works together with an intelligent competitive strategy. Magretta's view of a business model is, at root, that it is a story that explains how an enterprise works. Like all good stories, the business model should have well-described characters with plausible motivations, and a plot plausibly founded on an insight about value.

Summary

The process of business development within the construction industry is a complex activity. The business environment is complex and dynamic making it more difficult for businesses to succeed. Construction markets are complex and require careful segmental analysis.

Business development is intertwined with the strategic decisions a firm takes. The business strategy the firm adopts sets out the path of business development activity. Business development is also tied into the business model of the firm. This model set out how value is going to be created, the markets, the financial proposition and network that are going to deliver the product or service. It defines the constraints and targets that are placed upon the business developer.

Business development is not an isolated activity. It requires interaction with both internal and external sources. Interaction with primary and secondary stakeholders is essential given the pressure that they bring to bear on the firm and their ability to influence success. Business success is complex activity that requires individuals to have a sound understating of the organizations they are developing.

References

Ansoff, H.I. (1965) *Corporate Strategy: An Analytical Approach to Business Policy for Growth and Expansion* (New York: McGraw Hill).

Chesborough, H. and Rosenbloom, R. (2002) *The Role of the Business Model in Capturing Value from Innovation: Evidence from Xerox Corporation's Technology Spinoff Companies.* Working-paper Harvard Business School.

Freeman, R.E. (1984) *Strategic Management: A Stakeholder Approach* (Marschfield, M.A: Pitman).

Hamel, G. (2000) *Leading the Revolution* (Boston, USA: Harvard Business School Press).

Linder, J. and Cantrell, S. (2001) What make a good business model anyway? Can yours stand the test of change? Outlook. *Accenture.*

Magretta, J. (2002) Why business models matter. *Harvard Business Review* May.

Wood, D.J. (1990) *Business and Society* (New York: Harper Collins).

3

Marketing planning – planning the way ahead

Philip Collard*

Introduction

Why is it, that firms within the construction industry who excel at working in complex, rapidly changing environments, sometimes committing to deadlines (years in advance), fail comprehensively when trying to organize and administrate basic marketing activity?

The real problem stems from our enjoyment in *tangible* activities which requires us to be reactive, responsive and decisive. Guess what! project work fulfils this criteria exactly. Sadly, marketing is often perceived as an *intangible*, non-measurable activity, primarily an overhead and any time spent on non-fee-earning activity is essentially 'wasting' resources.

Yet marketing, if carefully planned and implemented, can be extremely effective and utterly accountable for its annual budget. If the management team can agree in advance their exact financial targets and the specific but quantifiable marketing objectives they wish to realize over the year ahead, then marketing strategies can be developed to achieve them. However, it is essential that the management team shares this desired direction and is willing to contribute time to individually drive forward and report progress on their assigned objectives.

In this chapter on marketing planning we will examine what constitutes a marketing-led client-oriented organization. We will also consider marketing objectives, strategy and the structure and process to ensure successful implementation.

Strategic approach

There has to be an emphasis on taking a strategic approach to marketing. This entails understanding the organization's wider goals and understanding how they were going to be achieved; setting marketing objectives in relation to those corporate goals and corresponding marketing strategies to deliver on those stated marketing objectives.

* Marketing Works Training and Consultancy Ltd, UK

Only by adopting such a logical and reasoned approach can marketing rationalize its right to be at the heart of the management decision-making process, a cross-functional discipline that '… *is too important to leave to the marketing department*' By being both logical and strategic in nature, it will help to dispel its current image held by many in the construction industry of it being about advertising, public relations (PR) and general promotional activities.

Project manage your marketing

Careful thought must be given as to how each marketing objective can be achieved, and just as in project work the overall tasks can be broken down into strategies, initiatives and specific actions and their associate costs. Clear identification as to who is responsible for each step must be made so that staff and managers alike know what is required of them to implement their part of the overall plan. Furthermore, a programme must be established which shows when specific campaigns or marketing initiatives need to be completed.

Outline steps for marketing planning:
1 Analyse the changing business environment
2 Identify the options relevant to the firms' core competences
3 Establish firm business strategy and define marketing objectives
4 Set marketing strategies and performance targets
5 Confirm achievable by undertaking market and client research
6 Formulate tactical initiatives and action
7 Seek individuals' commitment to implementing their part of plan
8 Create monitoring controls to evaluate performance.

The process described above is *project management* – marketing style. Project management as a generic management tool has proved to work rather well in the construction industry over the last twenty years. So if your board is convinced that project management has helped to improve the control and efficiency of project administration, it will not take much to get them thinking of what it could do for their marketing activities.

Let us start with the basics.

What is a marketing plan?

It is a formal management process. All marketing resources are allocated to meet specified marketing objectives. The marketing plan should knit together the strategic cornerstones of the corporate/business plan. It is a standard against which day-to-day marketing decisions are made. In being able to 'knit together' both strategic and tactical elements, the marketing plan should correspondingly include both strategic and tactical aspects.

For purposes of implementing the marketing plan the strategic and tactical elements can be differentiated by time frame. Any planning process needs to take account of both the long and short term. The broad three-year marketing plan should be treated as the strategic plan; the first year as the tactical short-term plan.

One of the first things to say about marketing plans is that they should be a focus for the whole business unit and/or firm and should not therefore be restricted to the marketing department. Secondly they should be based on the market(s) in which the business unit is operating. This is a simple but important point.

Marketing plans should take account of budgets and other financial measures but should not be based on them. Similarly sales-led organizations may base their planning and budgeting around sales targets. These might be overly optimistic to motivate a sales force rather than a realistic assessment of what the market will bear.

Marketing plans and budgets arising therefrom should necessarily be founded on careful, realistic assessments of what the market is doing in terms of both its external environment, e.g. economic conditions, market sector growth versus saturation/stagnation, competitor activity, etc.

What the firm can do in response to those external factors, e.g. new service launches, service extensions or improvements, improvements through new distribution (new offices, new locations), better promotion (hospitality, mailshots, campaigns, etc.) and increased sales force (often not required as easier and cheaper to get existing staff to take on a small degree of marketing responsibility).

Numbers and quantifiable targets (actually measurable and not just wish statements) are a central aspect of any professional and comprehensive marketing plan. Targets must be tangible and realizable so as to not demotivate. However the use of numbers, financial or by volume, is not enough on its own. Soft factors that require written explanation are similarly just as much a prerequisite as the quantifiable elements.

The approach to marketing planning should not be a formalized system, but should be one that complements the wider corporate aims and strategies of the organization as a whole. To that end marketing planning is at the heart of the firm and its planning, and is accordingly cross functional. It is not simply a tactical description of how marketing resources will be allocated over the forthcoming twelve-month budgeting period.

It follows on from this that if a marketing plan is founded on solid, factual information about the marketplace itself, then the starting point for constructing the plan will be the search for data organized in such a way as to become useful information.

The marketing audit; where are we now!

We saw in the previous section, the overall process of marketing planning. First, we will now start off with the key issues of the marketing audit.

In reality a marketing audit is really a detailed assessment of:

1 Who we are
2 What we offer – the number and extent of service ranges
3 Our current client base
4 The main feature of services
5 What we offer as benefits
6 The competitive advantages we provide above our competitors
7 Market segments/key sectors we work in
8 Geographical coverage
9 The diversity of business
10 The degree of vertical integration.

All these issues help determine structure and culture and in short, it is a full picture of where we are *now*!

If we are able to understand where we are at this current time, and can articulate where we could be at some future time, it is this that gives us our true direction.

The marketing audit

If the marketing audit is simply the collection of data to be converted into useful information for further distillation in the final marketing plan, there is as much need to formalize or systemize this process as there is for the marketing plan itself.

An outline framework of the type of areas a firm should be examining and the questions it should be asking is contained below.

Factors to be examined in the external business environment

1 The wider business environment can be summarized through STEEP analysis where STEEP stands for Sociocultural, Technological, Economic, Environmental, Political (also including legal and fiscal/taxation matters).
2 The narrower business environment is the market the business unit is competing in. Factors to be examined here are its total size by value and volume; whether it is growing; declining or not moving; the different customer/client groups that go to make up the market, e.g. segments and niches; the range of services/products purchased by these customers/clients in this marketplace, e.g. direct and indirect competitors; prices of services offered; the range of channels open and finally any industry/trade bodies and regulation that may be relevant.
3 Industry or market competitors. Examination of competitors can itself demand a framework of analysis. The best known in this regard is Michael Porter's five forces model, which is discussed in depth in many marketing and business management books. The constituent parts of the analysis at this stage include who the competitors are; whether they are direct or indirect competitors; their relative size by value and volume/market share; distribution channels used; brand image and values as seen by customers; profitability; structure and key (marketing) strategies; main strengths and weaknesses.

Factors to be examined in the internal business environment

This is a critical assessment of one's own firm or business unit's abilities and should include: sales – by service/product category/range, client segments, region/country (where applicable); market shares by value, volume and percentage in each service/product market; marketing strategies – channel strategies, promotional, pricing and service/product strategies (as applicable); marketing management/department; marketing information system and research plan(s).

It is easy to see that to conduct a thorough marketing audit is in itself a demanding task. The process above is described in list form only. The level of detail entered into each point will depend on the auditor and the size of the business or importance of that particular market to the firm.

What is more important is how the information gathered is brought together in some kind of meaningful framework, which can then be applied to the marketing plan. Two frameworks were mentioned in the audit methodology described, STEEP analyses and the Porter five competitive forces any industry will face. These types of frameworks are extremely useful in processing information and putting it into some form of perspective. McDonald, in his book *Marketing Plans* (1995), recommends drawing the entire constituent parts and multitude of information together through a Strengths, Weaknesses, Opportunities and Threats analysis or framework (SWOT).

This is particularly convenient because the McDonald approach, as that described above, fits perfectly together with a SWOT, as it differentiates between external and internal factors. Thus key points from the internal business environment analysis can be recorded under strengths and weaknesses while external environment factors go under opportunities and threats.

One further point on SWOT analyses should be stressed. Many companies use SWOTs for a variety of purposes. In this instance it is easy to record every single factor generated on the SWOT. This will make the whole framework unwieldy and defeat the object of its purpose. In contrast far more will be achieved by limiting the SWOT to key factors that have a direct bearing on competitive success in the following period. The objective should be to restrict each SWOT title to one side of text with each point there under summarized in bullet point form.

It is only when we have this full understanding of our scope of activities that we can match activities to the environment and match our activities to our possible capabilities. Yes, any future strategy is likely to require a modification of resources but it still must be a reflection of our attitudes and beliefs and these can only be distilled from a full audit.

Market segmentation

It is extremely important for firms to split their clients (or customers) into different segments, grouping together those clients with similar characteristics that have similar needs. This is not simply about size or sectors but more about what services are bought, by whom and why? The aim is to identify true clients' needs, which can be combined together to identify the best segments on which to focus your marketing efforts. This process is called segmentation and will identify your most attractive and profitable segments and also those with the highest potential for growth.

Operation of market segmentation strategy can offer considerable competitive advantage. Segmentation centres around are the best way to distinguish the main sectors you work in within the total construction market. The skill is in choosing appropriate segmentation criteria given the wide range of possibilities.

The criteria must refer to difference in demand by each of your client or customer groups. For example, the needs and requirements of development directors of retailers are different to development directors specializing in commercial office buildings. The features of your range of services clearly benefit different clients in different ways, and therefore you must distill the benefits they experience and promote tailored messages to each segment group.

Major segmentation criteria in the construction industry would be as described in Table 3.1.

Each of the industry classifications as shown in Table 3.1 must also be segmented into further categories such as commercial retail, commercial office or public health, education and private health and private education, etc. Again the same for geographical segmentation such as Midlands into East and West Midlands.

While clearly you must segment accordingly to your own customer grouping it is advisable to organize them in such a way that you are able to layer over data and research

Table 3.1 Major segmentation criteria in the construction industry

Industry segments	Geographical
Commercial	Scotland
Industrial	Wales
Public non-housing	North
Infrastructure	Midlands
Private housing	South
Public housing	etc.

findings from industry research bodies such *Construction Forecasting Research Ltd* or *ABI* to ensure consistency and compatibility. If you fail to ensure your segmentation forecasting is based upon quantitative research, it will not usually be easy to measure potential segment size or more importantly your progress. It is therefore critical to recognize that the full implementation of a segmented strategy demands an adequate flow of data for both planning and control purposes.

Without the use of segmentation the company pursues a homogenous strategy, which may lead to a product or service trying to be all the things to all people. This may work reasonably well while the company is dominant, or in a monopoly situation. However, this leaves the product or service vulnerable to attack by competitors who target their products or services more specifically at smaller sectors of the market – in time this could mean the 'homogenous' product or service appeals less and less to the total market whose needs are being satisfied elsewhere – and leaves them with a smaller universe of customers.

Constructing the way ahead

Constructing a three-year strategic marketing plan

The distinction between the three-year and one-year plan has already been made in the previous sections, with the longer time perspective necessarily addressing the main strategic issues the firm or business unit wishes to address. As we will see in a later section the shorter one-year plan correspondingly tackles more immediate and tactical tasks. The most important point is that the three-year marketing plan must precede the one-year plan, with the latter being a function of the former and not vice versa. Extrapolating the one-year plan into the three-year plan (as many businesses do) will serve no useful purpose.

The following nine-point plan describes the principal component parts of a professional strategic marketing plan. The author would like to acknowledge that this is a summary of the McDonald nine step process and readers who require a more detailed explanation, as well as all the forms to complete in carrying through the methodology, are recommended to refer to Marketing Plans, M.H.B. McDonald (published by Heinemann).

Step 1 – Statement of intent or mission statement
This statement should have been defined and set in the corporate plan; however, at the business unit level (as distinct from company or group level) a further mission statement

may be required. Mission/statements of intent should be differentiated from more esoteric concepts such as vision statements, these tend to be far more ideological or a long-term statement of strategic intent.

In this context the mission statement defines the role of the business unit as well as the business in which it should primarily be involved. It may also highlight its distinctive competence and give a broad indication of future direction without being overly visionary.

Step 2 – Performance summary

This section should examine past to present performance in terms of normal financial measures such as sales value and volume, margins/profitability, contribution, etc. By using an extended time period, e.g. the last two or three years, a broader picture will put the current situation into perspective. Effectively you are trying to identify what the reasons were for good or bad performance in the past as they may offer a number of key areas to address.

Step 3 – Financial projections

Having looked at past financials, so projected figures should be considered for the planning period under consideration. Similar measures as described above should be applied – sales projections by value and volume, contribution and profitability, etc.

Step 4 – Market overview

This section begins to draw on the information and analysis gleaned from the marketing audit. How a manager describes their own marketplace is to some extent a matter for personal opinion, however some of the key elements that should be included are market segments – how the market is divided into different segments and which ones the business unit primarily wants to do business with and secondly what is changing within this market, e.g. in terms of market segments and niches, competitors or even the legislative framework that may shape a marketplace.

Marketers need to provide a summary of the market in enough detail to be informative but not so detailed as to overbalance the marketing plan. McDonald recommends the use of visual aids wherever possible, e.g. bar charts, pie charts, service/product life cycle curves, etc.

Step 5 – SWOT analyses

The SWOT analysis is largely the conclusion of a great deal of preceding work. In assessing strengths and weaknesses, the business unit needs to be able to compare its own performance on a limited number of factors that are critical to success with how the competitors are performing. This necessitates listing the key or critical factors for success in order of priority and according each a weighting where the total of weightings adds up to 1, 10 or 100. This weighting in effect rates how important each factor is determining success in the marketplace.

The business unit can then assess its own performance on each factor, again out of ten or some similarly easy number, and then do the same for all direct competitors. By multiplying the weight of each factor with the score attained, a total weighted score can be calculated which directly compares performance with the competition and thereby quantifies strengths and weaknesses in a reasonably objective fashion.

The external factors, the opportunities and threats, can now be examined. Once again following the work completed in the marketing audit, a summary of the macro or wider business environment factors can be considered in terms of government policy, techno-logical developments, etc. (described previously as the STEEP analysis).

From this point the manager(s) concerned should be able to state the different assumptions to be made in each service/product/market segment and thereafter the main objectives and strategies to be followed in the same. This is based on the fact that the key issues will have been brought out from the analysis made above, e.g. SWOT points.

This should not be confused with the overall marketing objectives and strategies within the marketing plan, which have still to be set (these are considered under *Step 8* which will be detailed later).

Research is also necessary to examine the competitors' position described above, where critical success factors are weighted and the business unit's own performance is compared with competitors'. At this point the marketing audit can be further drawn upon to examine competitors' position more closely.

Each direct competitor should be examined separately to consider what their current position in the market is, what strategies they appear to be following to pursue what objectives and strategies they are likely to pursue in over the next three years. Once again the level of detail required will depend on the nature of the market and the degree of direct competition, as well as the amount of knowledge possessed about competitors, in terms of their intended broad marketing as well as product/market segment strategies.

Step 6 – Portfolio summary

The work conducted above to produce concise but meaningful SWOT analyses can be summarized by means of a Portfolio matrix, sometimes also labelled the shell directional policy matrix.

Market segments should have already been defined and ordered in terms of preference for doing business with. Segments at the top of the list are those that will be focused on being likely to deliver the best results, e.g. the most attractive market segments.

Having established the attractiveness of each segment, the business unit must now assess their own strengths in serving that segment vis à vis the competition. The pertinent questions in this regard should already have been answered, e.g. current market share; ability to grow; proximity to customers, etc. From this situation the manager should be able to plot the business unit's position on the portfolio matrix.

Equipped with this analysis an assessment can be made as to which market segments the business unit is best equipped to serve and which will render the most beneficial results. In the example in Figure 3.1 segment 1 may be very attractive but the business is least equipped to serve it, given its low strength rating. Segments 2, 3 and 4 can all be met with a high degree of strength but segment 2 has a low attractiveness rating. This leaves segments 3 and 4 as being the most likely for future focus.

McDonald takes this matrix system further replacing static positions marked as [3] in Figure 3.1, with circles where the diameter of the circle represents the proportion of total turnover that particular market segment accounts for.

This can be taken yet a step still further by plotting where these segments should be on the same matrix in a year or three's time. This is represented in Figure 3.2 with the white circle showing both a movement on the matrix and a growth in size of segment 3. This signifies both a shift in the attractiveness and the ability of the business to serve segment 3 in addition to forecast increase in sales.

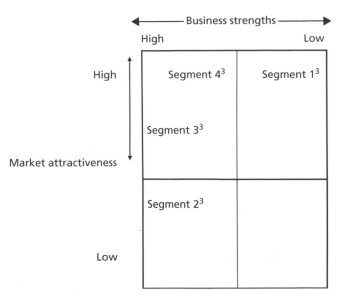

Figure 3.1 A basic shell directional policy matrix showing which market segment a business unit is best equipped to serve.

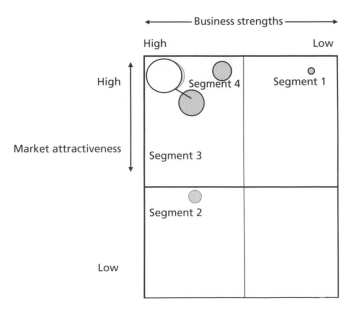

Figure 3.2 Shell directional policy matrix using McDonald's system using circles to represent the proportion of total turnover.

Step 7 – Assumptions (Ceteris paribus)

Ceteris paribus is Latin for *other things remaining equal*. Unfortunately in dynamic, ever changing marketplaces this rule very rarely holds true, very little remains equal. Given that so many things can change, it is logical to list any key points or assumptions on which the marketing plan is based. If these key criteria are not fulfilled then the marketing plan will not be able to deliver.

This should not be used as a caveat or loophole for the marketer to absolve him/herself of responsibility, rather a genuine reflection of external factors that may be beyond the control of the marketer, e.g. economic growth/decline, rising interest rates, the organization's access to capital investment or a competitor's withdrawal from a marketplace.

More detailed lists of assumptions may be made for individual product/services/markets; however the overall marketing plan should only include those key criteria that will directly affect its successful implementation.

Step 8 – Setting objectives and strategies

Having completed step 5 (SWOT analysis described previously) and step 6 (portfolio summary) as well as any outstanding assumptions, the marketing plan is now in a position to tackle objectives and strategies.

The distinction between objectives and strategies has already been made under product/service decisions, where an objective is the end goal and the strategy is the means to achieving the goal. It should be noted that many marketers mix the two up so as to make them indistinct (*'our strategy is to beat competitor X'*)

A further important point is made by McDonald:

> Marketing objectives … should be about products, services and markets only, since it is only by selling something to someone that the SBU's [Strategic Business Unit's] financial goals can be achieved. Advertising, pricing and other elements of the marketing mix are other means (the strategies) by which the SBU can succeed in doing this. Thus pricing objectives, sales promotion objectives, advertising objectives and so on should *not* be confused with marketing objectives.

On this basis McDonald cites the interaction of products/services to market segments, e.g. selling existing products/services to existing or new segments as marketing objectives with a corresponding marketing strategy of *'improve product/service functional performance and perceived value in conjunction with new communications campaign'*. This would require both new production and communications substrategies, which will complement the marketing strategy.

In finalizing marketing objectives and strategies McDonald recommends referring back to the portfolio analysis and using the labels developed originally by the Boston Consulting Group in order to simplify the position of different market segments or product/services/markets. The idea here is that each quadrant of the matrix has its own label describing their combination of attractiveness and strength. These are self-explanatory when shown in their respective quadrants (Figure 3.3).

In its most simple terms any business unit needs to have some kind of balance in the product/services/markets it serves. Cash cows deliver positive cash flow but will not last forever. Dogs are a drain on cash flow and unless they can be developed into question marks or stars then there they should be divested. Question marks, also known as problem

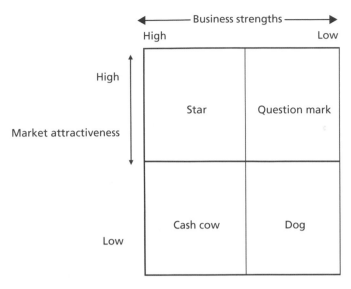

Figure 3.3 Shell directional policy matrix using labels developed by the Boston Consulting Group.

children or wildcats have the potential to become either dogs or stars. Stars are obviously very desirable but are difficult to cultivate, etc.

This BCG approach to portfolio management should be viewed as a facilitator and not a scientific end in itself. It simply aids the decision-making process providing a useful framework in which to plan an approach to the market, which takes account of both the market's needs and the firm or business unit's skills and core competences.

Step 9 – Financial projections

At this point, *marketers* should be able to provide three-year projections for the key financial markers, as described earlier – sales by value, gross profit, contribution, etc.

Only now can we consider how to implement the lengthy process of strategic planning by developing a practical one-year implementation plan.

Implementing the way ahead

This is the final part in marketing planning let us first review the whole planning process. While doing so please note the tactical plan will encompass steps 6–8 below.

Outline steps for marketing planning
1 Analyse the changing business environment
2 Identify the options relevant to the firms' core competences
3 Establish firm business strategy and define marketing objectives
4 Set marketing strategies and performance targets
5 Confirm achievable by undertaking market and client research
6 Formulate tactical initiatives and action
7 Seek individuals commitment to implementing their part of plan
8 Create monitoring controls to evaluate performance

The one-year tactical or operational marketing plan

Having waded through the lengthy process of constructing a strategic three-year marketing plan, the marketer at least has the consolation that the one-year plan is relatively simple by comparison, given that all the hard work has been done. All the quantitative analyses, portfolio matrices and competitor analysis have been completed.

With this solid foundation the one-year marketing plan can be put together in very little time. However, it is not underestimated as indeed implementation is actually the most important and critical part of the entire planning process. We have helped many large and small firms implement this cultural change and have found it takes around eighteen months to realign all the business units and profit centres so that they are all focusing on achieving the global corporate objectives locally. Far too often when we start this off we have asked management teams from the board or partnerships if they have a marketing plan. Yes, many claim to have one but in reality on inspection it is just a list of financial targets. I also spend days with such teams developing a three-year plan, but in truth this is all a waste of time if it is not actually implemented through a carefully managed process.

The main point of a one-year tactical is to create an action plan, which identifies all the strategies and tactical steps for the first year of the three-year plan. It is fundamental if you really want to adopt a marketing culture in your organization and make life easy for yourself. If you can plot actual financial progress along a predetermined route you are able to spot potential problems and short falls early on and action predetermined contingencies.

Let us look at the main elements needed:

1 *Overall objectives* These should include financial objectives, e.g. sales volume/value targets, gross margins, etc. They may also state targeted increase in market share or the goal of becoming market leader in terms of share/sales, etc. Some form of brief commentary should accompany the objectives.

   Overall strategies How the objectives will be achieved by targeting which customer/client segments and with which services or products/new services or new products, and how will all this be communicated, etc. with the clients using which various activities of the marketing mix.

2 *Detailed subobjectives by segment, client/customer, etc.* With large industrial or business-to-business markets this may go down as far as setting sales targets by client/customer or new accounts that will sought. Hopefully it will also detail your client action plans and who from your company will be pursuing whom from the client.

   Substrategies and action tactics How the subobjectives will be met – details, timing and responsibility for achievement. This should include indications of new advertising, sales promotion, PR, seminar programmes, events or direct mail campaigns, sales incentives as well as any other tools that may be employed in order to deliver the subobjectives set, such as linking these activities with your website.

3 *Summary of marketing activities and costs* This should cover the whole marketing budget for the year and include everything from advertising to entertainment and travel costs.

4 *Contingency plan* As was discussed above in the strategic marketing plan, a list of assumptions is made and the implications for the business need to be discussed and considered if those assumptions not met. Clearly if some of your tactics are not actually working and getting the desired results then what new tactics and actions have been previously identified to implement. This is crucial.

Having identified key assumptions, the financial implications can be easily modelled on a spreadsheet to demonstrate two or three different scenarios. For instance what if the firm's most valued client account were to be lost? What could be put in its place and how long would that take?

While comprehensive contingencies cannot practicably be planned for, identifying key assumptions and how the marketing department would deal with the resulting scenarios of a failed assumption is a requisite fall-back position.

5 *Operating results and financial ratios* This should summarize the main financial ratios as preferred by the firm. In addition to sales, gross margin, marketing costs, and the forecast return on sales, investment or even capital can be recorded. To some extent the content of this section will be dependent on each organization's own style of financial analysis.

6 *Key activity planner/schedule* A list of planned marketing activities that will take place, by month, throughout the year. If you want to keep it simple use Microsoft project as everybody in the construction industry can relate to such a programme of delineated activities.

7 *Other information* Any supplementary details such as sales targets by individual, realignment of sales territories or sales call plans can be contained in this section.

Although true marketing planning requires this integrated approach it does offer many benefits including ease of managing progress, as you can now assess actual progress against what is desired and peer pressure should ensure assigned tasks are completed. It also ensures that critical marketing objectives that the future success of the firm may depend on actually happen because of continuous review, so the usual excuse of 'too much project work' is simply not now acceptable. Such marketing initiatives will have variable demands on a manager's time and so he must get properly organized. Surely no current job can be more important than ensuring the firm stays in business in the long term?

Construction marketing in the future will mean firms are able to stand out from the crowd and have the ability to present themselves as offering something unique that not only differentiates them from the competitors but is valued by potential clients. Firms will need to innovate service products that not only fulfil and satisfy individual client's needs but also be able to identify the client earlier on to try and avoid the pressure and cost of competitive tendering.

I also believe in ten years from now marketing in the construction industry will have stopped being generally perceived as a non-measurable intangible activity, but a very valuable technique that wins you more profitable work, just as it has been for many other industries over the past decade.

Finally if there are a few members of senior management reading this who still have not bought into the marketing planning concept, think of this way … you would not start a project without a programme so why undertake expensive marketing activities without a plan. In other words all I have described in this chapter is project management, marketing style, and as a tool, has not project management been extremely useful to the industry? Just think for a moment what it could do for your business development.

I often note that there were various degrees of misunderstanding and confusion in use of marketing terminology. As it is essential that there is consistency in our interpretation among construction marketers and senior management perhaps the following could form the basis of marketing and business development terminology.

Construction marketing terminology

Business planning

The process of developing clear corporate objectives, identifying the desired level of profitability and growth.

Mission statement (statement of intent)

A statement of the firms overall business intentions. One is also required for each business unit in terms of the benefits, competencies and competitive differentiators they provide and their chosen future direction.

Corporate objectives

The financial profit and turnover targets that the firms overall business and those of its business units aims to achieve over the next three years.

Marketing planning

The process of predetermining a course or courses of action based on assumptions about future conditions or trends which can be imagined but not predicted with any certainty. Planning includes developing marketing objectives, tactics and strategies that will achieve the corporate ends.

Marketing objectives

A statement of goals or targets that the business and/or business unit wants to achieve through marketing activity over a three-year and one-year period where progress can be measured through accomplishment of pre-agreed milestones.

Marketing strategy

Marketing strategies are intended actions to a pre-agreed direction. A strategy is the means of how the business or business unit will achieve success.

Implementation

Tactical marketing planning identifies all the actions, steps and tactics for implementation over the forthcoming one-year period.

Recommended reading

McDonald, M. (1995) *Marketing Plans* (Butterworth Heinemann Professional Publishing Ltd).
Kotler, P. (1999) *Marketing Management Analysis, Planning, Implementation and Control*, 9th ed. (Prentice Hall).

4

Case study of marketing in an SME in construction

Evelyn Vernea*

Introduction – background to the company

The organization was a group of companies providing a variety of building and maintenance services to a wide range of clients in both public and private sectors.

The construction division had been created to take advantage of the boom in grant funded rehabilitation work to tenements in Glasgow in the 1970s. A stone cleaning and restoration company had been acquired in order to complement this work and provide a full building service. A lands division had been created in the 1980s.

What were the company's objectives?

The departure of the Marketing Manager created an ideal opportunity to review the marketing strategy of the company. They had a number of objectives from the commission:

- Move away from their heavy concentration on public sector housing and break into new, appropriate markets
- Raise turnover and profit margins, especially through negotiating rather than competitively tendering for projects
- Overcome an image problem, which they believed they had and show that they were a professional, good-quality builder.

What methodology was used to assess the problems?

In order to address these objectives we adopted a tried and tested, classical marketing methodology involving:

- An internal audit
- An external audit

* RED Creative Marketing Solutions, Glasgow

- Market research
- SWOT analysis
- Establishment of marketing objectives
- Preparation of marketing strategy and plan.

Internal audit

This was conducted through a series of structured discussions with the directors of the company and looked at issues described below.

- Defining core services provided by the company
- Listing and quantifying all markets in which the company had recently or currently worked
- Examining which services were most profitable, which were least profitable and where did they think that there was most potential for profit
- Clarifying critical factors for success in the markets that they served
- Describing marketing activities previously carried out by the company and their effect
- Branding and corporate image.

External audit

This involved looking at issues external to the company but having a bearing on their activities, the main areas being: Clients' perceptions – tested through a telephone survey of a number of their current and previous clients and also consultants with whom they had worked. It was particularly important to test in this way clients' perceptions of the company in the light of the internally perceived image problems. What emerged was that they were rated highly for their building skills but not good at following up defects, linked strongly with Local Authority housing projects and known for excessive activity on the corporate hospitality front. Image problems identified were with potential clients or their consultants who actually had little knowledge of the company.

Competitors' activities were analysed, looking at their strengths, weaknesses and marketing strategies. It is often useful to identify, as we did, among competitors, one or two 'exemplars', i.e. companies who seem to be doing the things you would like to be doing and study how they have achieved this.

Market research

To supplement the information gathered above a variety of on-line sources, trade publications, newspapers, directories were reviewed and telephone based research carried out. An in-depth analysis of the sectors in which the company had been or would like to be active was then conducted.

An opportunity analysis was carried out on each of these, looking at the likely future trends, especially growth prospects, major players, typical forms of procurement and so forth, with a view to identifying where the best prospects for future project opportunities lay.

SWOT

All of the information was gathered and analysed in order to draw out the essential strengths, weaknesses, opportunities and threats facing the company over the next few years.

Marketing objectives

The SWOT was discussed with the company in order to determine 'SMART' (specific, measurable, achievable, realistic and timed) marketing objectives for the next three years.
   These were to:

- increase turnover by 50 per cent, to £20m a year
- increase profitability from barely 1 to 10 per cent by maintaining low overheads and pursuing and securing higher margin types of work
- reach a position where only 50 per cent of projects were obtained through competitive tender by pursuing partnership opportunities. This would be a significant drop from the previous year's figure of 75 per cent
- spread the geographical coverage of the company across the central belt
- diversify into other, appropriate industry sectors, away from an over-concentration on housing
- create and project a public image of the company based on a reputation for high-quality construction in a variety of fields, rather than as 'a medium-sized building company that does a lot of work for the council'.

Marketing strategy and plan

In order to achieve the objectives described, it was agreed that the company had to build on its strengths and address its weaknesses in order to combat the threats and explore the opportunities summarized in the SWOT analysis.
   However, what also had to be taken into account was the fact that there were limited resources available to implement the strategy. A system of prioritizing and carefully focusing activities on areas that might best meet the objectives had to be found.
   This was based on the following key principles:

1 An active marketing campaign aimed at raising the company's profile, making contacts, developing relationships and pursuing opportunities in market sectors where clients would be more amenable to joint ventures and other forms of partnering. Explore sectors where the specialist skills of the company, e.g. in stone restoration might be demonstrated. From the detailed research undertaken a few key target areas were identified.
2 A more passive marketing approach in sectors which normally would require competitive tendering while still ensuring that the company was on approved lists and contacting the clients at appropriate points in the year, e.g. when new budgets were available or if specific projects were known to be coming up.
3 Support the first two principles and raise awareness of the company, its activities and strengths through good quality, up-to-date promotional materials and selective advertising.

4 Develop 'packages' of services for targeting specific markets, e.g. property maintenance.
5 Develop a 'client-care' policy covering pre-, during and post-contract stages.
6 Recognizing that knowledge is now the key resource available to any company. Set up systems to manage marketing information, not only to keep abreast of opportunities in key target sectors but also to monitor competitors' activities and trends in the market place generally.
7 Develop a 'marketing culture' within the company whereby all staff, both office-based and site operatives, would be encouraged to understand and play their role in the marketing of the company.

These key principles were developed into a twelve-month, detailed and costed plan of action for the company to carry out. The plan also indicated who should carry out which activities.

An essential element of the marketing plan was the built-in requirement for regular marketing meetings at which progress would be reviewed and the impact of various activities on meeting objectives would be evaluated.

At the end of the year, a larger-scale review would assess the success of the strategy, carrying over any uncompleted tasks into the next year's plan. This would also determine those activities that had been useful and those that were not working towards the objectives, allowing the useful ones to be repeated.

Implementation

Following acceptance of the report, strategy and marketing action plan, the author was further commissioned to assist with the implementation of the plan, based at the company's premises for a few days per week, acting effectively, as their part-time marketing manager. A number of activities were initiated and developed in parallel, including the following.

Promotional material

A professional design consultancy was commissioned to produce a new corporate brochure and update the company's image. The brief was to provide background information about the company, incorporate its values statement and client-care policy, and provide information about each of its services, all in a way that was easily updateable. The positioning and image to be projected was to be of good quality, professional, client friendly and innovative. Top quality photos were commissioned to help achieve the desired look and to provide an interesting variety of types of projects that the company had completed. Care was taken to ensure that a good balance of projects was incorporated to create the perception that the company had been fairly active in all of its key target markets (even if it actually only had one or two projects in these).

Along with the brochure, a presentation portfolio was compiled, using the same headings, photos and summaries of the text. This presentation portfolio case was produced in order that it could be used in introductory meetings with potential clients. The intention was that the presentation should take around 7 minutes to run through.

To further raise the physical profile of the company, a number of site boards and banners were purchased with only the newly improved logo and the company's phone number displayed. Concerted efforts were made to ensure that these were placed at high visibility locations on all project sites.

Client-care policy

Discussions involving all of the company's directors were held to clarify their attitude to client care and to encapsulate this in a statement that could then be communicated throughout the company.

This covered pre-tender, execution and post-contract work with an emphasis on post-contract work. The need to move operatives away from sites which were nearing completion and on to new projects often meant that they, in common with many contractors, were guilty of not always attending to snags and post-contract defects as quickly as clients would like. There was recognition that the last impression is what clients remember, even if the rest of the contract has gone like a dream. The company pledged to improve this area of their performance and enshrined this in the client-care policy. The policy statement, akin to a mission statement, was included in the brochure, circulated to key staff and posted on notice boards in the main and site offices.

Programme of visits

While the promotional material was being produced, specific identification of companies that offered opportunities in each of the target sectors was undertaken. Recognizing that consultants are often asked to suggest builders, architects and project managers involved in these sectors were also researched. In all cases, key individuals were identified and called by phone with the aim of obtaining short introductory meetings for the company. Thereby, a programme of visits was drawn up and added to in an ongoing fashion and, without waiting for the brochure and portfolio to be ready, a director of the company and the marketing manager undertook a series of short visits, usually of around 30 minutes.

Though naturally taking the opportunity to introduce the company and its services, we were careful to apply the 2:1 rule – 'two ears and one mouth' and listened hard to what the potential clients could tell us about their development plans and how and when they would be letting building contracts. All meetings were followed up with a brief 'thank you' letter and details of the discussions recorded in a computerized database. When the brochure and portfolio presentation were ready, these were used at these meetings.

'Passive marketing'

An exercise was mounted, involving in-house administrative staff to ensure that the company was listed on appropriate public sector approved contractors' lists, i.e. all local authorities, health trusts and the like across central Scotland. Since the company was unclear which lists they were on, each was written to asking how application might be made and then followed through receipt of application forms, completion and return of these, and confirmation that the company had been included.

Changing corporate culture

In successful companies, marketing is not just something carried out by the marketing manager, it involves everyone from the person answering the phone to the bricklayers on site. It was agreed that it was important that everyone in the company should have the opportunity to be told about the new strategy underway and to think about how they might contribute through their own roles.

A half-day seminar was arranged for a Saturday morning in a local hotel to which all office-based staff plus all site managers and foremen were invited. Presentations were given by the marketing manager and the director driving the marketing agenda. The presentations invited discussion of the client-care policy. After these, we broke into small groups to discuss what marketing meant in the different roles which people had and how they could contribute. A feedback session recorded all the main points of discussion and suggestions on the way forward. The main points to emerge were written up and circulated to all staff who had been present and displayed on the staff notice board. Suggestions, which were implemented, included:

- regular bulletins on marketing activities and priorities, new projects and the like to be placed on the staff notice board
- a suggestions box to be provided for staff to offer marketing suggestions
- all site managers and foremen had the responsibility to communicate to their workers the importance of being tidy and courteous on site
- more care to be taken on snagging and post-contract defects.

Corporate events

The company had had a reputation for hosting fairly lavish corporate events for local authority staff, councillors and the like at which 'raffle' prizes ranged from colour televisions to foreign holidays. As part of the plan to change the image projected, it was planned to host a small dinner in the private dining room of an upmarket local hotel. In all twenty-two people attended, six of whom were staff, the others being a handpicked selection of repeat clients, consultants and 'prospects' with whom relationships were being developed.

The emphasis was on creating an atmosphere of low key and relaxed comfort with fine wine and good food to signal a change in image. These changes were very well received with some clients claiming they were pleasantly surprised at the lack of sales talk. Directors regularly would take it in turn to invite a few guests for a round of golf and lunch at Gleneagles. These were always popular events and led to many sales leads being provided by happy clients and their consultants.

Having made a considerable investment in producing the new brochure, it was agreed to launch this in a fitting way and mark the shift in image and attitude that it represented. A lunch was hosted in a nearby cultural centre for a large number of clients, consultants and prospects. The managing director delivered a short speech on what the event represented before a buffet lunch. The atmosphere was consistent with the company's changed image. And, of course, everyone left with a copy of the new brochure.

Information gathering

Information gathering was an ongoing activity, using a variety of sources, including trade and professional journals, newspapers, business publications and project-tracking digests. Some of these were taken in-house and others reviewed in the Mitchell Reference Library, a huge information resource. A planning leads service that had been taken in paper form was now taken electronically. Through carefully tailoring the type of information required and using the cross-referencing facilities it had, allowed a great deal of useful information to be accessed. Added to this was the information gathered from attending appropriate business networks and, of course, the contacts being made on a daily basis in the target market sectors.

Database

To support the various activities being carried out and record information, a computerized database was set up in which details of all current and past clients and prospective clients were stored and added to as new information was obtained, e.g. through the programme of visits. A scheduling facility allowed dates to be programmed in for follow-up actions and next contacts and the system was networked between myself as acting marketing manager and all directors so that we all had access to the most up-to-date information when talking to a client or prospect. The company proved time after time the marketing adage that you will have contacted a prospect an average of seven times before an opportunity to bid for work with them appears.

Outcomes

This is not an exhaustive list of activities carried out in the first or subsequent years of the strategy but they do provide a flavour of what was done and the direction that was taken. And the outcomes more than achieved the planned objectives:

- Year on year turnover and profit have been increased: at the end of the three-year strategy, turnover exceeds £20m and profit margins are higher than industry averages.
- They are now known as a good-quality, reliable builder with a good attitude to client care.
- Although housing, public and private, is still a large part of their portfolio, they are also active in leisure, education and many commercial markets.
- Profile and 'brand recognition' is extremely high with their banners being seen on all sorts of building projects all over the west of Scotland.
- Only 25 per cent of contracts is now competitively tendered, with 40 per cent being negotiated under various forms of partnering arrangements (others are either for their own development company or design and build).

Why was it successful?

Apart from the hard work put into implementing a focused plan of action, a number of other factors added to their success:

- The commitment and willingness of the directors to invest the necessary resources of time and money and to take a long-term view on the development of the company.
- The shared desire to 'professionalize' the company and change an image that they knew to be an unfair reflection of their work.

- The existence of good relationships with their staff and high staff loyalty, which created the atmosphere of trust necessary to the introduction of cultural change in the company.

Above all, the best marketing that any company can do is a job well done – on time, within budget and to the client's specification. The company recognized that they were already doing this but now made a virtue of it and enshrined it in their client-care policy. Satisfied clients will always come back and will tell others. Unsatisfied clients will tell even more: according to research, on average, eleven times more!

5

Marketing of civil engineering consultancies in the United Kingdom

Paul Macnamara*

Introduction

In 1981, Bell considered that marketing in construction organizations was in its infancy, reactive rather that proactive. However, since the period of recession of the early 1980s construction organizations have adopted more extensive and positive marketing. Consultant practices have had to become more market oriented due to the lifting of codes of practice to allow competition, the increasing involvement of overseas based consultants and the increasing use of non-traditional forms of procurement (Newcombe *et al.*, 1990).

In addition, when there was enough work for each company to share, long-term, steady and stable relationships between client and contractor were developed (Pettinger, 1998). Companies then focused on product and technological excellence, but now that is not enough. The attitude and understanding towards marketing appears to be changing.

Marketing

In addition has been defined in many ways. In terms of civil engineering consultancy services, 'marketing' and 'selling' can be described as those activities undertaken to get the opportunity to bid, and how the bid is delivered. Although Smyth (2000) considers there to be no common definition for marketing, the definition often adopted, by, for example, Newcombe *et al.* (1990), Pearce (1992, 1998), and Lancaster and Reynolds (1995), is that put forward by The Chartered Institute of Marketing (CIM).

> Marketing is the management process responsible for identifying, anticipating and satisfying customer requirements profitably. (CIM 2001)

* Halcrow Group

Pearce (1998) highlights the important messages in this definition: the 'management process' involves the way in which the firm operates, by 'identifying, anticipating and satisfying customer requirements', the focus is clearly on customer needs, and without operating 'profitably', the organization does not remain in business to satisfy its customer's needs. In addition, when considering 'customer satisfaction', it is also important to recognize this gaining of credibility and the building of a long-term relationship with the client, must be the primary concern of all staff (Pettinger, 1998).

Modern marketing is said to have begun in 1955 with Peter Drucker's statement, 'Marketing is the distinguishing, the unique function of business ... It is the whole business seen from the point of view of its final result, that is, from the customer's point of view. Concern and responsibility for marketing must therefore permeate all areas of the enterprise' (Drucker, 1955). This raised marketing to a position of paramount importance and launched 'marketing orientation', that is, viewing the business from the customer's standpoint and placing the customer at the very centre of an organization's endeavours (Brown, 1995).

An all-encompassing definition of marketing adopted here is, '*All activities involved in obtaining future work*' (Macnamara, 2002), from the strategic analysis and planning, to staff enthusiasm and performance, the service delivery and customer feedback.

Wilson *et al.* (1992) refers to research by Hooley *et al.* (1984), followed up by Lynch *et al.* (1988), which demonstrated that the more successful organizations had a stronger market-oriented culture with dominant attributes such as a greater emphasis on identifying and meeting customers needs, more aggressive, expansionist objectives, and longer-term marketing goals rather than short-term financial objectives. In such organizations, the chief executive sees marketing as guiding philosophy for the whole organization, and great importance is attached to marketing training.

The better performing companies demonstrated a consistent implementation through their focused marketing structures and systems. Marketing practice characteristics exhibited included, a greater input from marketing to the overall strategic planning, increased evidence of formal, long-term marketing planning and more aggressively specified marketing objectives. They were prepared to attack the whole market and take on any competition and were more prepared to take calculated risks. Also, superior quality, high-price positioning strategies were adopted, competitive advantages were built through reputation and quality, and they were more active in new product development to achieve market leadership.

Marketing of the construction industry

The construction industry has been slow to appreciate marketing as a tool to improve market shares, and sales or profitability. The principal reason for this was the fact that from the World War II until the Oil Crisis, in 1973, the industry was never really short of work. Only during the recession of the 1970s, with the fall in demand of the public and private sectors, the industry began to recognize the benefit of increasing marketing efforts (Hillebrant and Cannon, 1990).

With the recession of the early 1990s, companies were forced to review their marketing strategy; firms withdrew to their core business, leading to a simplification of their business and marketing strategy (Cannon, 2001). Since then, the construction environment has experienced increasingly rapid change.

Political changes include the growing internationalization, greater privatization, the independence of former public bodies, such as the water companies, and the affect in the market due to mergers and takeovers. There have been changes in legislation, planning guidance, a demand for greater accountability (Whitehouse, 2001), the Latham and Egan Reports, and a number of Government initiatives, 'to place business in a broader context' (ACE, 1999: p. 20). Such initiatives include, Our Competitive Future: Building The Knowledge-Driven Economy (1998), A Better Quality Of Life (1998), Towards An Urban Renaissance (1999), Modern Markets: Confident Consumers (1999) and Regional Development Agencies (2000).

The UK construction market accounts for approximately 10% of the gross domestic product (ACE, 1999), with a trend towards private funding of construction output (69% in 1998) and a small increase in new construction (52% in 1998) in comparison with repair, maintenance and improvement work. Changes in the UK economy are represented by a general growth in service industries in the South and a shrinking industrial economy in the North. Globally, the unprecedented events in the United States of 11 September 2001 have directly affected the financial sector and the airlines; this will have major consequences on the construction industry, in terms of funding and projects. Other changes include the decline in speculative building, demand for new offices and out-of-town retail developments, new methods of procurement, PFI, emphasis on whole-life costing, sustainability and partnering (Cannon, 2001).

The UK society is changing demographically; the country is getting older, with fewer young people. This will change demands, consumption and working patterns, for example, it may accelerate the return to home working. As technology grows there are changing communications and requirement/expectations (Cannon, 2001).

With the predicted 'slow on the horizon', the changing world of construction marketing must address a number of issues (Pratt, 2001). The world is becoming less predictable, necessitating greater flexibility, and increased globalization means more international clients. The business environment and communication channels are changing faster requiring more rapid responses, segmentation of clients is needed to appeal to their different needs, and retention is driven by client satisfaction. Other current issues include supply chain positioning, brand values, CRM, e-commerce and marketing metrics.

Although competition is now intense (Hoxley, 2000), marketing remains, in many cases, piecemeal among both contractors and consultants (Smyth, 2000). Smyth concludes that unless changes are made in the construction industry, of which marketing and selling are a vital part, 'the fragmented market will become tougher' (ibid., p. 32). There is a need for additional investment, a move away from the, 'accountancy mentality that marketing and sales are costs', and a better balance between short- and long-term investment (ibid., p. 385). It is now a time for trust and commitment, and suggests that marketing, in particular relationship marketing, builds substance into service, 'job satisfaction and character into the individual and the organization' (ibid., p. 386).

It is suggested that a paradox exists, as the functions of marketing, which require a strategic and analytical process, and sales, with its intuitive 'seat of the pants' approach, are often co-ordinated by the same person. However, since most people have not been taught to cope with this 'schizophrenia', one of these two approaches is neglected, and for cultural reasons this is likely to be marketing. While it is suggested that, 'It is time to move from sales to marketing' (ibid., p. 32), it is believed that marketing and sales activities are merging.

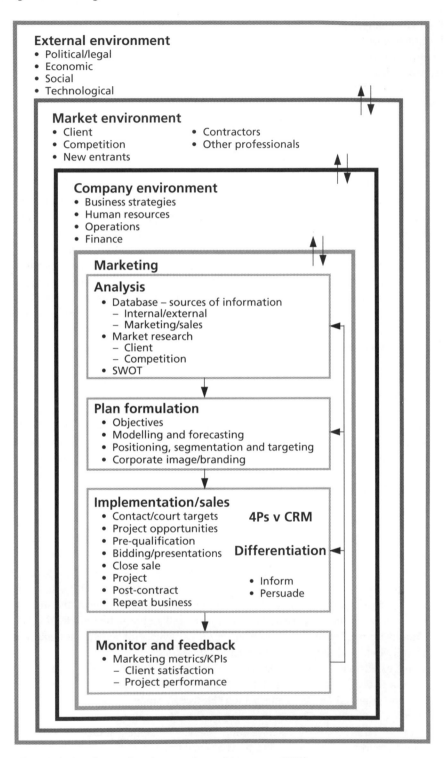

Figure 5.1 Marketing of an engineering consultancy (Macnamara, 2002).

Figure 5.1 (Macnamara, 2002) provides a model that illustrates how the marketing function operates in engineering consultancies, based on the work of Fisher (1986), Scanlon (1988), Wilson *et al.* (1992), Pearce (1992), Preece and Barnard (1999), Smyth (2000) and Collard (2001). It links the firm's marketing system, from the marketing analysis and planning to implementation and monitoring, to its environment, company wide, in the market place and nationally/globally.

Engineering consultancies and the changing client

The provision construction professional services is found to amount to £6 billions in 1999, being approximately 10% of the total construction activity, shared as shown in Figure 5.2, with engineering attracting 2.4 billions (ACE, 1999).

Although 93% of construction clients are not in the Construction Industry, they have become more 'sophisticated' (Newcombe *et al.*, 1990; ACE, 1999). They require that products and services that are delivered to time, budget and quality, work from day of handover, add value and reduce business risk (Williams, 2001). In addition, their expectations in terms of service quality (Pettinger, 1998), and their involvement in the procurement process,[1] have increased (Hoxley, 2000). The industry's performance has not been good: 70% of projects over budget, 73% delivered late, procurement has emphasized lowest price rather than long-term value, and contractors winning work on low price, recoup through changes, which leads to poor relationships (Whitehouse, 2001). The client must be confident in their construction investment. Egan (1998) stressed the need to focus on the end user, which clearly requires all in the chain to know 'who is the end user' (Pratt, 2001a), it is vital to understand what they do, what they want, what services they require (Crane, 2001).

Smyth (2000) highlighted client service expectations of consultants; these include, personal trust sought, understanding of the clients, common interests, reactive and spontaneous, and lack of tangibility. Specific areas where clients have reported dissatisfaction with consultants are their lack of understanding of client needs, lack of flexibility and innovation, and poor value for money.

Pettinger (1998) raises criticisms directed at all consultancy practices, not only in the construction industry, who are considered to be too prescriptive, operating without sufficient attention to the clients' requirements, and being too expensive which puts clients under pressure to accept recommendations. There is also the perception that clients tend to only hire consultants that will support their viewpoint.

'Marketing in all aspects of the construction industry is therefore concerned with mixing high levels of professional expertise and capability with the willingness to present these to the best advantage in terms of particular clients or client bases' (Pettinger, 1998, p. 237). Yet, construction is still perceived to be failing to meet the needs of modern businesses and rarely provides value for clients (Smith, 2001). This must be addressed especially as clients becoming more knowledgeable and well informed, better able to define their needs and more selective as to whom they award work.

Traditionally, professional firms obtained new work by being well known in the community (Pearce, 1992) and among their professional peers and not necessarily by making

---

[1] That is, rather than in a traditional contract where the architect or engineer acts as a surrogate client (Newcombe *et al.*, 1990)

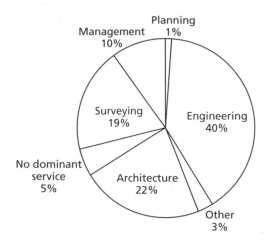

Figure 5.2 Share of construction professionals' fees (ACE, 1999, after Construction Industry Council, 1997).

overt approaches to potential clients. In fact, marketing was generally viewed with much scepticism (Scanlon, 1988).

A major change in the consulting environment was the abolition in 1982 of set fee scales[2] (Langford and Male, 1991) and the professional rules limiting consulting engineers from undertaking any blatant marketing practices (Pearce, 1997). This forced the consulting professionals to make strategic decisions concerning how to cope with the increasing competition and to consider how to respond to a changing business environment (Langford and Male, 1991).

The attitude and understanding towards marketing however, is changing; the 3rd International Conference was held in London, 2002, and there are now short courses for construction professionals (Thomas Telford, 1998, 2001; Madge Associates, 2002). Yet, when a client-oriented restructuring offering the client a 'one-stop-shop' should win the lion's share of the market, this has not occurred (Smyth, 2000).

A service, not a product

Engineering consulting is a professional service (Fisher, 1986) rather than a product and therefore cannot be marketed 'wrapped up' as a product (Forsyth, 1996; Young, 1998; Lovelock, 1999). Yet, services marketing is still considered to be a recent development that has not yet been fully embraced by UK professionals (Marshall and Murdoch, 2001).

Services are intangible, inseparable, variable, total and perishable. They are intangible as they cannot be seen, tasted, felt, heard or smelt before they are bought. Clients have to look for other signs and evidence of quality and value, for example, reputation, track record and prices charged. Services are inseparable as they are normally provided and consumed at the same time. The service provider has the capability to offer the service at all

---

[2] The Monopolies and Mergers Commission Report, in 1977, recommended that the mandatory fees set by the Association of Consulting Engineers (ACE) and the Royal Institution of British Architect be abandoned (Langford and Male, 1991)

times, but the only time it is delivered is when and where the client requests. Their variability stems from their being offered as generic but the nature, level, volumes and quality of the service will vary widely. There is also the totality of the service on offer and the totality of the service demanded by the client; the combination of expertise and support services provided, and the capability and willingness to tailor these to meet the demands of the client. Finally, as services cannot be stored or stockpiled they are perishable. They must be available when clients demand and if clients cannot, or will not, wait for the service provider, then they will go elsewhere and the opportunity is lost.

Marketing of a service must therefore be achieved through the corporate brand and building a strong reputation, the full understanding of the clients' requirements and the embodiment of the service experience, and the creation of tangibility, for example, the conduct and demeanour of the staff. The client must be guided through the process, the service delivered meets the clients' requirements, and a sense of value must be built through the creation of differentiation (Young, 1999).

It has been suggested that clients may place greatest emphasis on the more tangible areas of the service, such as office appearance, company vehicles, brochures and advertising material, as an indication of the service provider's business and ability to provide a quality service. However, it is has been found that for any consulting engineer to successfully market their services they provide they must be seen to produce quality service and drive for quality in all aspects of the business (Marshall and Murdoch, 2001).

Pettinger (1998, p. 140) summarizes this stressing that, 'The key to being an effective service provider lies in having high quality, expert, flexible and responsive staff'.

Construction marketing literature

While construction marketing is still considered to be only at an embryonic stage with very few academics working in this field, the industry is very interested in the subject and it would appear that the UK is leading the way in the research; this field is the focus of the CIB W065 Task Group 1 (Preece, 2001a; Bakens, 2001). One of the challenges is that while it is still difficult to define the 'product', it will be difficult to market. It was also recognized that the engineer is often too involved with the engineering to see what is it the client really wants.

There is, however, a growing understanding of this subject captured in literature. Much is aimed at the contractor rather than the consultant, with the occasional reference to the differences in attitude and approach between the 'mud on the boots' builder and the 'professional discipline' of the consultant (Fisher, 1986). Although the edges between these functions are beginning to become blurred (Pettinger, 1998), the marketing approach must therefore be different. The clients are different, indeed the contractor is often the consultant's client, and so the market is different, the culture is different, a design office background compared with a construction site, and the service is different, advice, information and design compared with the construction of the structure/works.

Marketing for the Construction Industry: A Practical Handbook for Consultants, Contractors and Other Professions (Fisher, 1986), aimed generally at the whole industry, was the first book to comprehensively consider the marketing of the construction industry, explaining the required client-focused approach of marketing and the benefits of an effective marketing strategy. *Marketing of Engineering Services* (Scanlon, 1988), provides practical guidance for consultant, contractor and public service civil engineers, discussing the different roles, future trends, the key results areas and marketing themes. He believes that, 'the need is not for marketing specialists, but for technical specialists with a high degree of marketing competence' (ibid., p. 70) developed by a change in attitude towards marketing, and both formal and experience training.

An Appraisal of The Marketing Development in Engineering Consultancy Firms (Morgan and Morgan, 1991), believed to be the first study to consider the marketing of engineering consultancy firms in the UK, was based upon previous studies undertaken by Morgan (1989, 1990) of other professional services. *Construction Marketing: A Professional Approach* (Pearce, 1992), and the papers for the Institution of Structural Engineers (1997) and The Chartered Institute of Building (1998) based on the book (1992), provides guidelines for all construction professionals.

Marketing Function in UK Construction Contracting and Professional Firms (Yisa *et al.*, 1995), covers survey of the UK construction and professional companies, aimed at certain strategic issues: marketing planning, organization of the marketing function, and resourcing. *Marketing for Architects and Engineers: A New Approach* (Richardson, 1996), states that, although architects and engineers, 'must develop a marketing agenda' to face the changes, challenges and increasing competition of the next century, their 'creative and visionary mindset' does not lend itself to traditional marketing methods.

Construction Marketing: Strategies for Success (Pettinger, 1998), is principally an introduction for students, covering client requirements, perceptions and values, an overview of marketing strategy, and focusing the market mix from a contractor's view point. *Report on the State of Marketing in UK Engineering Consultancies* (Preece and Barnard, 1999), proposed a Programme as a possible structure for a consultancy's marketing process, comprising five concentric activities focused on the targeted client, and describes the survey undertaken to test the proposal.

The ACE Client Guide 2000, was prepared with the principal purpose, 'to help the supply side understand their clients' business needs and equip to invest appropriately for current and future market developments and take advantage of emerging opportunities' (*ACE Guide, 2000*) provides a background to the engineering market, current trends, government initiatives, and a wealth of further sources of information. *Marketing and Selling Construction Services* (Smyth, 2000), which emphasizes the client interface, highlights research, 'that the most critical activity in winning a major project is developing person-to-person relationships with potential clients'. The book is aimed at the senior management of larger contractors undertaking major projects, yet the consultant is also well documented. It is stressed that although in theory and in practice marketing and selling are distinctive, they must be seamless to be effective in practice.

Winning New Business in Engineering Consultancy … the Critical Success Factors (Harris, 2000), details the research undertaken to establish the critical success factors in developing new business. The study compares attitudes and practises between different professional consultancy services, and between engineering consultants of different bid conversion rates. *Effective Marketing of Civil Engineering Consultancies in the United Kingdom* (Macnamara, 2002), reviews the current literature and with reference to a case study undertaken, concludes that the environment in which engineering consultancies operate is increasingly competitive, success and its measurement is becoming more clearly defined by Key Performance Indicators (KPIs), and although marketing is becoming formally adopted by many engineering consultancies, this is primarily by the larger organizations.

The most common theme of all the literature is the need for an organized, client-focused approach to marketing, selling client satisfaction. The benefits of an effective marketing strategy are increased profits, reduced uncertainty and generation of new business (Fisher, 1986). Scanlon (1988) covers the importance and benefits of marketing, and the necessity for a strategic, structured approach and how it can be achieved in civil engineering.

Pearce (1996) describes how the importance of marketing is slowly growing in the construction industry with the realization that its principles can be applied to this industry. Although, traditionally, the professional marketed its services by building relationships within clients and professional circles, given the intense competition, marketing requires a strategy, relationship marketing, the creation and maintenance of mutually beneficial, trusting relationships between supplier and customer.

The slow uptake of marketing stems from a perceived clash with professional ethics, and a belief that by simply providing a better service, 'the world will beat a path to the door' (Fisher, 1986). In addition to their 'creative and visionary mindset' struggling with traditional marketing, Richardson (1996) believes that the greatest barriers to the adoption of marketing by architects and engineers are resistance to cultural change, misperceptions and misunderstanding, and the reluctance to adapt to social and economic changes.

Pettinger (1998) raises a number of different issues to be reconciled when the consultant presents its service to the client. The distinctive high-quality professional expertise has to be presented without appearing to be too specialized or compartmentalized. The presentation of desired qualities of dynamism and responsiveness must be without being too generalist and 'all things to all people (and therefore nothing to anyone)'. The ability to adapt both expertise and flexibility to any situation must not appear to be too bland or prescriptive.

By focusing its marketing activities, a firm can protect its existing customer base and win new client business. This can be achieved through the proper understanding and management of the client base, and in enabling the tailoring of corporate messages, this would improve the chance of winning work and the profitability of that work (Smith, 2001).

Construction marketing theory

The marketing process proffered by Smyth (2000) follows the same general pattern as that of Wilson *et al.* (1992). It is considered that, 'information is the lifeblood of effective marketing' (Bullock, 2001), and should permeate all areas of a firm's business and marketing activities (Fisher, 1986). Market research helps build this information so that the organization can understand how the market works and is performing, identify marketing opportunities and formulate its marketing plan (Fisher, 1986).

Pearce (1992) and ACE (1999) in particular provide a wealth of sources of information on clients, competitors, government initiatives, market trends and potential work. This information must, however, be meaningful and stored in a manner that it facilitates retrieval (Scanlon, 1988; Pearce, 1996; Bryans, 2001).

A thorough understanding of the whole environment (Figure 5.1) is vital; the scrutiny of the information gathered and its assimilation to feed into the formulation phase. This analysis includes the history, changes, trends, demands, constraints and key influencing factors with regard to external PEST factors, the construction market, the clients and competition, and the business itself (Fisher, 1986; Scanlon, 1988; Pearce, 1992; Pettinger,

1998; Cannon, 2001). A popular technique used to undertake this assessment is SWOT analysis; see Wilson *et al.* (1992).

Marketing Plan Formulation is the next stage in the procedure to establish 'where do we want to be?' (Wilson *et al.*, 1992) which this direction will originate in the business plan, and how to achieve them. This involves the consideration of different options and an assessment of which options to adopt.

Richardson (1996) proposes the use of a combination of scenario planning and synthesis marketing. Scenario planning is, according to Schwartz (1992), 'the art of the long-term view', a method for dealing with uncertainty and a common element of successful practices. The advantages of using scenario planning over traditional marketing and planning methods being that it (Richardson, 1996):

- Provokes more options and possibilities than would have been revealed
- Encourages imaginative and creative thinking
- Highlights interconnections, which may not have become evident
- Facilitates later decision making by 'crossing many bridges' earlier in the process
- Helps identify critical success factors.

Richardson states that synthesis will shape marketing in the twenty-first century rather than traditional analysis, and suggests that successful strategies will be based on:

- A synthesis of social, cultural, economic environmental factors
- A demonstrable ability to bring things together and manage a wide variety of project elements
- A clear articulation of the benefits of intangibles such as design quality and purpose.

Strategic mapping is then recommended to identify strategic options available and to map options over the duration of each scenario plan. The strategic preference is then translated into a synthesis-marketing programme.

In starting with the business objectives, Smyth (2000) develops a model that identifies the six basic market positions as shown in Figure 5.3. It is suggested that consultants will tend towards positions E and F, where selling is through non-company networks, reputation is a 'key plank', the client wants the involvement of senior personnel, and selling is through technical and professional means, demonstrating the most appropriate solution. The value orientation, from Practice to Corporate, is the primary driver of the organization; the emphasis is either on being 'professional', or on competent and effective performance, to achieve financial success.

The model adopted for growth will depend on the market position; expansion in existing markets, market penetration, expansion in new markets, service differentiation, and expansion by takeover or merger. Research highlights that many organizations believe that service differentiation in existing markets and diversification into new markets is currently seen as the appropriate approach. This approach requires detailed marketing analysis of the market position, segmentation and client targeting; this means investment (ibid.).

Segmentation is the division of a business into manageable parts where each part has a strong client-group focus (Scanlon, 1988), the purpose being to understand the nature of that particular segment of the market, its needs and wants, so that the capabilities of the business can be presented to take greatest advantage (Pettinger, 1998). Table 5.1 shows a segmentation matrix for consulting engineers.

**Technology and
methods**

	A	B
Routinized	Low risk	Medium risk
	Low profit margins	Low profit margins
	High turnover	High turnover
	High market share	High market share
	Medium competition	High competition
	Separate sales function	Separate sales function
	Medium potential for repeat business	Low potential for repeat business

	C	D
Analytical	Medium risk	Medium-high risk
	Average profit margins	Average profit margins
	Average turnover	Average turnover
	Average market share	Average market share
	Low-medium competition	Medium competition
	'Door-opener' sales function	'Door-opener' sales function
	High potential for repeat business	Medium-high potential for repeat business

	E	F
Innovative	Medium-high risk	High risk
	Medium-high profit margins	High profit margins
	See-saw turnover	See-saw turnover
	Low market share	Low market share
	Low or no competition	Low or no competition
	No separate sales function	No separate sales function
	Low potential for repeat business	Low-medium potential for repeat business

Paternal/practice   Corporate

Value orientation

Figure 5.3 Typical key features of marketing positions (Smyth, 2000).

Table 5.1 Outline market segmentation (Scanlon, 1988)

Client groupings	Service offerings				
	Engineering design	Preparation of bids	Resident engineer	Feasibility studies	Multi-client reports
Public sector ● Government agencies ● Local government ● Specialist authorities					
Private sector ● Mining and resources ● Energy and utilities ● Manufacturing ● Retail and distribution ● Transportation					
Consortia ● Design and construct ● Investment					

Following segmentation, the procedure is continued to breakdown, in a similar manner, on the selected segments to clearly identify target companies and/or projects (Lancaster and Reynolds, 1995).

All organizations have an identity, 'whether they recognize it and whether they like it or not' (Fisher, 1986). Marketing has the role of creating and projecting an organization's image, that is 'truthful, appealing, unique, and consistent with reputation' (Scanlon, 1988). The image can be projected as the 'brand', representing recognizable products/services, it conveys what the company does and symbolizes and standardizes expectations, and guarantees satisfaction. Successful branding provides market penetration, profit, communications, staff/recruitment, quality/standardization/reduced systems costs and work (Marsh 2001).

Brand is especially important when selling a service; 'marketing must help manage your brand to support your organization's position in its chosen markets' (Williams, 2001). It must also be dynamic and as the organization grows and transforms, it is important that the image develops abreast with these changes (Pearce, 1992; Gospel, 2001).

In considering marketing implementation and sales, Smyth (2000) states that the service offered must provide added value, that being the sum of knowledge, expertise and relationship value, the unique combination of these features creates the unique selling proposition (UPS). Harris (2000) stresses the need to differentiate the company and its services to win the opportunity to bid to work. In the increasingly competitive market, 'being the same is not good enough' (Crane, 2001).

The concept of the market mix and the 4Ps is outlined in Wilson *et al.*, and covered comprehensively by Pettinger (1998). The strategic approach of the market mix is explained and compared extensively with that of relationship marketing by Smyth (2000), who concludes that the latter is more appropriate for contracting and consultant services (Figure 5.4). The market mix is considered to be inappropriate as the *product* is an intangible service, influenced by market position, service quality and specific added value, *place* is irrelevant, *promotion* remains relatively under-explored, leaving *price* as the only

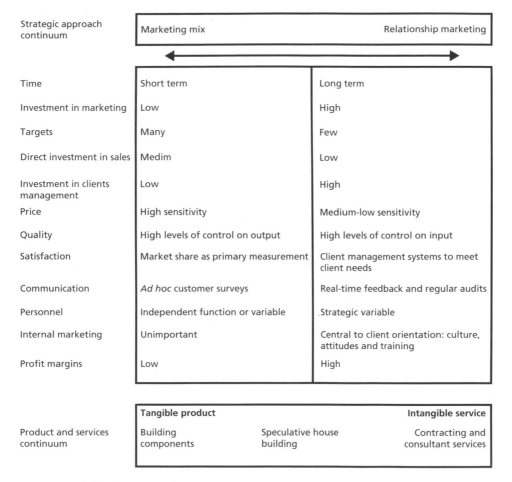

Strategic approach continuum	Marketing mix	Relationship marketing
	←	→
Time	Short term	Long term
Investment in marketing	Low	High
Targets	Many	Few
Direct investment in sales	Medim	Low
Investment in clients management	Low	High
Price	High sensitivity	Medium-low sensitivity
Quality	High levels of control on output	High levels of control on input
Satisfaction	Market share as primary measurement	Client management systems to meet client needs
Communication	*Ad hoc* customer surveys	Real-time feedback and regular audits
Personnel	Independent function or variable	.Strategic variable
Internal marketing	Unimportant	Central to client orientation: culture, attitudes and training
Profit margins	Low	High

	Tangible product		Intangible service
Product and services continuum	Building components	Speculative house building	Contracting and consultant services

Figure 5.4 Idealized conception of marketing theory (Smyth, 2000).

dominant variable, although this is a complicated issue, inextricably linked quality and service.

Key characteristics of a relationship marketing approach are an understanding of the client business, the understanding client needs, the development of close relationships, inducing trust, the delivery of promises and giving satisfaction, fostering of loyalty and hence repeat business (Smith, 2000).

The relationship marketing model, which provides the, 'linkage between perceived value and resultant relationship profitability' (ibid., p. 193), is shown in Figure 5.5. Built on vision, expectations, authority and trust, relationship marketing is a more appropriate approach to sales, as the management process to secure competitive advantage.

Pearce (1997) refers to Kotler's suggested steps to establish a relationship marketing programme (1994). Key customers are identified as meriting relationship marketing, and a skilled Relationship Manager with a clear job description is then assigned. An overall manager is appointed to supervise the Relationship Managers and to prepare the long-range and annual customer-relationship plans.

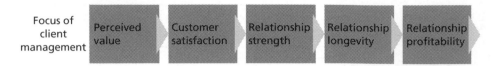

Focus of client management

Perceived value → Customer satisfaction → Relationship strength → Relationship longevity → Relationship profitability

Figure 5.5 Pipeline of relationship marketing management (Smyth, 2000).

Smyth (2000) emphasizes the importance of robust sales systems, including strategies designed for specific market positions and segment, systems established from top-down, and feedback systems to ensure that the marketing plan and sales practice evolve dynamically and appropriately for the market and organization.

While it is believed that sales are 'alive and well', marketing is frequently carried out in a limited and fragmented fashion due to self-imposed constraints due to attitude and thinking, low levels of creativity, lack of management understanding, and limited range of promotional tools. Harris (2000) emphasizes the need to get close to the client, to understand what is really required by the client/project, and the criteria used by the client in assessing bids.

Bidding involves both tangible skills and soft skills, including creativity, to develop a solution, to understand an issue and its influencers, and an organization, to empathize/to see and feel from the client's perspective, to communicate, to inform and convince, problem anticipation and problem resolution (White, 2001). The bidder must understand the clients: the needs and drivers, the constraints within their business and within their industry, the internal and external influences, and the processes. What the client needs, in general terms, is quality, service, comfort, cost, time and value, in specific terms:

- A building which gives investors confidence
- Achieve planning permission in high-profile location
- Handover of completed project on time
- Maximize benefits of whole estate
- Demonstrate adherence to cultural agenda
- 99.99% resilience
- A building which demonstrates financial clout
- Deliver increased capacity
- Rationalization of several sites into one
- Community acceptance
- Minimal interaction with facility during occupation

The bidder must gain an understanding of the clients' selection criteria. The ACE Guide points to specific competence, availability of key staff, 'make up' of team, creative input, methodology proposed, general reputation, financial stability and price.

It is important to manage the bidding processes; this requires leadership, management and ownership to establish responsibilities, and a programme for the tasks and activities. The use of checklists is recommended (ibid.) for compliance and for protocols, in terms of bid budget, approvals and reviews, and forms; a suggested framework for the proposal includes:

- Technical proposal
- Fee bidding

- Delivery
- Negotiations
- Project resourcing
- CV management
- Presentations
- Learning

The structure of the proposal must demonstrate, in a clear and logical manner, that the bid is both compliant and client-focused. This should include details of the understanding of the requirements, the proposed approach to the project, the team and its experience, and the proposed basis for fees. The drafting and presentation should:

- Be reader friendly
- Use graphic presentation
- Be consistent use of names, tense, layout
- Propose solutions not only identify problems
- Use of standard forms
- Be persuasive
- Use proposal vocabulary
- Communicate your understanding of key issues
- Show 'why this team'

Once the project is won, its execution must be aimed at client satisfaction and post-project contact maintained to continue the developed relationships and ultimately obtain repeat business. This 'aftercare' is perhaps a particularly neglected area (Preece, 2001a).

Scanlon (1988) provides practical guidance on the promotional activities, presentations and submissions, and Pearce (1992) takes 'getting the enquiry' to 'getting the contract'.

As the external, market and company environments are dynamic, plans must be keep current by monitoring performance and feeding this back into the marketing information, analysis (Fisher, 1986) and the 'Where are we now?' (Wilson *et al.*, 1992). Monitoring must be undertaken consistently and regularly, covering all major areas, both quantitative and qualitative including organization targets (business and marketing plans), sales targets for segments and niches, account-handler targets and satisfaction targets (Smyth, 2000).

A particularly subject for an engineering consultant is the success of bid delivery; this must be reviewed on completion to understand reasons for the outcome and to establish the lessons for why the bid was whether won or lost; the main aspects to consider are technical, management, communication, and the cost/price. The review can point to opportunities for the future and gives vital market information; this learning must be shared (White, 2001).

Performance analysis has historically focused on financial measures and business growth (Scanlon, 1988). With the increased recognition that construction has been failing the client, emphasis is now being placed on client satisfaction which has culminated in KPIs developed from Egan (1998). The 'softer' marketing metrics must, however, be fully understood and appreciated by the organization's board (Pratt, John 2001).

Client satisfaction can be measured using the KPIs and the SERVQUAL model and can help improve results and directly assist in ISO 9000 success (Pratt, Jennifer, 2001; Marshall and Murdoch, 2001).

The adoption of marketing by engineering consultants

The extent to which engineering consultants have embraced a marketing-oriented approach has been assessed in research by Morgan and Morgan (1991), Yisa *et al.* (1995) ACE (1999), Preece and Barnard (1999), Harris (2000), Marshall and Murdoch (2001), and Macnamara (2002).

In 1991, Morgan and Morgan found that, although there was limited marketing organization, those firms that had adopted such an approach were set to develop or at least maintain their marketing structures. Preece and Barnard established that in 1999, it was mainly the larger companies have a greater formalized marketing function, although as the size of the firm increased some felt that centralized marketing department was too distant so the marketing efforts were dispersed to, 'allow greater focus, while maintaining contact with other marketing personnel to maximize the use of combined knowledge and ideas' (ibid., p. 15).

Yisa *et al.* (1995) reported that that the majority of contractors had a structured marketing department headed by a marketing executive, whereas most consultants and architects had a partner/director managing the marketing function in addition to other responsibilities. Yisa *et al.* and Preece and Barnard (1999) also showed that few consultants employed individuals with marketing qualifications.

Similarly, marketing planning was found by Yisa *et al.* (1995) to be more important to contractors than to consultants and architects. The responsibility for marketing plans in contracting organizations, where the marketing tended to be more formalized, was found to lie with the marketing function whereas greater responsibility for marketing plans rested with the managing directors/partners of the consulting and architectural firms. Contractors also had longer-term marketing plans, while almost half of the consultants did not plan beyond year-one and a quarter did not have any marketing plan.

By 1999, Preece and Barnard found that 84% of consultancies had established company objectives, 74% of firms had developed a formal marketing strategy, and 58% had produced formal marketing plans. All of the large and major firms (see Table 5.2 for size categories) had developed a formal marketing strategy, compared with only 43% of the medium-sized and 80% of the small companies. Even in accounting for difficulties in guaranteeing a direct comparison, this is still a very significant increase from 1991.

In considering the use of marketing information, Morgan and Morgan (1991) revealed that only a quarter of the respondents had a market research unit and, when frequency of use of certain types of marketing research was considered, were surprised by the high incidence of firms never using these marketing research activities. It was concluded that the use of marketing information was uncoordinated, and this remains the case (Yisa and Egbu, 2001).

Preece and Barnard discovered that marketing analysis was far more developed by 1999. The large and major companies used use the SWOT technique regularly, particularly to

Table 5.2 Size of companies interviewed (Preece and Baynard, 1999)

Number of qualified engineers	Size category	Number of companies
1 – 29	Small	5
30 – 199	Medium	7
200 – 1199	Large	4
1200 +	Major	3

develop marketing plans and strategies, while the small and medium companies tended to only use it to focus on a specific problem. This difference in approach by the smaller firms was attributed, to be in part due to reduced resources, but also to the likelihood that managers were in closer contact with company performance due to its reduced size and complexity.

All companies were found to undertake some form of market analysis, such as existing market sectors, the amount of work in theses sectors, and client profiles. The finding that more firms analysed potential markets than those examining their existing markets was considered surprising; it was suggested that more effort was expended on potential markets due to difficulties in obtaining reliable information on markets in which they did not currently operate. There was found to be little formal competitor analysis, most companies taking a 'keep an ear to the ground' approach rather monitoring activity in journals, financial performance, tender lists or communication with relevant people.

In terms of annual marketing expenditure as a percentage of annual turnover, Yisa *et al.* (1995) found that while most contractors and architects spent less than 2% on marketing, half of consultants spending between 3% and 7%, although this point is not drawn out in the report. Conversely, Preece and Barnard (1999) found that the total expenditure on marketing activities was, however, almost completely unknown.

With regard to marketing communication, while most consultants were registered with national registration systems such as Constructionline, few maintained contact/client databases providing, 'more informed communications and more accurate targeting of materials' (ibid., p. 22).

Popular marketing strategies for increased market share were found by Morgan and Morgan (1991) to be new service development in existing markets and development of new markets with existing services. The specific marketing strategies highlighted as very important (Figure 5.6) were professional reputation and technical service excellence, as well as the image of the firm and personal staff contacts. The level of fees was also considered important; it was noted that the then recent introduction of fee competition was making a significant impact on marketing strategies.

However, promotional literature was thought to be less important, and advertising was not considered very important by any consultant. Morgan and Morgan commented that when

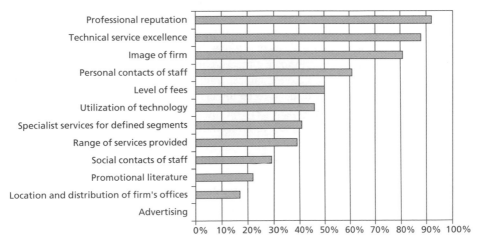

Figure 5.6 Elements of marketing strategy (Morgan and Morgan, 1991, reproduced with permission from Taylor & Francis Ltd, http://www.tandf.co.uk/journals).

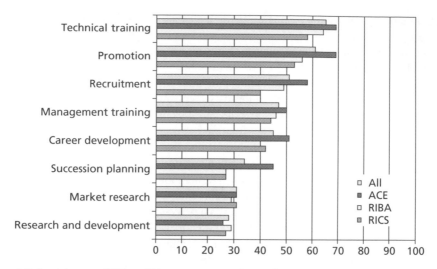

Figure 5.7 Special responsibilities within construction profession firms (ACE, 1999).

firms clearly wanted to raise awareness of their professional image, reputation and technical service excellence, why was so little attention given to marketing communications strategy?

Preece and Barnard (1999) concurred with the findings that the people factor has the greatest importance in terms of staff competence and suitability, suggesting that, 'staff are the greatest assets' (ibid., p. 17), and highlighting the significance of recruitment, staff motivation, promotion and training. Reputation with both clients and the other construction team members was considered very important to consultants, with awards and service quality and journal items to support this. Similarly, while promotional material was tailored by most firms to the individual clients, to provide the client with information specific to their requirements and to give confidence to the client of the understanding of their specific needs, advertising was considered very unimportant with many undertaking limited or no such activities. However, articles in journals, recruitment advertisements and the Internet, three quarters of companies having a web site and the remaining planning to develop one, were seen as useful methods of advertising the firm.

Another survey, by the ACE (1999), considered a number of issues including, services provided and used, the contribution made by professionals, different methods of the procurement of professional services, and performance measurement. When considering inward investment, there was a clear emphasis on technical training due to the nature of the business (Figure 5.7). Promotion was also found to be important, whereas functions such as market research and research and development were far more limited; ACE suggests that the small and medium sized firms were less likely to invest in resource-intensive, non-core activities.

Morgan and Morgan (1991) deduced that marketing was becoming considered as a 'legitimate' management function within some firms, although there is evidence that that the 'trappings' prevail rather than the 'substance'. Marketing information needed to be coordinated and communications strategies developed; there are also cultural barriers to overcome. It was concluded that market-led and customer-driven orientations are fundamental to the implementation of the marketing concept.

By 1995, Yisa *et al.* had established that marketing had become a top management priority, all respondents practicing some form of marketing, either formally or not, and

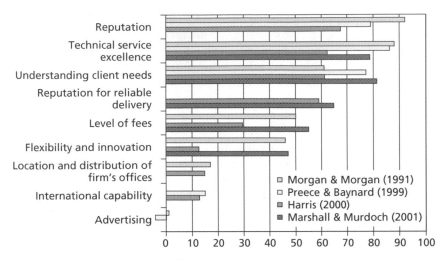

Figure 5.8 Comparison of the importance of different consultancy activities/features (Macnamara, 2002).

investing in marketing, 'a very considerable amount when one considers that fact that the profit margining low in the UK construction business' (ibid., p. 32). However, the marketing function lacked proper planning and control, with most consultancies managing the marketing function as a secondary responsibility by a director or partner, with non-formal marketing plans, monitored on an *ad hoc* basis.

Preece and Barnard (1999) considered that the size of the consultancy had a major affect on its marketing activity. Larger consultancies had a more developed marketing function although required more complex communication and information management systems, whereas the smaller firms tended not to undertake a formal marketing management process which it was suggested would, 'provide structure and improve the efficiency of the whole marketing process'. Smaller firms often adopted an alliancing approach to overcome drawbacks associated with finance, resources and previous experience in such firms, see Hill and Wright (2001).

Company size also affected their marketing environment attracting both advantages and disadvantages: smaller businesses provided a more personal service for clients, though this may be limited geographically due to financial and resource restrictions, while larger companies could provide a wider range of specialisms although communication and management became more complex as a consequence.

With reference to Figure 5.8, although is it clear that reputation, technical excellence and client relationships are still the most important aspects of the consultants' service, the emphasis is clearly shifting from the former to the latter; compare Morgan and Morgan (1991) with Marshall and Murdoch (2001). There is still little value given to advertising, yet Smyth (2000) considers that there is great potential.

Consultancy performance and measurement

With the growing dissatisfaction of the UK construction industry (Whitehouse, 2001), there have been a number of initiatives over the last few years to promote change, and tools and issues central to the development of the industry (ACE, 1999). The three key bodies in the process of this change are the Construction Industry Board (CIB), original centred on the recommendations of the Latham (1994), the Movement for Innovation (M^{4}I), which focused on the performance targets of the Egan (1998) and the Construction Best Practice Programme (CBPP), established to assist the construction industry and clients identify routes for best practise development, supporting the adoption and maintenance of a best practice approach (ACE, 1999).

Egan (1998) stated that, 'The industry must replace competitive tendering with long-term relationships based on clear measurement of performance and sustained improvements in quality and efficiency'. Macnamara (2002) considered the degree to which engineering consultancies monitor their performance is assessed, methods to establish the level of success are reviewed, and factors considered 'critical to success' (Harris, 2000) are analysed.

In 1991, Yisa *et al.* found that monitoring was only considered in terms of the evaluation of marketing activities, with few consultants supervising their marketing programmes. Preece and Barnard (1999) assessed marketing management and control in greater depth, establishing that some form of marketing management control was undertaken by most firms. Client assessment of performance was undertaken by half of firms during the contract and by most after completion. This was usually established through interviews aimed at obtaining a more open and honest response to form a basis for improvement. Other methods of monitoring performance included project evaluation, generally done informally, and quality assurance, including complaint procedures, although this was not found to assist consistency of service to the client.

Other areas of performance reviewed to lesser extent included profit, marketing or business plans, and project enquiries received in terms of repeat business, and marketing channels effectiveness and conversion rate. To determine an organizations level of success, company performance has not only to be monitored, it must be compared with that of the competition. Benchmarking has been the only method of formal competitor analysis adopted to any significant degree (ACE, 2001, 2002), although this was found to be generally only undertaken by the larger companies (Preece and Barnard, 1999).

In 2000, Harris undertook a survey to establish the 'critical success factors' in developing new business for engineering consultants. The study was part of a larger project considering professional consultancy services, the others being accountancy, advertising, management consultants, IT/communications consultants, marketing and public relations consultants, and solicitors. Respondents were divided into two categories: the most successful, 'those that win more than half of their pitches to bid for new business', and the least successful, those that do not.

The results from these two categories were compared to establish differences in approach; Figure 5.9 shows that only 20.2% of consultancies fall into the 'successful' status. The survey covers many different dimensions of business performance and marketing, yet the key to the measurement of success is only based on success in bidding; this emphasis is also opposed to the direction recommended by Egan (1998) that promotes long-term relationships rather than competitive tendering.

Therefore, although bidding performance is acknowledged as important in developing new business, this gauge of overall 'success' is considered too narrow. Other factors must include financial status, quality of staff and client satisfaction. The ACE (2001, 2002) sets out KPIs and Additional Indicators (AIs), of which bidding success is only one, developed

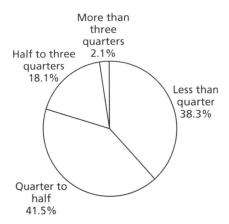

Figure 5.9 Proportion of successful pitches for new work (Harris, 2000; policypubs@kbnet.co.uk).

from Egan (1998) by the ACE, RIBA and RICS, with support of the UK Government, the ICE and the Construction Industry Council.

The principal focus of the ACE KPIs is on client satisfaction; the ability to meet the project elements of value, time, quality and health and safety awareness. The other KPIs relate to company performance, in terms of training (days per FTE employees), productivity (value (£) added per FTE employee), and profitability (pre-tax profit as a percentage of turnover). The AIs also centre attention on client satisfaction, considering speed of response, overall capability, technical innovation, understanding clines need and the identification of problems, along with fee bid performance and percentage of repeat business.

These indicators are then plotted on charts to establish a benchmark score, and then this score is plotted on the KPI radar chart. The nearer the plotted line is to the outer perimeter, the higher the overall performance. Consultants are encouraged to repeat the process regularly with the aim of prompting action for improvement, 'doing more than just keep pace with its peers'.

It is considered that the KPIs form a particularly useful structure to determine a firm's success, highlighting the critical factors and providing direction for improvement.

Success factors

The ACE Client Guide (1999) was prepared with the principal purpose, 'to help the supply side understand their clients' business needs and equip to invest appropriately for current and future market developments and take advantage of emerging opportunities'. Surveys were undertaken to establish clients' perceptions of consultants' roles and performance compared with those of the consultants; the three principal themes to arise from these surveys were:

- *Procurement:* the need was identified for fewer interfaces in the supply chain, integration of design and construction, closer working between all suppliers, single point responsibility, and teams that understand their culture and their customers

- *Performance:* the emphasis is on improvement, which therefore necessitates 'robust and consistent mechanisms', and introduces the Business Excellence Model, KPIs, and Benchmarking
- *People*
- *Employees:* there are 1.4 million people employed in the UK construction industry; these people 'need to be nurtured by the construction industry if it is to improve its image and its long-term prospects', based on shared goals, culture, learning, effort and information
- *Everyone else:* effective marketing is considered vital, yet 'is not particularly widespread among firms of construction professionals'; customer focus and an understanding of clients' businesses, cultures and their customers' needs is essential

The ACE survey concluded by considering the development of the client/consultant relationships, and issues to be addressed. A comprehensive list included the requirement for construction professionals to develop their companies as businesses and, in so doing, increase profitability and attract and retain high calibre personnel, focus on clients' needs and understand clients' business drivers. To achieve this there is a need to be prepared to take responsibility, to minimize the impact of construction on clients' businesses, to predict and forecast changes in workload, to seek new opportunities and invest in marketing.

In the Harris report (2000) undertaken to establish the 'critical success factors' in developing new business for engineering consultants, it is clear that all firms focus primarily on the growth of profit, Figure 5.10. However, there is major difference between the two different success groups in terms of staff utilization and development, and entry into new markets and increased penetration into existing. Harris concluded, 'it pays to be a good employer'; having highly motivated staff helps build and maintain a strong reputation. It is interesting to note that these two issues feature as company KPIs; training, profitability and productivity (ACE, 2001, 2002). Harris also suggested that the more successful companies are more adventurous and eager to pioneer into new areas of the market.

Whilst it was found that all consultancies relied heavily on existing clients for new work, this was notably greater for the more successful companies. There was also a larger difference in terms of frequency of receiving business from previous clients and referrals from

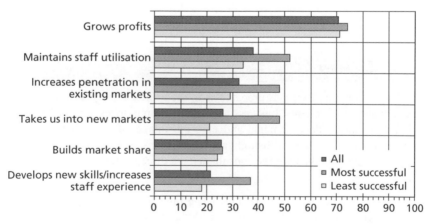

Figure 5.10 Reasons considered very important for developing new business (Harris, 2000; policypubs@kbnet.co.uk).

clients. Harris suggested that the variation could be due to a distinction in quality of service and individual relationships; these elements also feature as the principal KPIs of client satisfaction, and the AI of repeat business (ACE, 2001, 2002). The most successful firms used specific marketing activities as a good source of new work at 33% compared with 22% of the least successful companies.

It was concluded that, with regard to the research into the development of new business, the key actions were:

- Start differentiating from the start
- Activate your contacts network
- Focus effort where it counts
- Understand your market
- Listen to your clients
- Develop strong client relationships
- Fuse leadership and commitment.

In considering winning an invitation to bid, the areas of attracting invitations to bid and issues relevant to winning new opportunities to bid were analysed. Figure 5.11 shows that all firms rate image and reputation very highly, and although the quality and experience of their people was also important, it was held greater by the most successful consultancies. Other significant issues were relationships with clients, reputation for reliable delivery and track record in similar projects. These factors are covered by the AIs featured in ACE (2001, 2002).

Although fee levels were a notable factor, they were not such a major issue for the most successful consultants. Harris made no comment on this specific contrast, however, the research had shown that engineering consultancies in general considered fee twice as important as the other surveyed professionals did, suggesting that clients of the engineering consultancies were tougher on fees due to a greater tangibility of the results of their work. Another interesting issue was the large difference in the attitude towards having expertise in the client's area of business. It was put forward that the least successful firms were more risk averse, whereas the other group were more willing to consider work outside of their traditional area, hiring expertise as necessary.

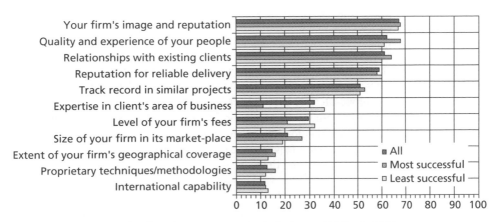

Figure 5.11 Issues considered very important attracting invitations to bid (Harris, 2000; policypubs@kbnet.co.uk).

The issues of greatest relevance in winning bid invitations were, not surprisingly, the development of personal industry contacts/networking, which was particularly so for the most successful firms, and the seeking new projects from existing clients. Although marketing materials and the monitoring potential clients were adopted by many companies, they were considered less important, with other marketing activities, such as cold calling, advertising and sponsorships, were though to be of little real value.

Harris concluded that the key points for securing the opportunity to bid included:

- Differentiate your consultancy
- Enhance your reputation
- Value your contacts
- Upgrade your marketing materials
- Keep networking
- Investigate the Internet

When selecting the best prospects, key issues were found to be the potential return from the project, type of project, relevance of own skills and risk, especially with the most successful firms. Areas attracting less import to the most successful firms included size of client, prestige of the competitors and the cost of making the bid. Reasons for declining invitations to bid were conflicts of interests with existing clients, doubts about client/project ethics and concern about project risk.

Having won the opportunity to bid, the factors considered in making the bid were the consultants' understanding of the client, communication with the client,[3] and the construction of a winning team. It was found that the most successful firm were significantly more satisfied with their level of understanding and communication with the clients, although this level was not particularly high suggesting an area where there is much room for improvement.

There was much more accord between the most and least successful firm when building the winning team. The only major difference was the emphasis placed on the leadership from the senior partners/directors, demonstrating commitment to the project at the top level.

The key points regarding preparing the bid included:

- Focusing on the client
- Establishing a dialogue
- Fostering teamwork
- Using existing knowledge
- Selling the individual.

Finally, both of the groups were generally in agreement regarding the important issues in making a bid proposal. The inclusion of the senior partner/director in the team and the provision of a detailed proposal, were very important, along with factors relating to the support of visual aids, notes and rehearsals for the presentation, and the selection of the team members. Then when in the negotiation stage, there was also concurrence, with the principal points were having clear position on fees, service guarantee, the development of good relations, and giving confidence regarding timescales.

---

[3] The validity of the questions regarding 'communications' must be queried, as discussion with the client during the tendering period often forbidden.

In concluding, Harris proposed ten key principals established from the study; the most successful consultants:

- Get it right from the start
- Work to differentiate themselves at every stage of the bid process
- Build client relationships more effectively
- Treat their contact network as organic rather than static
- Work harder at understanding and communicating with the client
- Make every opportunity to bid count
- Recognize that business development is a skill in its own right
- Recognize that winning new business is a 'means to the end' of creating the kind of consultancy they want to be
- Put the client at the centre of the universe
- Work smarter at the negotiating end-game.

Marshall and Murdoch (2001) also undertook research, using the SERVQUAL model proposed by Parasuraman *et al.* (1991), to determine key success factors by analysis which issues were most import to the client, in terms of tangibles, reliability, responsiveness, assurance and empathy. The results were analysed to determine the relative importance placed the five dimensions of service quality, and the most important aspects used to judge the quality of service (Figure 5.12). Reliability, the ability to perform the promised service dependably and accurately, was clearly of most importance while the tangible aspects were of little importance. This is also in accord with the ACE KPIs (2001, 2002), matching reliability with the client satisfaction KPIs relating to project performance, and responsiveness, assurance and empathy with all of the client satisfaction AIs. The results were also compared with those of Parasuraman *et al.* (1991), to discover a consistency of trend; Figure 5.12 incorporates these findings.

Marshall and Murdoch extended the survey to considered other aspects covered by the ACE Client Guide (1999), which were beyond the scope of the SERVQUAL model. Although it is clear from the results that delivery to the promised date is very important to the client, more so than delivery to budget or value for money, the greatest importance is placed on technical ability and requirement to understand the clients' needs. In this

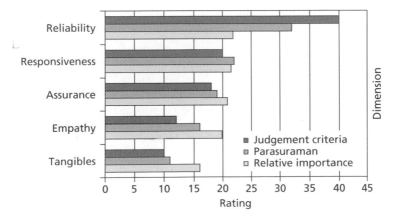

Figure 5.12 Service quality dimensions (Marshall and Murdoch, 2001).

Figure 5.13 Importance ratings for aspects of service provided by the consulting engineer (Marshall and Murdoch, 2001).

instance, the client satisfaction KPIs were relegated below the AIs of technical innovation and understanding client needs.

There are, therefore, notable differences; Figure 5.13 shows the client's requirement of understanding is highest, whereas Figure 5.12 indicates that empathy is not rated to the same degree, and yet Figure 5.13 demonstrates that technical competence and delivery to time are ranked second and third when Figure 5.12 clearly illustrates the importance of this reliability.

Marshall and Murdoch state, in terms of the marketing mix, it has been suggested that productivity and quality are one element of the mix, however, that the provision of quality is interlinked with the other elements of the service marketing mix. 'The customer's expectations and perceptions of quality are formed by the interaction of all elements of the mix. The elements of the mix affect the expectations of quality in different ways and to differing extents.'

It is important to fully absorb Marshall and Murdoch's conclusion that for any consulting engineer to successfully market their services they provide they must be seen to produce quality service and drive for quality in all aspects of the business; 'The essence of service marketing is services. When the product is a performance, nothing is more important than performance of quality' (ibid., after Parasuraman *et al.*).

It is clear therefore that the KPIs (ACE, 2001, 2002) are in accord with the findings of ACE (1999), Harris (2000), and Marshall and Murdoch (2001). It is also transparent that the Harris gauge of success is insufficient, as 'success' is more than bid performance.

The KPIs do not focus on any specific marketing activities but facilitate long-term relationships through client satisfaction; success can only be achieved by providing a quality service consistently across all measures of performance.

Conclusions and recommendations

Consultants traditionally obtained new work through professional relationships. More recently, consultants have had to cope with increasing competition, especially since the abolition of set fee scales, yet marketing remains piecemeal. This reluctance to embrace marketing stems from a perceived clash for professional ethics, and a resistance to change. Engineering consultants most recognize that they provide a service, rather than products, so their marketing must reflect this by building a strong reputation, creating tangibility, ensuring delivery of a quality service that meets the client's requirements, and demonstrating real value.

It has been highlighted that the benefits of an organized, client-focused approach to marketing have been defined as increased profits, reduced uncertainty and the generation of new business. The more successful organizations have a stronger market-oriented culture with dominant attributes such as an emphasis on customers needs, more aggressive, expansionist objectives, longer-term marketing goals, and the importance attached to marketing training.

Although there is a movement away from competitive tendering, bidding remains particularly important. This process has been described highlighting that it is essential to understand the client, the project requirements, and the selection criteria; a well managed approach and structure is strongly recommended. As the marketing function is organic, it must be continually nourished with feedback in terms of financial results, bidding successes, client satisfaction, and lessons learnt.

The model proposed by Macnamara (2002), outlines the marketing structure of an engineering consultant, linking its relationship with the national/global, market and business level environment, with that of the strategic marketing functions of analysis, planning, implementation and monitoring.

It has been established that the marketing process has become far more formalized in engineering consultancies, particularly in the larger companies. The small to medium organizations, which could particularly benefit from the discipline introduced through a formalized marketing approach, have yet to appreciate the need and are reluctant to invest in non-core, resource-intensive activities. The recruitment and retention of well-trained and highly motivated staff is very important; 'it pays to be a good employer'.

There is still little value given to advertising, yet this is an area of great potential; marketing communication is vital to raise awareness of professional image, reputation and technical service excellence.

The KPIs set out by the Association of Consulting Engineers (2001, 2002), developed from Egan (1998), focus on client satisfaction, in terms of project elements of value, time, quality, and health and safety, and the company performance metrics of profitability, productivity and training.

Factors found to be particularly important to the success of an engineering consultancy include:

- A fundamental understanding of their clients' needs and business drivers built on long-term relationships
- The ability to recognize opportunities and predict workload changes based on well coordinated information systems and analysis
- A strong image/reputation and differentiated services founded on demonstrable quality
- Focused and well-organized bidding and negotiation
- Highly skilled and motivated staff
- Clear business objectives and effective business management.

The fact that the first four of the above are principally marketing functions is stressed.

Bid performance alone is deemed insufficient as a gauge of success. It is proposed that a more appropriate gauge of success should include for growth, profit and client satisfaction, as encapsulated in the KPIs. Nevertheless, Harris has provided a very useful insight into the adoption of marketing activities and areas of strengths and weakness in the marketing of the profession.

Work is not awarded for 'good marketing' *per se*, yet marketing is the function that manages the client relationships, develops and conveys the corporate image, and provides the monitoring, information, analysis, and therefore, evidence to demonstrate quality.

The principal recommendations are that since effective marketing promotes success, it should be embraced by all; long-term relationships should be developed and maintained, with existing clients, potential and within the industry.

There is evidence that bid preparation can be improved by adopting a more structured approach, with set timetables to allow communication with the client and for checking. It is also recommended that KPIs should be adopted throughout the profession, as a consistent measure of performance for clients and to highlight areas for improvement for the organizations.

References and Bibliography

Association of Consulting Engineers (1999) *The ACE Client Guide 2000* (London: Thomas Telford).

Association of Consulting Engineers (2001) *Striving for Business Excellence: A Handbook of Performance Indicators for Construction Consultants* (London: ACE).

Association of Consulting Engineers (2002) *Achieving Business Excellence: A Handbook of Performance Indicators for Construction Consultants* (London: ACE).

Bakens, W. (2001) CIB and re-engineering. In: Preece, C. (ed.) *2nd International Construction Marketing Conference: Academic Proceedings 2001*.

Bell, R. (1981) Marketing and the larger construction firm. *Occasional Paper No. 22*. Englemere, Ascot: The Chartered Institute of Building.

Brown, S. (1995) Life begins at 40? Further thoughts on marketing's 'mid-life crisis'. *Marketing Intelligence & Planning,* **13** (1), 4–17.

Bryans, A. (2001) Effective database implementation and use. In: Preece, C. (ed.) *2nd International Construction Marketing Conference: Academic Proceedings 2001*.

Bullock, D. (2001) Information is the lifeblood of effective marketing. In: Preece, C. (ed.) *2nd International Construction Marketing Conference: Academic Proceedings 2001*.

Cannon, J. (2001) Formalized research improves the strategic thinking process. In: Preece, C. (ed.) *2nd International Construction Marketing Conference: Academic Proceedings 2001*.

Chartered Institute of Marketing (2001) (Online) Available at http://www.cim.co.uk/libinfo/index.htp (accessed 3 September 2001).

Collard, P. (2001) An introduction to strategic marketing planning. In: Preece, C. (ed.) *2nd International Construction Marketing Conference: Academic Proceedings 2001*.

Crane, A. (2001) Welcome and introduction. In: Preece, C. (ed.) *2nd International Construction Marketing Conference: Academic Proceedings 2001*.

Drucker, P. (1955) *The Practice of Management* (London: Heinemann).

Egan, Sir J. (1998) *Rethinking Construction* (HMSO).

Fisher, N. (1986) *Marketing for the Construction Industry: A Practical Handbook for Consultants, Contractors and Other Professions* (London: Longman).

Forsyth, P. (1996) *Marketing Professional Services* (London: Pitman Publishing).

Gospel, J. (2001) Global re-branding – challenges, adventures & results. In: Preece, C. (ed.) *2nd International Construction Marketing Conference: Academic Proceedings 2001*.

Harris, N. (2000) *Winning New Business in Engineering Consultancy ... the Critical Success Factors* (Bedford: Policy Publications in Association with the Association of Consulting Engineers and the University of Luton).

Hill, J. and Wright, L.T. (2001) A qualitative research agenda for small to medium-sized enterprises. *Marketing Intelligence & Planning*, **19** (6), 432–443.

Hillebrandt, P.M. and Cannon, J. (1990) *The Modern Construction Firm* (London: Macmillan).

Hooley, G., West, C. and Lynch, J. (1984) *Marketing in the UK – A Survey of Current Practice and Performance* (Cookham, Berks: Chartered Institute of Marketing).

Hoxley, M. (2000) Are fee tendering and construction professional quality mutually exclusive? *Construction Management and Economics*, **18** (5), 599–605.

Kotler, P. (1994) *Marketing Management*, 8th ed. (Prentice-Hall International).

Latham, Sir M. (1994) *Constructing the Team* (HMSO).

Lovelock, C., Vandermerwe, S. and Lewis, B. (1999) *Services Marketing: A European Perspective* (London: Prentice Hall).

Lynch, J., Hooley, G. and Shepherd, J. (1988) *The Effectiveness of British Marketing*. University of Bradford Management Centre.

Macnamara, P. (2002) *Effective marketing of civil engineering consultancies in the United Kingdom*. Unpublished MSc dissertation, University of Bath.

Marsh, C. (2001) Value propositions in the construction industry. In: Preece, C. (ed.) *2nd International Construction Marketing Conference: Academic Proceedings 2001*.

Marshall, G. and Murdoch, I. (2001) Service quality in the marketing of consulting engineers. In: Preece, C. (ed.) *2nd International Construction Marketing Conference: Academic Proceedings 2001*.

Morgan, N.A. (1990) Marketing in UK accounting firms. *Service Industries Journal*, **10** (3), 599–613.

Morgan, N.A. (1989) *Marketing – UK Law Firms*. Cardiff Business School Working Paper in Marketing and Strategy, 1989/1.

Morgan, R.E. and Morgan, N.A. (1991) An appraisal of the marketing development in engineering consultancy firms, *Construction Management and Economics*, **9**, 355–368.

Newcombe, R., Langford, D. and Fellows, R. (1990) *Construction Management 2: Management Systems* (London: Batsford).

Pearce, P. (1992) *Construction Marketing: A Professional Approach* (London: Thomas Telford).

Pearce, P. (1997) Marketing professionally. *The Structural Engineer*, **75/1** (7 January 1997).

Pearce, P. (1998) Marketing construction. *Construction Papers No. 94* (Englemere, Ascot: The Chartered Institute of Building).

Pettinger, R. (1998) *Construction Marketing: Strategies for Success* (Basingstoke: Macmillan Press).

Pitcher, M. (2001) Understanding your customers' needs. In: Preece, C. (ed.) *2nd International Construction Marketing Conference: Academic Proceedings 2001*.

Porter, M. (1980) *Competitive Strategy* (New York: Free Press).

Pratt, John (2001) Ten points from today for action tomorrow. In: Preece, C. (ed.) *2nd International Construction Marketing Conference: Academic Proceedings 2001*.

Pratt, Jennifer (2001) Measuring customer satisfaction. In: Preece, C. (ed.) *2nd International Construction Marketing Conference: Academic Proceedings 2001*.

Preece, C. and Barnard, L. (1999) *Report On The State Of Marketing In UK Engineering Consultancies*. Construction Management Group, School of Civil Engineering, University of Leeds.

Preece, C. and Male, S. (1997) Promotional literature for competitive advantage in UK construction firms. *Construction Management and Economics*, **15**, 59–69.

Preece, C. (2001a) Academic forum. In: Preece, C. (ed.) *2nd International Construction Marketing Conference: Academic Proceedings 2001*.

Preece, C. (2001b) The benefits from academic research for construction marketing. In: Preece, C. (ed.) *2nd International Construction Marketing Conference: Academic Proceedings 2001*.

Richardson, B. (1996) *Marketing for architects and engineers: a new approach* (London: Spon).

Scanlon, B. (1988) *Marketing of Engineering Services* (London: Thomas Telford).

Schwartz, P. (1992) *The Art Of The Long Term View*. Century Business.

Smith, K. (2001) Building relationships, building success. In: Preece, C. (ed.) *2nd International Construction Marketing Conference: Academic Proceedings 2001*.

Smyth, H. (2000) *Marketing and Selling Construction Services* (Oxford: Blackwell Science).

Thomas Telford (1998) *Improve Your Profession By Effective Marketing*. Course notes.

Thomas Telford (2001) *Selling Skills Workshop*. Course advertisement. (Online) Available at http://www.t-telford.co.uk/HTML/ (accessed 14 November 2001).

White, S. (2001) Success through bidding. In: Preece, C. (ed.) *2nd International Construction Marketing Conference: Academic Proceedings 2001*.

Whitehouse, M. (2001) Modernising construction. In: Preece, C. (ed.) *2nd International Construction Marketing Conference: Academic Proceedings 2001*.

Williams, A (2001) The general challenges UK construction marketeers face today. In: Preece, C. (ed.) *2nd International Construction Marketing Conference: Academic Proceedings 2001*.

Wilson, R., Gilligan, C. and Pearson, D. (1992) *Strategic Marketing Management* (Oxford: Butterworth-Heinemann, in association with the Chartered Institute of Marketing).

Yisa, S.B., Ndekugri, I.E. and Ambrose, B. (1995) Marketing function in UK construction contracting and professional firms. *Journal of Management and Engineering*, 11 (4), 27–33.

Yisa, S.B., Ndekugri, I.E. and Ambrose, B. (1996) A review of changes in the UK construction industry. Their implications for the marketing of construction services. *European Journal of Marketing*, 30 (3), 47–64.

Yisa, S.B. and Egbu, C. (2001) Improving marketing skills, Competence and innovations through knowledge management. In: Preece, C. (ed.) *2nd International Construction Marketing Conference: Academic Proceedings 2001*.

Young, L. (1999) *Services Marketing* (Reading: Chartered Institute of Marketing Meeting).

PART 2

Tools and techniques

6

Customer relationship management

John Pratt*

What is CRM

For many marketers who have been around for some time, customer relationship management (CRM) is a bundling together of familiar marketing techniques. There are two drivers that have given CRM particular impetus. Firstly, there is the power of data warehousing to hold information that enables these techniques to be used. Then, more importantly, the need for such analysis and decision-making has increased as competitive forces have turned many markets into commodities, where the buyer has a wider choice and is less loyal. The objectives behind implementing CRM should be to manage the relationships with customers in such a way that it delivers more value to the enterprise. This is spelt out by Prof. Adrian Payne (from CRM, CBI November 2000), 'CRM is concerned with the creation, development and enhancement of individualized relationships with carefully targeted customers and customers groups, the desired results being to maximize the total customer lifetime value.'

An overview

There has been a lot of hype about CRM but do people in the construction industry really understand what it is? Patently not! Although research like that done by Cap Gemini found that 65% of companies were aware of CRM and its benefits, many fail to take advantage of them. With the cost of retention, one-sixth of the cost of winning a new customer, we should all be planning how to get closer to our best customers.

Why CRM is important

With the intensity of competition in the industry and globalization, using the information about your customers effectively will have a significant effect on a company's profitability.

* Leading Edge Management Consultancy

However, the crucial word here is effectively. The information needs to be analyzed to give a deeper understanding of how customers think. Then those that think in a similar way can be grouped together and your product or service offering can be shaped to meet their needs. This is simple marketing theory. It might identify, for example, which contractors want to buy cheap, which clients need helping through the process and which consultants want fast information at their fingertips. Then the way you handle these groups can be planned and your pricing strategy can take account of these needs.

Segmentation powers real CRM

However, it seems, that according to anecdotal evidence in the UK, even with sophisticated CRM software working out the segmentation of the customers is too difficult. The more popular 'old-economy' view of CRM is still to some extent database enabled, but the accent is on the word *relationship*. This makes it more like a cousin of key account management, where the relationship with selected customers is structured around a segmentation strategy and objectives. This drives the scale and level of contact management. And it is preceded by an in-depth analysis of how customers want their relationship with their supplier to work. At the end of the day, facilitating better relationships is what CRM is all about.

Software enables CRM

The tag CRM is confusing because it has come to mean different things to different people. It is heavily promoted by the software industry, which is selling big systems with a running cost of typically $15–30 million per annum. The CRM software market is worth around $7 billion, and Cap Gemini Ernst and Young reckon that 74% of European companies either have or are in the process of implementing CRM. The pitch was that you could identify the customers who gave you profitable business and so direct your marketing effort to win more from them.

The key areas served by the software products are:

- Customer service and support, enabling companies to manage incoming queries, orders and complaints from customers over a variety of channels like telephone, fax and e-mail
- Marketing automation, managing the outgoing promotion of goods and services to customers
- Sales force automation, enabling an organization's sales people to manage their contacts, schedule appointments, and identify and respond to sales leads
- Customer analysis to provide data analysis facilities.

CRM success is hard to achieve

However, in practice it appears that very few such systems have delivered on the promise. Research by the Gartner Group (*Marketing*, November 1999) concluded that in some CRM sectors, up to 65% of projects failed to deliver and many over-ran or came in over budget. Research by vSente suggests that 80% fail to meet expectations and Forrester

Research in the USA suggests that companies are using it tactically and failing to achieve the return on the enormous investment. Specifically there is a lack of co-ordination and structure in many organizations' approach to CRM.

The CRM-Forum (www.crm-forum.com) undertook a survey in 2001 in conjunction with the CRM Institute of the University of Strathclyde and Caledonia Business School. The report is called, 'Improve the ROI of CRM: A Report of the Factors Impacting on the Success and Failure of CRM Projects.' It was based on a survey of CRM-Forum members in 2001, with over 700 respondents. It examines the factors which impact the success of CRM projects from the perspectives of companies implementing CRM, consultants supporting those projects, and companies supplying software products and other products and services to the CRM industry.

The report concludes that companies think their CRM projects are significantly less successful than either consultants, or suppliers, do. The report says, 'Assuming that the companies implementing CRM have the more realistic view, this seems to imply that consultants are seriously under estimating the lack of success of their CRM projects. We find this rather disturbing and it has to raise the question as to whether the consultancy companies, and particularly the Big 5, are successfully supporting their clients in the implementation of CRM programmes. At its worst, one has to wonder whether or not they are part of the problem. Of course, the gap is usually even wider when one considers the suppliers' understanding of success, but to a certain extent this is less worrying. We know that the supplier of a software product has a vested interest in the success of the use of his product and we accordingly adopt an attitude of 'caveat emptor' in our dealings with them.'

But how do you start the process of managing better customer relationships and what are the implications for the construction industry? An audit of current practice and efficiency would be the first step leading to a strategic view of how to move forward at a scale and level appropriate to your business needs.

Find out in the next section how to find out who should be your target customers.

The issues

In the previous section, we looked at what CRM is. Here, we are looking at beginning the process. We see CRM as an over-arching concept which creates the platform on which you can build a customer focus programme within your organization. For many organizations, however, large complex software systems can sometimes get in the way rather than help. It is the philosophy of putting 'customer' information at the heart of the business is fundamental. The key to this is knowing what information you need to manage and what processes to put in place.

The construction industry has special needs

Customer relationship management came into being as a natural extension of contact-tracking systems, based on relational databases. From a construction industry viewpoint, the simplest contact management systems cannot handle the complexity of the supply chain, where there are a large number of participants. Typically, if you are a contractor or materials supplier, you will want to find the most active architects working in your area; then you will want to find the other projects that they are working on, then the QS's working on them – and so on. So, system selection is an issue if you want to be sure that you can capture and manage the contact and project data that you need.

Collecting the right data

With any such database, there is a huge onus on collecting data and keeping it clean. Salesmen are notoriously reluctant to input all their customer knowledge, with many still believing that it is their own intellectual property and that it enhances their worth to the company. So there may be issues to be overcome, especially if a call centre takes on part of their role.

I have worked with many clients to help them make better use of their customer data. For example, you can use sophisticated software tools to analyze it for trends and segmentation. This can cover the market size, growth and project characteristics and customers' buying behaviours. What is it that spurs a customer to buy your particular product or service? You may think it is because of your superior customer care and the image of the product, but perhaps it is just because of a small detail you could not predict. To be sure, you have got to get inside their minds – to understand what motivates them, which shapes the way they behave, so that you can harness this.

For example, at the simplest level, some customers are willing to be serviced by a 'call centre', which can reduce the sales costs, but others demand that a representative calls. This is a simple view of the differences that exist and the scope for cost saving. But getting it wrong could lose you business. Specific analysis techniques can take the guesswork and risk out of this. I would strongly endorse research to collect quantitative data and qualitative data for analysis using clustering software, like SPSS. If you classify the qualitative responses, it is usually possible to find three or four segments of customers who are driven by the same needs, behave in the same way and will respond to specific offerings from you. It is a matter of looking at the way that your customers buy rather than just what they buy. Sophisticated clustering analysis can enable you to re-define your markets into new logical segments of customers that can be targeted according to their specific needs.

Segmentation is the first step, so that marketing messages and service offerings are tailored towards the different buying behaviour of different segments. Knowledge of the customer is everything. Anyone buying into CRM needs to really understand how it can be used to integrate sales and marketing before spending serious money on software.

In addition, the CRM data warehouse should contain market data from other sources. For example, planning application information can reveal architects' and contractors' market shares and how much each of them is winning. This is vital marketing knowledge, to find out who is letting most work and, therefore, the contacts that are crucial to business development. This helps to identify which sectors and which customers to target.

Then there are straightforward marketing techniques for prioritizing customers according to both their potential and the competitive issues involved in winning more of their business.

It is worth mentioning that eCRM that can change the paradigm. The customer enters their own information, and if your offering is compelling, they will keep it clean for you, by making changes to their personal information. You may be able to obtain better quality data on the customer this way. However, while this is fine for consumers (the financial services market has mopped it up), it is less likely to be cost effective in a business to business, or a construction market context.

Using CRM to target segments

You could, for example, target opportunities in sectors that are growing, before your competitors get to know about them. The crucial step is to review what service level is appropriate to each customer segment and review the resources committed to them – whether it's a call centre, technical support or field sales. You should certainly set realistic individual short-term targets for the split of sales calls for each territory and customer segment.

Issues may surround the purpose, size and shape of the sales organization. Misconceptions, bad design or even bloody-mindedness, can disconnect it from being part of a CRM project. So preliminary research and analysis to segment the customer base and establish what their service needs are is the first step. Find out in the next section how to approach the full implementation.

How to approach the implementation

Should we really sack customers if they are not profitable or retain them if they are profitable and then have other products or services 'cross-sold' to them? This appears to be the CRM software vendor's concept. But the marketer's way of looking at customers is as partners in a long-term relationship, which means not exploiting them. It is more about how you relate and deal with customers (to understand how you can meet more of their needs), not how you sell more to them. It is the difference between push and pull. Excessive push can drive your other customers away. But loyal evangelists can spread the word for you. Customer retention and loyalty should be key metrics, as well as sales volume.

CRM hinges on the customers' motivations and behaviours

The data has to have enough detail on behavioural and motivational issues, so that you can marry the customers' needs to your offerings for the product/service. Groups with common behaviour patterns can then be targeted together, so that you can identify the needs of those for whom you have a suitable offering. The acid test for segmentation is if you can define and describe the customer segments easily, so that you can classify all your customers in this way.

Deciding how to analyze CRM data

On-going analysis can be a real issue. A sales force with antennae tuned to the market will understand what is going on, but to expect the same recognition of signals through analysis of customer data derived from an eCRM system is hopelessly optimistic, unless there are sophisticated metrics on the key drivers of business. Selecting the variables to measure is all-important, although on the more highly specified systems, the 'analytics software' is getting easier to use.

The behavioural issues of why people buy from you are as important as what they buy and when. No one in the insurance industry thought you could sell insurance over the phone but then came Direct Line. No one thought you could sell building materials over the Internet, but look at Screwfix. It won e-tailer of the year at the Retail Week Awards 2002. The judges, fifteen high-profile business and media personnel from the retail industry, felt that the Screwfix Direct website, Screwfix.com, combines 'a vast inventory with a high degree of usability' and was making the most headway in a highly competitive retail environment.

The claimed benefit of CRM is improved efficiencies, less complaints from customers and the right hand knowing what the left is doing. But getting CRM to work for you depends on having a pragmatic view of what it can do for you, not a gigantic wish list, which will never be fulfiled. A simplified approach may be less risky, but it still means that management may have to define some processes to be simpler and match the IT capability.

Get your needs sorted before plunging in

The confusion surrounding CRM is because it has grown from simple contact management systems to all-singing, all-dancing large systems, leading to the mistaken belief that it is the answer to everything.

The key lessons of users are:

- Do you really need the 'full-house' solution or are you seeking just some of the benefits
- Do some analysis of the customer base to segment it first
- Get the buy-in of employees
- Go for a modular solution that is scaleable
- Start small and grow on the back of extra revenue generated
- Do not hand over your business to self interested software vendors and IT consultants.

Using independent advice

Customer relationship management failures have all the hallmarks of the dotcom failures – companies and their bankers have been seduced by promises that are unattainable. Whatever level you are at in the CRM game, the chances are that you can always do it better and you could easily do it worse. So, are you prepared to take the risk of moving forwards without independent advice?

The CRM-Forum survey concludes that, 'Companies undertaking major CRM programmes, might well find it valuable to take a leaf out of the oil industry's approach when building offshore oil platforms. Oil companies do appoint an "implementation contractor" to take responsibility for the building and hook-up of the oil platform, equivalent to the role the Big 5 play in building and system integration of major IT environments. However, the oil companies also appoint independent "project engineers" to monitor the development of the project, to keep the project vision alive, and ensure the earliest possible delivery of oil (ROI) from the platform. Those project engineers do not come from the implementation contractor. Independent CRM practitioners with experience of delivering the business benefits from CRM, and sufficient understanding of IT to monitor the detailed technical implementation could play a similar role in CRM programmes.'

The decision-making process

The key to successful CRM implementation depends on two things. Firstly, recognizing that apparently similar customers may behave in different ways according to their culture – so, segmenting them is necessary, but not easy. It requires data on soft, behavioural issues as well as the regular classifications of size, sector, SIC code, etc. Secondly, with such a high failure rate and high cost, you need to go into this with a well thought through plan and a high level of preparation, before even thinking about potential consultants and vendors of CRM systems.

The headlong rush into new CRM systems was driven initially as a by-product of IT departments facing up to Y2K compliance problems. But with the ensuing lack of success, it is clear that marketers need to be driving the process, to ensure that customers are put at the focal point. There will be many vested interests from field sales, call centres, IT and finance departments, each with its own way of working and own systems. This means that you have to take a holistic approach – it is not a bolt-on situation or a quick fix.

CRM – the decision points

So, as a marketer, what decisions have to be taken? The following journey list is put forward more as a menu, than as a serial process to be followed. It all depends where you are on the journey; different companies will be at different points (Table 6.1).

How does CRM sit with your brand values

The impression left with the customer from CRM activity can impact heavily on the brand. The 'brand' is not just the name and logo of the organization, but in modern marketing terms is thought of as more like the impression left behind after any contact with the company. It is, therefore, dependent on a whole range of variables that are involved in each customer transaction with the business.

Customers and prospective customers rely on experience and their often long held attitudes about a brand. These are developed from their experience of dealing with the organization, however, remotely. Their attitude can be expressed simply as a set of adjectives that describe the 'brand values' that the company stands for in their eyes. It is important that the contact and transactions with customers is sufficiently good that it will enhance the brand values of the whole enterprise. It is all too easy for a failure, like failing to carry out a promise, i.e. a breach of trust and certainty, to create a dissonance, which erodes the brand. The implication of this is that all CRM activity should be designed within the framework of the brand values that the organization aspires to.

CRM has to live the talk

Brands used to be the preserve of consumer goods manufacturers, but today even the smallest construction organization must be aware of the value of their brand image – for this is how clients see you. The company's brand values should set the operating style for

Table 6.1 The CRM implementation checklist

Decision point	Action
How does the concept of and competencies required for CRM sit with the company's brand image and culture	Define brand values and assess staff and customers' perspective of brand image. May need external help with this
Create a climate for acceptance of CRM	Communicate intent internally, form steering group of internal stakeholders chaired by marketing function
Decide how to segment customers according to their service needs	Survey customers and analyze to identify groups who want to be treated similarly. May need external help with this
Evaluate the value of different customer groups	Identify profitability and loyalty of segments
Define the customer data needed and what it will be used for	Specify all the fields needed to define the customers and manage all communications/ transactions with them
Decide how to service different customer segments	Create an outline marketing plan for each segment
Resolve the issues of who owns the customer contact	Consult with internal stakeholders, hold workshops with them and establish ground rules. May need external help with this
Evaluate the implications for optimizing business development, marketing and other customer service in a customer-relationship focused way	Review the resources and organization appropriate to the new CRM environment. Plan how to introduce change. Run re-skilling training workshops
Decide how to prioritize customers according to appropriate criteria	Define methodology for prioritizing according to scale of opportunities and other criteria
Plan the resources needed	Review the resources appropriate to the new CRM environment
Write a brief for a system provider	Prepare an outline brief of how customer relationships are managed and operated, including field lists
Find suitable systems for the construction industry	Specify the particular requirements of the industry
Decide how to populate with clean, appropriate, vital, data	Establish how to clean the data and who is to do it initially and then ongoing. And prevention of data collection for its own sake
Write the CRM sales and marketing action plan	Develop the marketing plan to show all the campaigns and ongoing activity logs, with briefs, responsibilities and timeframes
Define the customer touch points where data can be collected continuously	Identify how the customer can interact with the system to provide self-cleaning and engage with the organization
Treat the web as an integral channel for CRM	Review how the web can be used as a channel and prepare a brief for the web master to implement change
Ensure all databases are co-ordinated and synchronized – in real time	Cover this as part of the CRM system brief
Achieve organizational change to leverage efficiencies/effectiveness of the CRM system/ culture	Consult with staff, prepare job descriptions, use workshops and counseling to introduce change. May need external help with this
Train customer facing staff to recognize which segment a customer fits into	Use training workshops to 'up-skill' staff and provide scripts, templates. Set performance targets. May need external help with this

(*continued*)

Table 6.1 *continued*

Decision point	Action
Define the data sets and reports needed to measure and control CRM	Establish reporting levels and criteria
Keeping ahead of the game. These segments are a snapshot today	Develop a plan to regularly check whether these segments are still relevant and monitor where and when customers needs change (remember Direct Line). May need external help with this
The next stage to NPD	Now it's up, developing a process to develop new ideas, products and services for your current segments or moving into new ones. May need external help with this

the organization in all its customer facing activity. You only have to look at an untidy disorganized building site, a mucky building materials lorry or be played 'Greensleeves', while being kept on hold by the switchboard, to know how it can affect a company's brand image. The difficulty is that, while a great deal of effort has to go into creating a brand, it can be destroyed very quickly. For that reason, every brand should have a brand strategy that is communicated and lived throughout the organization. That means defining what your organization is doing to support these brand values and understanding what it is doing to destroy them.

The trick for CRM is to find out what features and benefits members of the target segment want, make sure the product, or service, has them and then communicate it in a way that enhances the brand. So, we find, for example, that being fair and honest with customers is not only CRM, but part of branding as well. The two are inextricably linked.

Chapter summary

1 Marketers should exert leadership of the project to represent the customers.
2 Engage with all the other stakeholders to get their 'buy-in'.
3 Take a holistic view of CRM as it affects all parts of the business.
4 Learn from the experience of others who have not achieved success – define success and bear in mind that vendors and the implementing consultants will have an optimistic bias.
5 Spend time planning how the system is to be used to identify all the consequences for the organization and to prepare a tight brief for the vendor and consultants.
6 Opt for a scaleable solution that you can manage, consider whether you need all the 'bells and whistles'.
7 Make sure that the way you treat customers meets your brand values.
8 Recognize that successful CRM is more about understanding customer motivations and behaviours than IT. Research them first before designing the system.
9 Make sure that you understand what all the different eCRM, web and other CRM products can do.
10 Ensure that all customers are treated in accordance with the organization's brand values.

Further reading

Harvard Business Review on Customer Relationship Management. *Harvard Business Review*, 1 January 2002.

Don Peppers, Martha Rogers. (January 2002). *The One to One Managers: Real-World Lessons in Customer Relationship Management* (Peppers and Rogers Group).

Merlin Stone, Bryan Foss. (1 July 2002). *Successful Customer Relationship Marketing* (Kogan Page).

Simon Knox, Lynette Ryal. (27 June, 2000) Customer relationship management. *Financial Times* (Prentice Hall), Paperback.

Zingale, A, Matthias Arndt. (30 June 2001). *New Economy Emotion: Engaging Customer Passion with eCRM* (John Wiley and Sons Ltd).

Tony Cram. (23 November, 1994) Relationship marketing. *Financial Times* (Prentice Hall).

7

Customer care

Christopher Preece* and Krisen Moodley*

Introduction

Organizations in construction have been slow to develop customer- or client-care programmes, which may provide a number of important benefits. It may help to differentiate them from the competition in highly competitive markets, improve perceptions of their clients and their professional advisors, increase client satisfaction with the services provided, encourage loyalty and create a reputation for being a caring and client-orientated organization. Internally, the construction company may benefit from improved staff morale, increased employee participation and foster internal customer/supplier relationships.

By introducing a client-care programme, a construction organization may bring about continuous improvements to the operations of the organization.

Focusing on the customer/client

The 1980s saw an increase in interest in customer care in the UK. Organizations found it increasingly difficult to differentiate their products and services from those of their competitors. Consequently, excellent service to the customer became a way of seizing a competitive advantage. Companies can confront their competition better if they can move from a 'product' and 'selling' philosophy, to a 'customer' and 'marketing' philosophy. They can win customers and outperform competitors by doing a better job of meeting and satisfying customers' needs.

It is from this need to focus more upon the customer or client that the interest in Total Quality Management (TQM) has grown. In comparing customer care with TQM, Daniels (1993) states that the aim of customer care is similar to that of a quality improvement programme, which is to consider the customer's perception of the service (which is often quite different from that of the supplier) and to use those perceptions as the basis on which to make improvement. Clutterbuck and Kernaghan (1991) take a slightly different view. They assert that while the two concepts make use of many similar techniques, particularly in 'team-based problem solving', '... total quality is almost entirely about systems and procedures with the aim of producing consistency', while customer care focuses on changing the system and 'establishing customer supportive attitudes and behaviour' and 'controlled

* School of Civil Engineering, University of Leeds

flexibility'. Many companies that have embarked upon total quality programmes have subsequently launched customer-care initiatives as well.

Client-care initiatives or 'programmes' are designed to:

- assist companies in differentiating themselves from their competitors
- improving their image in the eyes of clients
- increasing client satisfaction with the company's performance
- encouraging word-of-mouth endorsement from satisfied clients
- delivering 'products' that are 'right first time'
- creating a reputation for being a caring and 'client-oriented' company
- making the company more profitable.

It is argued that through wide-spread application of the client-care principle, construction firms will do much to improve their image and ensure repeat business from a more satisfied client base.

Issues that may frustrate development of client care

Management of marketing, quality and the human resource are relatively underdeveloped areas in the construction industry. Firms have generally been 'product' or 'sales' oriented as opposed to 'customer' or 'marketing' led. Emphasis has therefore been on quality of the end product, i.e. the building or structure rather than on developing services, which meet the expectations of the client.

The standard of service in providing construction projects is often affected by major conflicts and disputes between the parties, rather than a partnership culture focusing on satisfying the clients' needs and wants. Much of this conflict is associated with the professional culture of the industry which has traditionally divided design from construction and has perpetuated mistrust on all sides – the 'them' and 'us' syndrome.

The people in contact with the client in construction change during the course of a project. This is often due to the time it takes to move a project from initial inception through the prequalification and tendering stages and beyond. This places great emphasis on all a firm's personnel being trained to be 'caring' to the client team. In addition, subcontracting and outsourcing of responsibilities, makes it more difficult to control the way the client team is being served.

Clients' perceptions are 'coloured' by the overall image of the industry. Attempts to introduce client-care initiatives are likely to be dismissed as purely marketing gimmicks, and not taken seriously by the client team.

Given the low profit margin in contracting, client-care programmes are likely to be viewed as too expensive to implement.

What is client care?

A review of the general literature established a range of views on the definition of customer or client care.

Cook (1992) considers customer care to be about management of 'the total consumer experience of dealing with the producer.' This involves the producer in controlling and managing 'customer confidence', from the moment they are aware of the product or service to the point where they become part of it. Customer care is about 'managing perceptions as well as realities'. Daniels (1993) asserts that these perceptions need to become the 'base point' from which to make improvements to the service provided.

Clutterbuck (1988) assert that customer care is a fundamental approach to standards of service quality, covering every aspect of a company's operations from design, packaging, delivery and service. Client-care initiatives need to permeate every part and activity of an organization (Bee and Bee, 1995). It involves a complex series of relationships between customers, individual employees and the organization. It is a means of 'establishing customer-supportive attitudes and behaviour' (Clutterbuck and Kernaghan, 1991). Customer or client care can be defined as the identification and management of critical incidents in which customers come into contact with the organization and form their impressions of its quality and service. The organization's aim is to provide customer satisfaction (Thomas, 1987).

Wellemin (1995) introduces the variety of tangible and intangible elements of customer care. Tangible elements include physical features of a product, i.e. its size, colour, etc. Intangible elements are more difficult to define and are related very much to the service provided. For example, making the customer feel secure, trusting and well disposed towards the supplier and individual members of staff.

Smith and Lewis (1989) support these views and consider customer care to be a 'philosophy' of treating customers and clients well and keeping them informed. They also introduce the notion that implementation of the customer-care philosophy is dependent on a change in the way that employees are cared for by the company, in terms of management style and working conditions.

From these broad definitions of customer or client care it may be seen that company initiatives need to integrate not only product and service quality, but also marketing and personnel practices if they are to be successfully implemented. In essence, customer care is not only about improving systems and procedures but needs to become a guiding philosophy, part of the shared values, culture and mission of the company.

Client care in other industries

The concept of customer care has been widely used in manufacturing, service and public sector industries. Blackman and Stephens (1993) recognize that the use of customer- or client-care initiatives in the public sector is on the increase due to the introduction of market forces. A paper by the Audit Commission (1988) argued that customer care would be essential if local authorities were to become 'competitive' and questioned whether councils viewed the public as customers with 'views and choices' which should be used in policy planning and implementation. The whole privatization of public utilities has created a new emphasis on the customer. Major parts of the National Health Service (NHS) have undertaken quality and customer-care programmes intended to re-orientated traditionally hierarchical and paternalistic-based cultures into commercial enterprises (Cook, 1992).

According to Clutterbuck and Kernaghan (1991), 'sooner or later, effective total quality management programmes run into the problem that most customer complaints are to do with the quality of service. Customer care may be regarded as the next phase in the evolution towards a customer-oriented company.'

Contents of typical client-care programmes

For client-care initiatives be successful they need to span the entire organization (Woodruffe, 1995). Training of employees on a piecemeal basis will not be effective. It needs to be supported whole-heartedly by top management. There are typically six common elements to be found across successful customer-care programmes (Clutterbuck and Kernaghan, 1991).

1 *Decide the objectives and structure of the programme* This is where top management should establish what the programme is supposed to achieve and outline its own role in making that happen.
2 *Audit the current situation* The organization attempts, usually through market research, to find out what customers think of the quality of service provided, both in absolute terms and vis-à-vis the customer. It also looks internally, asking employees what they consider would be most unsettling for the customer in doing business with their departments.
3 *Planning the programme* This is frequently carried out in workshops that also present useful opportunities for team-building and for some problem-solving that will provide visible initial success.
4 *Defining policies and objectives* This should occur at an early stage of planning and involves looking at the most obvious barriers to customer care.
5 *Preparing the ground through internal marketing* In general, the bigger the change in culture and behaviour required, the greater the cynicism the employees will exhibit. To overcome that cynicism, top management has to communicate its intentions strongly and with conviction.
6 *Devise an appropriate training programme* This is aimed at all levels of management and staff, particularly those in direct contact with customers.

Organizing an effective client-care programme

According to Clutterbuck and Kernaghan (1991), the main reasons why customer-care programmes fail is that the company does not enter them with a full appreciation of, and commitment to, the scale of change that is required. Customer care, like TQM programmes have to start as top-down exercises. This is essential for role models to be provided and to ensure overall direction and commitment to enforce the level of training and participation required to make the programme a success. Cook (1992) adds that many businesses discover that a campaign to merely enhance staff skills, to tackle service quality improvements from the bottom up, does not go far enough because it does not change the prevailing attitudes at management level.

An alternative view by Daniels (1993) is that adopting a customer-care approach makes an organization concentrate on the frontline staff (normally at the bottom of a pyramid management structure), and work back through the customer chain, involving the internal customer–provider relationships, developing more effective means of providing and enhancing the various products or services in line with customer needs.

According to Daniels (1993), in a company there is a front line in which staff have direct contact with the final purchasers of the service, and then a series of interfaces within the organization where one member of staff (or a team) provides an internal service to another. There is thus a 'customer–supplier' chain which stretches back from the end (external) customer to the point at which a product or service is designed and specified. The frontline service can be improved and maintained only if all other service points are improved and maintained. The frontline service is the nearest to the customer, but is not necessarily the largest determinant of perceived good service.

Cook (1992) also asserts that it is important that the customer-care initiative should not be seen to be emanating from any one particular department, i.e. marketing or training but that it should be positioned very much from the overall strategic level.

Implementing client care

Clutterbuck and Kernaghan (1991), emphasis that the whole customer-care process must start with a clear vision. This has to be gradually built and enhanced through gathering information from four key sources: customers, employees, competition and other business sectors. A customer-oriented strategy is the first building block in remaking the company. The ultimate aim is to have an operation, which responds rapidly to changing customer needs, is proactive, anticipating or creating needs and having a planned approach to meeting them. The organization has to be staffed by people who think 'customer service'. Clutterbuck and Kernaghan (1991) assert that the organization will need to change its structures, systems and standards in line with this vision. This has to be matched by attitudinal and behavioural changes in the workforce.

Management, customer and system interfaces

Management needs to create a service strategy which distinguishes the company from its competitors. This needs to be clearly communicated to both the employees and the customer. Management must also ensure that the organization structure and system are customer oriented.

Undoubtedly, the frontline staff have the highest level of contact with customers. They should be aware and understand the customers' needs and expectations on an individual basis. The customer will asses the companies service on the basis of the staff they come into contact with. The staff who do not come into direct contact with customers need to realize that they are supporting those who do and therefore need to be viewed as internal customers.

The interface between management and staff internally is crucial to the level and standards of service delivered externally. Training in customer-care skills internally, as well as externally, is essential.

The external customer comes into contact with the company system and procedures. The system needs to be user-friendly and take into account how the customer will use it and not be designed purely at the convenience of the company.

Management within the company needs to seek improvement to its systems and procedures. Identifying those elements that must be performed in the customers presence will ensure that non-essential elements be carried out away from the customer. The layout of any premises used for the service, has a profound effect on the atmosphere, which is created within the service organization.

Operating procedures, recruitment, attitudes and behaviour

Clutterbuck and Kernaghan (1991) suggest three golden rules which will normally help maintain a balance between bureaucracy and slackness:

- keep the rules short and simple and focused on priorities
- involve employees in drawing up and monitoring procedures and in explaining these to new recruits to the company
- express the rules in a positive language.

Changing the attitudes and behaviour of staff is very difficult. Critical in creating customer-oriented attitudes for people already within an organization are;

- a feeling of responsibility, of being valued and supported
- an understanding of who the customers are, what they need, what the organizations customer-oriented strategy is and their individual plan to achieve it.

A company embarking on a customer- or client-care programme needs to first gather information on the attitudes of its employees. An 'attitude audit' needs to establish whether the company is creating the kind of climate where customer care can flourish. Is the organization listening to what customers and employees are saying?

Piloting, steering, introducing and servicing the programme

Cook (1992) claims that research into organizations that have successfully applied customer-care programmes reveal that the approach chosen to introduce the initiative often determines its success. One means is to introduce a pilot scheme, which may be useful in dealing with initial resistance. Through identifying a part of the organization, which is typical in structure, to be used as a model, an illustration can be made of the success that may be brought about through the entire enterprise. A steering group of influential and representative members should be drawn from all parts of the organization whose role it is to implement the programme. In finally introducing the programme a number of techniques are identified including:

- workshops and seminars with senior management
- day or half-day events where all management and staff attend
- team meetings
- staff announcements
- videos.

Clutterbuck and Kernaghan (1991) recommend a series of measures in order to build a genuine customer-oriented organization including the need for effective communication and for top management to evaluate how the programme is progressing.

A small number of studies have been conducted into the application of client-care initiatives in the legal profession, local authorities, banks, building societies, insurance companies, retailers, and the leisure and travel industries (Smith and Lewis, 1989; Blackman and Stephens, 1993; Witt and Stewart, 1996). These studies have provided guidance on the possible subjects of research and the type of data collection methods to be used when applied to construction.

The only construction-related study identified from this literature search was the work of the Pollock Nisbet Partnership (1994). This research was carried out for Scottish Homes and involved identifying the 'state of the art' in client care in housing management. The scope of the project was a review of client-care initiatives carried out in the North and South District of Scottish Homes and included examination of initiatives carried out by other housing managers and across industries.

In the context of client care in housing management, the sample frame consisted of a sample group of customers, i.e. tenants, owner-occupiers, people on the waiting list and internal customers within Scottish Homes. The Pollock Nisbet Partnership also examined studies in four other service industries, Royal Mail, Scottish Power plc, Customs and Excise and Strathclyde PTE (public transport) and adopted a research methodology, which involved qualitative surveys to determine important aspects of service and index measurements of performance.

The Scottish Homes assessment measured the level of satisfaction with specifc aspects of their services as follows:

- communications with tenants (by telephone, face-to-face, etc.)
- area office environment
- personalizing of the service (badges, photo directory, etc.)
- complaints procedure and handling.

Who is the client in construction?

The clients in construction are not 'uniform' or 'average' organizations. The objectives of one client organization may be quite different from those of another. Turner (1997) considers clients across five categories: property and development companies, investors, occupiers, local and central government authorities, and quangos. Each type of client has different priorities, needs and expectations of the construction service and will require different approaches. An aim of client care must be to add value to the client and their business.

In addition to the 'end-user', the construction client team includes many different types of consultants who offer design and cost control services. It is important to establish their 'buying behaviour'. The involvement of the client team provides for a much greater involvement in the service than in other service industries.

Contractors need to know how their services, marketing efforts, managers and staff, facilities and brand image affect clients and their advisors perspectives. They also need to know how the competition is perceived. The firm in practice needs to establish why the client continues to negotiate and place contracts with them. Is this merely a repeat business and just how loyal is the client? This information needs to be incorporated into the client-care programme.

The only way to find out whether a company has met, or indeed exceeded client expectations, is by asking them. This should identify strengths and weaknesses in the service experienced, and will aid in improving processes in the future.

Who's on the 'front line'?

Essentially, anyone who comes into contact with the client and/or their advisors may be considered to be in the 'front line'. Contact with the client commences with early meetings, telephone conversations, interviews and presentations during the prequalification phase of a projects and continues through negotiations and tendering procedures, the award of the contract, construction stage, completion of the building or structure and during the after-care phase. The 'frontline' staff in contracting will change throughout the different stages. Unlike other industries, 'client-contact' staff will be at almost all levels in the company, from director level down to labourers on site.

The front line is drawn from a variety of different functions and departments of the business which need to be co-ordinated and view each other as internal customers. The client-care initiative will need to be driven from director level down if the required level of change to attitudes and behaviour is to be achieved, and if an 'internal marketing' culture is to be established. The client-care initiative would aim to improve the quality of services provided by the project and site managers and others during their interface throughout these processes. It would involve identifying the needs of clients during these phases and where improvements were necessary in the service provided by frontline and support staff.

From the literature search conducted only one published example of the application of these techniques was identified. This was the case of McNicholas Construction (*Contract Journal* 1998). This organization launched the 'McNicholas CARES' initiative, which urged employees of the company to be more proactive. 'CARES' is a mnemonic from the words customer, awareness, respect, enterprise, excellence, enthusiasm and solution. McNicholas formed a series of focus groups of customers to identify their needs. The aim was to try and get 'close to the customer' and to give a better service particularly to the firm's clients in the water industry. The firm was reported to be winning work in Europe due to its established reputation for commitment to serving its customers.

Concluding comments

Client care begins from the moment clients and their advisors come into contact with the construction company, to beyond the point when they become part of the service. It is a philosophy that needs to pervade every part of the construction enterprise and requires an emphasis on training if it is to be effectively implemented.

Client care involves complex relationships and interfaces between clients and their advisors, individual managers and the organization, covering every aspect of the organizations operations throughout the life of a construction project.

The aims of client care are to increase the satisfaction of clients and their advisors to ensure repeat business and client loyalty. This image will improve word-of-mouth endorsements of the contractor and should ensure success during the prequalification stage.

Most contractors have applied quality assurance procedures and many would seem to have identified the need to develop this further towards a total quality approach. However, there is little indication that the philosophy of client care is being implemented through comprehensive client-care programmes, or that the benefits of such an approach has been identified and appreciated by companies.

It is important to note that despite the significance of customer care to service companies such as contractors, very little has been written about the subject in construction. This ongoing research aims to explore the topic further, partly through surveys of contractors to establish whether they are developing client-care programmes and the type and level of training they may be using.

The principles of customer or client care outlined in this chapter can be applied to companies operating in the construction industry, taking into account the specific nature of the 'client', the market and competitive environment. As stated earlier, customer- or client-care initiatives require an integrated approach to marketing, service quality and personnel (human resource) management. These areas are underdeveloped in the construction industry and it will require a significant change in the business culture of construction organizations for implementation of client care to be successful.

References

Anonymous (1998) Launch to boost contractor's profile. *Contract Journal*, 14 January.

Audit Commission (1988) *The Competitive Council* (London: HMSO).

Bee, F. and Bee, R. (1995) *Customer Care* (London: Institute of Personnel and Development).

Blackman, T. and Stephens, C. (1993) *The Internal Market in Local Government: An Evaluation of the Impact of Customer Care, Public Money and Management*, Vol. 13, No. 4 (Oxford: Blackwell Publishers), pp. 37–44.

Clutterbuck, D. (1988) *Developing Customer Care Training Programmes, Industrial and Commercial Training*, Vol. 20, No. 1 (Bradford: MCB University Press Limited), pp. 11–14.

Clutterbuck, D. and Kernaghan, S. (1991) *Making Customers Count: A Guide to Excellence in Customer Care* (London: Mercury Books).

Cook, S. (1992) *Customer Care: Implementing Total Quality in Today's Service-Driven Organisation* (London: Kogan Page Limited).

Daniels, S. (1993) *Customer Care Programmes, Work Study*, Vol. 42, No. 1 (Bradford: MCB University Press Limited), pp. 12–13.

Smith, A.M. and Lewis, B.R. (1989) Customer care in financial service organisations. *International Journal of Bank Marketing* **7** (5), 13–22 (Bradford: MCB University Press Limited).

The Pollock Nisbet Partnership (1994) *Customer Care and Housing Management: A Research Report*, Scottish Homes, Edinburgh.

Thomas, M. (1987) Customer care: the ultimate marketing tool. In: Wensley, R. (ed.) *Reviewing Effective Research and Good Practice in Marketing* (Warwick: Marketing Education Group), pp. 283–294.

Turner, A. (1997) *Building Procurement* (2nd ed.) (Hampshire: Macmillan Press Ltd.).

Wellemin, J. (1995) *Successful Customer Care in a Week* (Northants: Institute of Management).

Witt, C.A. and Stewart, H.M. (1996) Solicitors and customer care. *The Service Industries Journal*, **16** (1), 21–34 (London: Frank Cass).

Woodruffe, H. (1995) *Services Marketing* (London: M&E Pitman Publishing).

8

Bidding and winning strategies

Simon White*

Introduction

Understanding where bidding fits into the bidder's business and growth strategy is important in preparing to bid for work. Bidding is an investment in a specific opportunity, and brings a need to bring diverse skills and aptitudes together.

In responding to the invitation, the bidder needs to recognize the complex nature of the procurement, and how this has changed over the recent years, and be prepared to devote focused effort and resource to their response.

Managing the process becomes critical as increasing pressure is put on both clients and bidders in order to deal with increasingly complex procurements.

The need to understand the client and his objectives are key issues in bidding for and winning work.

There is some conflict and tension in that bidders would wish to avoid bidding, yet clients seek benefits from competition.

Where does the process start?

In an ideal world, as suppliers of services, works or goods, bidders would not be bidding. We would all seek direct and/or negotiated appointments based on the relationships arising from customer management activity, from client care programmes, and from working collaboratively with clients to deliver their projects. Bidding takes people out of their comfort zone, frequently gives onerous processes to follow, and usually a requirement for responses within a tight programme.

Clients, on the other hand, seek competition as a means of identifying the best team to entrust their project to obtain competitive fee and cost proposals; to receive value for money, and increasingly these clients are obliged to maintain an audit trail to demonstrate that they have achieved this to others.

* Arup

There are four main starting points to the bidding process:

1 The client has a project or has taken on a project, and needs to identify, select and appoint a team or individual to provide specific services in order to deliver it. A competitive process is identified and established, and an invitation to prospective bidders is issued. The stages that the client navigates to get to this point naturally vary, according to whether it is a public or private sector client, project scope, services required, programme, etc. The procurement strategy that is chosen should also be considered – 'appropriate procurement strategies are needed to help achieve optimal solutions in terms of cost, time and quality' (Kumaraswamy and Dissanyaka 1998). The process should also reflect the client's attitude to risk – a key factor in bidding – which the procurement and contract strategy seeks to minimize or to transfer specific risks elsewhere (Merna 1998).

2 The respondent or prospective bidder will see an invitation, whether in the form of an OJEC notice, arrival of the tender documents, invitations to submit particulars, received either from the client or through an intermediary or work-giver.

3 The bidder establishes and develops a relationship with a prospective client, building up their knowledge of the client, their business and drivers, and sometimes early knowledge of the project – achieving this through a formal customer relationship programme or equivalent, or through general business development or networking. Where this does not result in a direct appointment, it is then likely to result in a place on the list to receive the invitation.

4 The bidder would, typically, have taken a conscious decision in their strategic plan to be in a market sector or segment that features competitive bidding. This might have been addressed within the marketing plan, where the infrastructure that needs to support their bidders in their activity would be identified and its development instigated. This could encompass identifying specific skills sets, people who will lead and manage bid responses, suitable promotional material and the investment levels required to sustain the activity, etc. It should also include:

● An overall strategy for the market and the strategy for bidding
● How you will position your firm to be invited to bid
● How you will identify suitable prospects and opportunities
● How much you will invest in their pursuit
● How much preliminary contact you seek to have with the client.

The plan might also set out a simple metric (Bid/No-bid) for identifying or prioritizing which opportunity to pursue, and which to decline. This would probably include issues of geography, sector, client relationship, service required, desire to do the project, and the degree of fit with the overall strategy.

Bartlett (1997) describes the conceptual sequence:

● Marketing leads to an invitation to submit a proposal for a new project
● A successful proposal leads to the client awarding your company the project
● A successful project gives you more material for the next round of marketing activity.

When does it start?

It is usually too late to start when an invitation to bid lands on your desk.

● From the client's perspective the project process and the process of selection has already started. Decisions will have been made on the needs, project, etc., the nature of the competition to be used, and from this the framework to determine who to invite to bid – whether informed by an open competition/OJEC response, or from formal or informal contact with colleagues, other clients, and suppliers of services, works, or goods. By this stage most clients will have also set out their marking system and looked at the weighting issues for specific sections of the response.

● From the bidder's perspective, then, this document as it arrives, is the result of many things – most of which start with a decision to be in a particular market or business. If you do not wish to bid for work, then you gravitate toward non-competitive and more collaborative markets. Clients usually will already know that you are prepared to bid, and have taken a decision, based on their contact with the market in various contexts, to invite you to be on the list.

Any incoming opportunity should be reviewed against the Bid/No-bid criteria set out in your bidding strategy and process (Figure 8.1). This process should assess whether it is worth pursuing, and provide a guide to allocation of bid investment, based on an estimate of response costs, potential fee and profit. In all probability this will not give a definitive answer, but will inform any decision that is taken.

But what is bidding?

There are many documents that can be embraced by the term 'bid' (proposal, tender, offer, submission, possibly also a pre-qualification or expression of interest document, etc.). The nature of the response might range from a business letter, through to major multi-volume documents that respond to a major PFI/PPP or outsourcing bid, where the bid costs alone can reach several million pounds.

A bid is a proposition or offer – a statement of what will be provided for what cost. Depending on your perspective it is a document to persuade the client to award you the appointment, or a document to close the sale.

In many circumstances the bid becomes the basis for the contract, and hence the delivery of the service. The more substantial responses will set out what is to be done, receivables and deliverables, who will do what, and when, and the basis for payment for the service; so it is not surprising that it takes on this contractual and commercial significance.

As a result of taking this role in persuading the client it inherits further roles, reinforcing your:

● ability to deliver the service
● desire to win the work
● key messages to clients
● differentiators.

Illinois University's defines a bid as a proposal that persuades the reader to improve or alter the existing situation. The University of Toronto's Engineering Writing Centre suggests that a successful proposal is one that convinces the client that the proposition is good and that the authors are qualified to accomplish the task.

At its most fundamental level, therefore, the bid document takes a highly focused and critical place in the client–bidder relationship; it is 'the main point of interface with the buyer – and therefore its primary means of influencing the outcome.'(Martin, 1997).

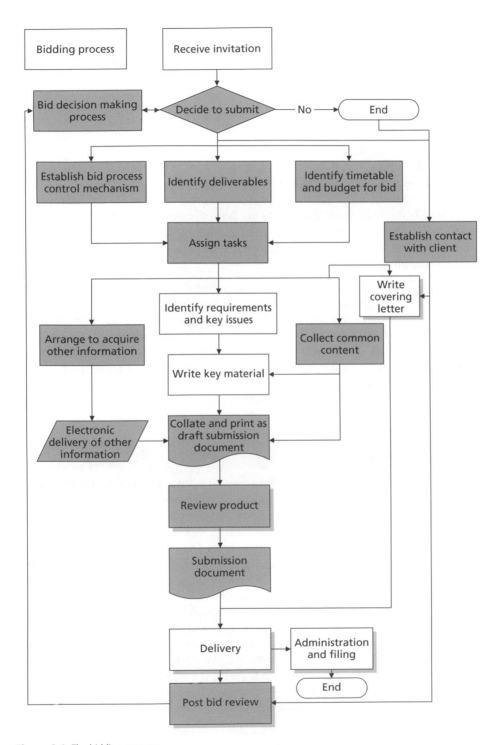

Figure 8.1 The bidding process.

What does this mean in practice

Being in a market that features competitive bidding (most of the construction industry) means being prepared to invest in the pursuit of opportunity. And this means accepting the waste of unsuccessful pursuit.

In addition to scope and service, three other factors come in to play when considering the scale of this investment:

- The client's desire for comparability – to be able to have a method of direct comparison of the responses of the various applicants on a like-for-like basis
- The client's need for auditability and a shareable audit trail; which in some circumstances leads to an increasing demand for more detailed information, and/or the application of simplistic metrics as the sole means to apply judgment or knowledge and
- The bidders desire to respond to the client's demands, their enthusiasm to win, and the need to be clear in their response (e.g. to emerging contract forms, or in understanding and responding to the risks that they inherit), results in increasingly complex and voluminous responses.

On the more sophisticated and substantial procurement processes, such as appointments for PFI/PPPs or design competitions – there is a fourth factor in considering the scale of investment – early input. This is where the process requires early creative contribution, such as the detailed development of options, sometimes solutions that will be delivered.

The more skeptical will recognize that competitive bidding is not an investment that should be made lightly – some contractors have announced their determination to withdraw from it. Due to time and effort that it needs, bidding should be planned, selectively considered, budgeted for and managed effectively.

Client focus

Perhaps the most important issue is to understand the client, particularly their objectives and process. It is prevailing good practice for this information to be included in the documents dispatched to the bidders, but there are many potential sources that can supplement this, e.g. an annual report or their internet site can provide useful information.

A key factor is the marking system to be adopted and how/who will be doing it. The client and bidder sometimes have different views of the significance of particular issues (1999). Most bidders encourage selection by quality rather than least cost, but this introduces subjectivity. The DTLR/Local Government Association, e.g. recommends that 'Local Authorities … should develop evaluation criteria which incorporate quality and whole life costs … They should be agreed in advance and should be published, transparent and auditable (DETR and Local Government Association, 2001)'. Recommended evaluation criteria have been developed and offered to clients by pan-industry bodies such as the Construction Industry Board (Construction Industry Board, 1996).

The use of pre-qualification and tender questionnaires and other common documents, proliferating over recent years, can have both positive and negative aspects:

- The client should receive a document in a form and sequence that facilitates comparison. This assists the auditability and marking processes.

- Questionnaires often fail to shed light on the client's real objectives for the project, particularly those drawn from other projects.
- Questionnaires focus on matters of fact and numbers – this results in a focus on the bidder. Since some questionnaires are shared between clients, most bidders will naturally develop suitable content for re-use, which lacks client focus.
- The questions used should be designed to set the scene, enabling the client to identify and select the bidder. They should be relevant to the stage in the process and scope of the project.

Some thoughts on numbers

There is increasing sophistication in procurement methods, with consequences on the response demanded from the bidder:

- The client has to deal with shortlisting a finite number of bidders to take to tender from an increasingly complex market, arriving at a meaningful evaluation criteria, and the relative weighting of each area, and then has to deal with the marking of the response. These criteria and their weighting need to be evaluated each time they are used.
- The bidder needs to evaluate their probability of success. Frequently this is based on the number of other bidders (20 per cent if there are four others). This informs setting a realistic bid budget, the numbers involved in arriving at a realistic and deliverable winning financial response, and where to place bid effort. Since clear guidance is not always available, effort is frequently focused in those areas that are perceived to be significant, whilst seeking not to lose points in other areas.
- Complex projects, with procurements running over a long period of time, such as PFI/PPPs, require early effort in the development and appreciation of options, and how they match to the stated client objectives. These also bring specific issues – e.g. whole life cost and value for money, neither of which are easily quantifiable – HM Treasury's definition of whole life is based on not just the cost of delivering and maintaining the facility, but also the influence of the facility on what is going on inside, bringing issues of productivity, efficiency, etc.

Other numbers games

Hit rate is a frequent conversation topic, often used as the measure of effectiveness (percentage of bids won), but there are other issues:

- How many responses does the client have to deal with? How can you differentiate and get through to the next stage? With major public sector clients receiving upwards of 100 responses to OJEC advertised open-competitions these are critical questions. And each bidder will have a response that fits them and their approach.
- How long should a long list be? How short should a short list be? Guidance varies – again according to scope and service, and with the process that is being used. Some procurements have a long list of 18, an intermediate list of typically seven, mid-bid interviews, with a shortlist of three or four who will go through to bid stage. Others, such as PFI may end up with two bidders at the penultimate stage, with the preferred bidder carrying through to financial close.

Multiple appointments to framework agreements are an interesting case – typically they are used by public and private sector clients with a significant on-going programme of capital works in either a sector or a geographic region. The bidder, seeing four appointments from a tender list of twenty, might assume that they have a 20 per cent probability (one in five). Is this a realistic assessment? How many bids should you go for in a year? How many bids should you aim to win in a year? There is probably no definitive answer – it depends on the project, service, location, and upon the client. You can win ten appointments in a year accounting for 50 per cent of your turnover, or win five projects for 80 per cent of your turnover, or 5 per cent of your turnover in the first year, but bring in 80 per cent of your turnover for the following year. How much you need to win depends on your strategy and thus on your business model – your targets, as set out in your plan, should not be crude numbers.

A number of strategic, tactical and practical issues inform the Bid/No-bid decision, with these issues themselves shaped by business plans, and also by consultation with others in the organization. These issues fall broadly into five categories as shown in Figure 8.2.

Lowest cost or best value? The trend away from lowest cost was crystallized in the Egan Report, where the expressed desire to modernize cited a number of areas, including: 'too many clients are undiscriminating and still equate price with cost, selecting designers and constructors almost exclusively on the basis of tendered price …. The industry needs to educate and help its clients to differentiate between best value and lowest price.' (DETR, 1998). The trend away from lowest cost towards value for money has started, with both broader and more specific issues being taken into consideration at the procurement stage, e.g. safety, quality, environment, but few of these can be easily quantified. And in the USA they have recognized that not accepting the lowest bid, perhaps because it is 'discordant', has public accountability issues associated with it (Crowley and Hancher, 1995). From this comes the need to be clear in defining the best bid in this light. Our own National Audit Office provides one view: 'Value for Money is about designing and constructing buildings for the best outturn cost likely to meet the operational requirements of users of the building to appropriate standards of quality' (National Audit Office, 2001). Many

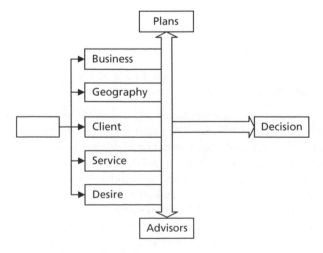

Figure 8.2 Bid/No-bid: issues for consideration.

public sector clients now seek to arrive at an evaluation framework that will provide them with the best team to deliver this.

Skills

Bidding requires a variety of skills and experience. Some of these may be strategic, others bring value in implementation. The important issues are having the right skills at the right time, deploying a team with the right blend of skills, and having access to expert and experienced advisors.

The skills requirement

Tied to the following tangible skills and competencies is a softer skills set – less easy to define – such as leadership, empathy, creativity, constructive listening and understanding, team working, persuasive communication, ability to visualize the solution. In short – the ability to arrive at and deliver the winning proposition.

Marketing

Bids and proposals are aimed at communicating to the client that you or your firm are the ideal people to meet their needs at the optimum level of fee and profit for both parties, and doing so efficiently and economically. It involves communicating to the client that you are interested in working for and with them in meeting their needs, and that their work is important to the business you represent. It involves developing and communicating an appreciation of the client and project requirements.

It is about giving the client confidence in the people and processes, their skills and attitudes, such that an appointment is the natural result; and seeking to achieve this efficiently and profitably.

Marketing provides a focus to encourage and facilitate the gathering and sharing of best practice, to encourage teams to bid more effectively through a focus on the client, on the project requirements, and to champion excellence throughout the bid process. The aim is that this input enables more profitable appointments to be won.

Communication

In bidding this remains a two-way process, conducted in a variety of environments; – reading and assimilating the requirement, responding to the brief and/or need, tender presentations, etc. This should also bring the ability to listen constructively, and through listening arriving at a greater understanding. It is about being positive, facilitating communication between others, and being persuasive.

Communication also takes place within the bidding team – team members are briefed, and specialist advisors are consulted. They take their lead from the bid leader and manager, and their contribution is dependent on the quality of communication.

Commercial

The nature of the win proposition can be shaped by good commercial people. This includes the fees, programme and scope. It is important to bring these skills early into the discussions to appraise the viability of the opportunity, and bring experience of working in particular geographies and markets.

Project, risk and value management

Bids are projects and should be managed as such – some major bids are larger than small projects. They therefore require planning, management, control and reporting in much the same way – a project manager would set out the project controls, and manage the process accordingly. They have their inputs and outputs, mobilization, briefing, negotiation and deliverables, and learning to inform subsequent activity. They also have value management in common with projects – the identification and prioritization of those issues that are important to the client in the context of the project. Increasingly, with many larger bids, particularly those involved in transferring risk from the client to the service provider, such as PFI and PPP, they also have formal risk assessment techniques applied to them.

Persuasive writing

The narrative style that is most successful in bidding is difficult to define. The body language of negotiating needs to be replicated in the written text. The essence is in communicating truth in a convincing and focused manner – this requires particular attention and skill.

Purpose-written text is always going to be better received by the client than boilerplate or generic text. Commitment, enthusiasm, understanding of the issues can be conveyed through vocabulary, e.g. with the use of positive verbs, the avoidance of jargon and technical terms which may or may not be understood, and the use of the client's vocabulary to demonstrate the understanding of the role; all demonstrate a willingness to engage.

And there is a significant body of wisdom that promotes the view that persuasion is a matter of structure – what are the significant issues, how can they be achieved. The primacy principle, expressed by Tom Sant and supported by others, is that you put first those things that are important to the reader, not those that are important to the writer.

Visual presentation

A well-designed document, clearly laid out, and focusing attention on the key elements of the proposition, is a far more attractive, and therefore winning, document. It will communicate that you have taken time to understand what is important to this client and this project, and that you are concerned that this is communicated clearly.

The use of colour, e.g. more so now that the technology is widely available, can help strengthen the document, even bring additional cohesion through matching sections of the response with the various themes or response. The look and feel can also be used to communicate an unambiguous and professional view of the firm presenting the bid.

The visual presentation of information and concepts can help reinforce specific points that you wish the reader to note – the eye is naturally drawn to colour and to images. Many documents, particularly those responding to onerous processes, become bogged down in the printed word – it is no surprise that interest in reading fades away after the first few pages.

Knowledge management

Bidding effectively is about learning – from previous wins and losses; gathering, sharing and establishing a body of knowledge for the future, and monitoring of processes to ensure that they continue to add value to the businesses, and those of the client. The investment made in bidding for work in the context of business continuity is essential, and should be learnt from.

Information management

Preparing to bid (whether putting in place the infrastructure that helps bidders be more effective, or researching the individual opportunity) is a necessary investment. Discussions and meetings with the client, visits to the site or premises, desk research on the client's market, etc. all build up the body of knowledge within the team, and will help them in developing their response.

There is a lot of common content in bids – particularly those run under such strictures as the EU Procurement regime. Having ready access to pre-prepared information is increasingly necessary, and can create time in what is typically a high-pressure programme to address the quality aspects of the bid. But this should be balanced with the recognition that superfluous information does not advance the cause, and clients prefer project specific responses.

Defining roles

The technical and management skills that are required to respond to the specific opportunity should be available within or to the responding team. Bringing these skills in to the bid team needs to be done on planned basis, with clear roles. Bartlett sets out the model for defining roles and responsibilities of the major players within the bid team (Bartlett, 1997). These should be clearly communicated and understood across the team.

Winning the bid

There is an increasing amount of published material on the subject of bidding: some of it prescriptive and process focused, some offering best practice sales hints, but there is little directly relevant to the construction industry. There is also a broad range of guidance and narrative that the bidder should be aware of.

This is a reflection of the complexities of our industry. 'The industry making box girder bridges is completely distinct from that making intelligent buildings on dense city centre sites or that repairing private houses' (Groak, 1996). Consequently we have many different clients in a wide range of sectors – construction is not of primary interest for some of these clients – it is a facility or environment that they give little thought to until they wish to expand or renew.

They may be regular employers and users of the construction industry, or maybe they see themselves coming to the industry once a generation or once a century (although they will be using a part of the industry to maintain the facility).

Each of these clients has projects that they feel are unique, are driven by unique objectives, in unique circumstances, and require a bespoke response.

What is the client looking for?

So, will what was successful on one occasion work on the next? Many bidders start by drawing from the last bid that they produced. This approach is unlikely to be a success – but there are some general lessons that can be learned.

Many of the issues for the client that shape whether a bid is won, can be summed up in the word 'confidence':

- Am I getting what I need?
- How will my needs be met?
- Can I work with this team?
- Can this team deliver to my budget?
- Can this team deliver to my programme?
- Does this give me value for money?

How bidders respond is shaped by their perspective on the implication of these issues, the understanding of the project and the abilities to respond. Success is determined by effectiveness in communicating this and instilling confidence in the client (Figure 8.3).

For the bidder:

- How do you decide which opportunities to pursue?
- How can you stand out from a multitude of interested parties?

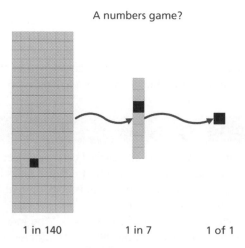

A numbers game?

1 in 140   1 in 7   1 of 1

Figure 8.3 How can you differentiate your offer?

- How can you differentiate your offer?
- What it your probability of success?

For the client

- How are you to find the best firm to meet your needs?
- What criteria do you need to get from a long list to the appointment of the most suitable respondent?

Some pointers

Among the published guidance there is much that seeks to encapsulate best practice in some key headline issues.

Early preparation 1

Having the infrastructure in place to be able to respond to invitations is essential. If entering a new market, e.g. it may be advisable that sample documents are obtained in order to estimate the level and depth of information that is required in order to respond. This then informs the development of the supporting infrastructure.

> Kennedy and O'Connor's research, conducted with successful bidders, identified some seventeen critical success factors, and it is interesting to note that seven relate to the depth of their understanding of the client and its players, eight relate to broader market and communication issues, and only two can be said to be bid-specific – the communication of value, and the offering of supporting or related services (Kennedy and O'Connor, 1999).

This may encompass case studies and images, standard responses to specific questions, identified bid and business leaders and managers, a model bid programme and cost plan, allocated war rooms for bid teams, agreed formats and templates, etc.

> KPMG's 10 Golden Rules provide one view of the core issues involved (KPMG, 1998):
>
> - Strategy
> - Organization
> - Joint Venture partners
> - People
> - Bid compliance
> - Innovation
> - Project management
> - Risk Management
> - Independent Reviews
> - Benchmarking.

Early preparation 2

Having received an invitation to bid, it is important to review and possibly develop your understanding of the client's organization and the key decision takers (or bid markers). This should be supplemented with a good understanding the client's business and the market in which it operates. There are many potential routes to this knowledge, and experienced information professionals should be able to source this effectively.

Checklists

Since bidding has several sub-processes, frequently running in parallel (technical proposal, resourcing, fees, drafting, etc.), and sometimes with inputs from several people, it is beneficial to have a clear and shared view of the process. This can be supplemented by using checklists for each of the various stages – review of the invitation, deciding to bid (Bid/No-bid), planning bid activities, briefing the team, reviewing the response, compliance and delivery, preparing for interview, preparing for negotiation, etc.

With the costs of bidding escalating perhaps as more prospects are pursued, projects grow in scale and scope, process issues start to pre-dominate, and the need to manage the process becomes even more important.

The above-mentioned checklists will assist in delivering the bid, and with there being constant opportunities or needs to explore particular issues, it is important that every member of the team is aware of their responsibilities. Proactive management is necessary to avoid many of the pitfalls that come from a lack of focus in this area.

Managing the response

The criteria for a successful project are typically delivery to cost, programme and technical specification (or quality) – in the case of bids this applies to both the bid and the solution proposed:

	Bid	Solution
Cost	Bid delivered within bid cost plan	Matches stated cost parameters as a minimum
Programme	Delivery to deadlines	Matches stated programme as a minimum
Technical specification	Compliant document as defined in the invitation	Matches stated objectives as a minimum

The larger the bid, the greater the need for effective leadership and robust management. There may be a team of people involved full-time with corresponding need for clear and shareable project procedures. Where the bid team, bringing skills from various organizations, has co-located there are obvious needs for the environment to be managed constructively. War rooms are a common feature of some organizations, and having a single secure space for the bid team is obviously beneficial, as well as sending a clear message about the value of bids to the organization.

There is also a clear benefit for the team that will deliver the project to be integral to the bid team – ideally they should be the same. Clients are clear that they do not wish to see sales or business development people who will not be involved in the project, and the team that delivers the bid will have the best understanding of the project and its needs later in the process, and when it comes to delivery.

Learn lessons

Best practice clients will give bidders the opportunity to receive feedback on their bids – it helps both client and bidder. It is important that advantage is taken of this opportunity – the Construction Industry Board (Selecting Consultants for the Team) recommends that debriefing is provided. Guidance by HM Treasury's Central Unit on Procurement (now the Office of Government Commerce) and Construction Industry Council endorses this recommendation. This intelligence can inform the bidder at strategic and tactical levels, and in relation to the market. And since bidding is a part of the marketing plan, the information from post bid discussion informs any assessment of bidding effectiveness.

Drafting: focus on

- Being clear about your differentiators
- Being clear and concise
- Avoiding jargon
- Being consistent in the use of terminology, names and tense.

Think about structure and sequence

The need to present a logical proposition is often forgotten in the pressure of looming deadlines, and many argue for various 'standard' or generic structures as being most effective.

> Sant recommends (Sant, 1992):
>
> - Identification of need
> - Benefits of arriving at solutions
> - Recommendation of solution
> - Supporting details.

One logical sequence is self-evident – the client's own sequence of questions and issues as provided in the invitation. On the assumption that this is organized in terms of their significance to the client, then it can be assumed that this is a reasonable sequence for the response. You may argue that this is naïve – the client issues are not often that transparent, and are frequently rationalized to thematic areas e.g. financial, health and safety, by an intermediary, yet it warrants serious consideration.

> Kantin recommends (Kantin, 2001):
>
> - Client background
> - Proposed solution
> - Implementation
> - Seller profile
> - Business issues.

References

Bartlett, R.E. (1997) *Preparing International Proposals* (Telford).

DETR and Local Government Association (2001) *Delivering Better Services for Citizens* (DTLR).

Groak, S. (1996) Project related research and development. In: Dunster, D. (ed.) *Arups on Engineering* (Ernst & Sohn).

Kumaraswamy, M.M. and Dissanyaka, S.M. (1998) Linking procurement systems to project priorities. *Building Research and Innovation*, **26** (4), 223–238.

KPMG (1998) *Bidding to win* (KPMG) Quote in full or extract from (this is extract).

Bartlett, R.E. (1997) *Preparing International Proposals* (Telford), pp. 78–81.

Construction Industry Board (1996) *Selecting Consultants for the Team: Balancing Quality and Price* (Telford).

Ng, T. *et al.* (1999) Decision-makes perceptions in the formulation of prequalification criteria. *Engineering, Construction and Architectural Management*, **6** (2), 155–163.

Martin, J. (1997) Winning the bid. *Project Manager Today*, April.

DETR (1998) *Report of the Construction Task Force (Egan Report) Rethinking Construction* (DETR).

Crowley, L.G. and Hancher, D.E. (1995) Evaluation of competitive bids. *ASCE Journal of Construction Engineering and Management,* **121** (2), 238–245.

Merna, A. (1998) Financial risk in the procurement of capital and infrastructure projects. *International Journal of Project and Business Risk Management*, **2** (3), 257–270.

National Audit Office (2001) *Modernising Construction. HC 87 Session 2000–2001* (Stationery Office).

Kennedy, C. and O'Connor, M. (1999) *Winning Major Bids … the Critical Success Factors* (Policy Publications).

Sant, T. (1992) *Persuasive Business Proposals* (Katz & Associates).

Kantin, R. (2001) www.salesproposals.com;http://www.salesproposals.com/default.htm; http://www.salesproposals.com/article2.htm.

Further reading

Holtz, H. (1990) *The Consultants Guide to Proposal Writing*, 2nd ed. (Wiley).

Hoxley, M. (1998) *Value for Money: The Impact of Competitive Fee Tendering on Construction Professional Service Quality* (RICS Research).

Joseph, A. (1989) *Put it in Writing!* (McGraw-Hill).

Lewis, H. (1992) The Consultants Complete Proposal Manual (PTRC).

Porter-Roth, B. (1998) *Proposal Development*, 3rd ed. (Oasis Press).

Walker, K. *et al.* (1998) *Creating New Clients: Marketing and Selling Professional Services* (Cassell).

Chapman, C.B. *et al.* (2000) Incorporating uncertainty in competitive bidding. *International Journal of Project Management*, **19**, 337–347.

Griffiths, F.H. (1992) Bidding strategy: winning over key competitors. *ASCE Journal of Construction Engineering and Management*, **118** (1), 151–165.

Herbsman, Z. and Ellis, R. (1992) Multiparameter bidding system – innovation in contract administration. *ASCE Journal of Construction Engineering and Management*, **118** (1), 142–150.

Lo, W. *et al.* (1999) Effects of high prequalification requirements. *Construction Management and Economics*, **17**, 603–612.

9

Public relations: business development's vital ingredient

Alan Smith*

Introduction

The changes within the construction industry over the past decade have been profound. The impact of those changes has been most clearly manifest in the fresh, more vibrant and collaborative culture that has pervaded almost all of those 'delivering' construction today. Indeed, such has been this attitude step-change that in many respects those within the industry today are already light years ahead of those outside observers, both academic and governmental, who are the most vocal in calling for the need for change.

Business development, as a function, has been at the forefront of converting this new culture into tangible form through managing relationships between the provider and the customer; establishing and nurturing communication, trust and understanding throughout the extended supply chain. But the whole environment within which this industry is evolving so dynamically is now being influenced, to a hitherto unprecedented extent, by a revolution in the delivery of comprehensive, co-ordinated public relations activities across the broadest range of issues. This impact, more than any other, will foster the continued development of an industry whose reputation has lagged so far behind its own dynamic reality. The industry is dependent entirely upon its people. 'People' is as much public relations as human resources in construction.

This chapter will echo many of the themes in other chapters: those of change, of culture, of relationships and of the dynamics of evolving business development. But it will concentrate here upon how those changes, both structural and cultural, have forced changes to the public relations function in its delivery and how, conversely, public relations has forced changes upon the industry. For it has indeed been a two-way revolution in the last decade. Reflecting the changes wrought upon the construction industry by the landmark reports of Sir Michael Latham and Sir John Egan, the public relations function at the start of the

* HBG Construction Ltd

twenty-first century, the roles it now undertakes within the management matrix, and the nature of the services it now delivers, are totally unrecognizable from the early 1990s. Moreover, never has the public relations function pervaded more deeply within the departmental structure of construction organizations nor linked more integrally with other outside participants within the supply chain.

In particular, this chapter will examine the range of key public relations activities that are now an integral part of the construction industry's business development. It will cover the conventional public relations functions in passing, briefly referring to press relations, internal communications, corporate affairs, customer liaison, supply chain liaison, communicating health and safety. However, it is not intended to review the whole plethora of the public relations remit or to even list what should or should not be part of the function in the construction industry.

What is important is to examine the most influential roles of the public relations practitioner in support of the business development function in the construction industry today and how recent developments have radically altered priorities in this interface. Thus we will look in some detail at the impact of Private Finance Initiative (PFI)/Public Private Partnerships (PPP) upon the function as well as examining community relations and its vital role in the business development context. By the same token, it will not look at the aspects of financial or investor relations as this sector of the public relations remit is seen to be a specialist issue that is influential upon, but not necessarily influenced by the business development environment. The topics, although examined through the headlines that have brought about change, including radically altered client perceptions, the impact of PFI and facilities management (FM) upon the industry and consolidation within the construction industry, will be of a generic nature, applicable equally to the civil engineering, building and property services sectors.

Finally, all of these issues will be brought together under an all-encompassing topic for the industry and its future: Corporate Social Responsibility (CSR), a concept embraced so wholeheartedly by the retail and manufacturing sectors but only weakly recognized by the majority of those in the construction industry. CSR will in the near future be a cornerstone or even a precondition to all business development initiatives. Those organizations not adopting a genuine CSR policy and strategy will be seen as the dinosaurs of the industry and will quickly become extinct.

An evolving industry evolves public relations

'Bodget & Scram Ltd, Builders of repute'. We have all met them. They have built our extension or our patio, rebuilt the kitchen or bathroom. And can we get them back to put it right or get our money back after they have left? No chance. But will we ask them back to do another job? Never. This realization seems only recently to have dawned upon the wider, some would say, larger, more professional industry. But whether it is a driveway you are having built or a £250 million hospital or dual-carriageway bypass, the same philosophy applies. The days of Bodget & Scram are, hopefully, in the past. The days of massive claims, confrontational contractual and legal wrangles over payments and delivery are also, we hope, disappearing.

Just so with public relations. The soft, remote and usually stand-alone public relations associated with the 'photo-shoot' and the cynical spin-doctoring characterized by political institutions never really manifested itself in the hard, men-only environment of the construction industry. By the same token, the industry has never tolerated the luxury of a public relations overhead cost within its traditional sparse operational budget unless that function actually contributed to the bottom line. That philosophy usually manifested itself in the function being simply the production house for glossy brochures, the provider of corporate pens, diaries and golf umbrellas, and the organizers of turf-cutting ceremonies, topping-out or tape-cutting events. Those days are, for most organizations, also disappearing along with Bodget & Scram!

Having said that, the public relations function has always been 'useful' in the context of basic press relations, providing corporate profile largely in the trade journals, promoting contracts awarded, innovative solutions to technical issues, project reviews and views on issues of the day. Generally press release led, backed up by the occasional site visit by one or more journalists, and the regular contracts awarded form-filling, the press officer function was usually reactive and, therefore, defensive. Any questions not initiated via an already approved and multiple-vetted press release were regarded with suspicion and met with evasive action rather than openness and honesty.

And why was this? For a start, in an industry where any and every contract was won by achieving the lowest price, regardless of the quality or stability of the provider, where was the point in investing in profile, in advertising your wares? By the same token, where every client views the press, or more precisely contact with the press, as a major contractual issue, how could the contractor be forward or proactive in talking to the press in anything but evasive or defensive terms?

This attitude also extended down the supply chain. If the client wants the cheapest and quickest building project undertaken, then the contractor will by necessity want the cheapest and quickest supplier of materials and services to complete that job. This simply breeds a culture that repels quality. More importantly, it repels value, and it repels positive relationships.

Moreover, within this environment one of the biggest sufferers was the public. Being very much a 'here today, gone tomorrow' industry, there was not a great deal of incentive for contractors to be good neighbours during the construction phase. The construction process does involve mud, dust, noise, vibration, traffic disruption and the presence of heavy vehicles and a transient workforce. If a road had to be constructed or a supermarket built, then the public simply had to put up with all the impacts of the process. After the original consultation/planning permission and compulsory purchase orders were through, the public could do very little in response to the reality of the construction phase. And why should the contractor care? He will get paid and will move on tomorrow to another job elsewhere.

So what has changed in the industry? On the one hand the Egan/Latham initiatives have undoubtedly thrown governmental and industry bodies into the fray to improve relationships, to reduce adversarial conditions, ease contractual straightjackets and encourage more respect for value rather than cost. This has certainly driven a step-change in attitudes from the client side.

Partnering, negotiated contracts, alliances, demonstration best practice and such like have all arisen from such initiatives. Driven on by the formation of M4i, the Construction Best Practice Programme and the plethora of other movements within the industry, this attitude change has been delivered in an almost academic way; a conceptual, theoretical approach that looks good on paper, sounds good on the conference platform and is politically correct.

The grim reality, however, is that the genuine, on-the-ground change of attitudes and relationships has been driven not so much by talk as by actions within the individual companies delivering construction services and individual clients procuring those projects. Indeed, it has been this process and the competitive edge gained by those entering into the new era of relationships that has galvanized the whole industry more than any other outside initiatives.

Construction companies, whether consulting engineers, quantity surveyors, structural engineers, contractors in building or civil engineering, are getting bigger, more professional. They have become a lot more concerned about reputation. The bigger the organization, the more susceptible it is to criticism, the more sensitive the Stock Market is to bad or controversial news. As companies have expanded, so they have been forced to adopt Plc attitudes, with more respect for the press and more consideration for the public. They have had to accept that a big problem among the press or public on one individual site can impact upon the reputation of the company on every single project it is working upon and can influence the perception of the organization among existing or potential clients globally. Big is beautiful, but big is also a bigger target.

Clients now look for reputable suppliers of construction services. Whereas the prequalification criteria used to be quite simply: have you built one before?, other elements have gradually crept into the fold, such as can you build it safely?, can you build it without going bust?, can you build it with environmental sensitivity?, can you build it with quality and value? And today, increasingly, a significant element of that prequalification criteria concerns public relations and community relations surrounding that project: can you build it while keeping the neighbouring population informed and content with your operations?

Clients are much more aware of the impact of construction upon their business. For British Airways to build its Waterside Development and the vast Prospect Park near Heathrow, it had to be very conscious of the new neighbours it was going to have. Not just in the consultation stage, but particularly in the construction phase. By the same token, Asda Stores realize that only by being considerate during the construction phase will their future customers respect them when the new store opens. In both cases, their public and community relations do not begin when they open their new doors, but goes way back to the planning and construction phases.

Of even more significance in the change of attitudes from the contractor side is the advent of Repeat Business and of Negotiated Tenders. A happy client that has seen a commitment to provide value as well as quality is now more likely to go back to that provider again. The old days of Lowest Bidder have not gone, but they are becoming fewer. Strategic relationships have built up between clients and a few trusted partners in the construction procurement process. Trust, openness, honesty and relationships are of fundamental importance to both clients and construction service providers. And this has extended down the supply chain.

An example of this is Asda. Having only four main contractors selected for all its construction work has had a massive impact upon its construction delivery programme. Safety has improved dramatically, store build-time has virtually halved, value has improved as manifest in contract values/delivery times and quality has demonstrably improved. Why? As each contractor operates on an open-book principle, each innovation is shared, each time and cost-saving element is shared and all examples of best practice are highlighted to all parties. The performance of each project is closely monitored and follow-on contracts are all determined by the performance levels of previous projects. It creates a circle of consistent, constant improvements.

A significant element of this appraisal is a consideration of how the contractor has handled the local community and local press during the construction phase. Controversy on site during the construction phase will have a direct and larger impact upon the business when the doors open for retail business. A serious incident involving the public during the building phase can and will directly affect the market on day of opening as local press is a powerful tool in the creation of reputation locally and can have major impact upon a business.

So client relations is, to a large extent, dependent upon community and public relations. Nor should this factor be underestimated. It can be critical to the success or failure of business development for future work. It is an area in which the marketing department needs to be totally appreciative of the public relations role.

The PFI/PPP influence on public relations

One of the biggest influences upon the positive evolution of the construction industry and its approach to public relations has been the advent of the PFI or PPP. Since 1995 there have been literally hundreds of PFI/PPP-funded projects and, suddenly, the big contractor is not just a contractor/constructor, but is the fund-holder, the landlord, the facilities manager, as well as the builder of the project.

More importantly, as the owner and manager of a facility (road, bridge, hospital, police headquarters, or school or college) the attitude to building that facility has had to be adjusted completely. Buildability has always been a key issue in construction. PFI has introduced new, critical criteria into the construction process such as maintainability, sustainability, heat loss minimization, natural light maximization, repairability and so on. As the owner and the maintenance contractor for the ensuing twenty-five or thirty years, the construction contractor has to be extremely sensitive about how it goes about constructing the facility it is about to manage for that period of time.

PFI has brought contractors into the grim reality of being client and provider! The construction industry has met its client in itself. How scary! When the PFI projects division of the company is dealing with the straightforward construction division, then the demands of the 'client' is suddenly an in-house problem. The mirror can be a shocking phenomenon to the traditional contractor when turned client! Moreover, if that same construction company has its own in-house FM division, as most now do, then this simply adds to the in-house pressure. The FM team will be determined to ensure that the facility, whatever it may be, is wholly maintainable, that light bulbs are reachable, that air conditioning systems are easy to maintain, that windows can be cleaned safely and so on.

If you are a construction contractor trying to go about your normal business of delivering a simple £18 million college complex in the middle of Livingston, West Lothian, the last thing you want is a colleague from your same company (PFI Projects division) giving you a hard time about cost, quality, specifications, variations at the same time as another colleague (FM division) bleating about access to the boiler room, the ventilation facilities, how the surface water drainage system is not manageable, parking facilities are a shambles and the like. But that is what PFI and PPP have delivered to our industry. Suddenly we are our own client. Suddenly we can see from the outside in. A lot more thought now has to be given in the design and construction phase to usability, maintainability, sustainability and whole-life value of a given project.

Whatever Egan, Latham, M4I, CBPP and the plethora of other such initiatives tried to do, in one fell swoop, PFI and PPP have delivered in real tangible terms. Suddenly all these initiatives become almost irrelevant. As the industry can see in itself what only its clients once saw. The industry does not need these governmental, civil service led initiatives any more, nor does it need the academics hurling principles at it any more. The industry has seen the light. It is now able to deliver in the fashion, which the traditional 'client' has always wanted. It is the gamekeeper and the poacher.

This fact has been of fundamental importance to the public relations function in the construction industry. Any construction organization that has not taken on board this revolutionary change in the whole character of our industry and the dynamic changes required in our public relations function will not survive in the new world of the construction industry. The role and scope of the public relations function have grown into one of the keystones of future business development, of client relations, of partnerships, of repeat business, of negotiated contracts and, of critical importance, of future PFI and PPP work.

Image, reputation, press profile have never been so important. And, in the new scenario of PFI and PPP in the construction industry, all these elements are not only critical in the corporate, national or global context, but, of more significance, is the need to have image, reputation and press profile on a local basis. Local is often now even more important than national, since a local issue in today's era of instant communications, quickly become global and one small local incident will very quickly become a major national or global incident. At the time of writing, the Jarvis situation in the wake of the Potters Bar rail crash in the UK is a typical example of the impact on a large company involved in a large franchise suffering globally from a horrible accident at one point in thousands of miles of a rail maintenance contract.

Public relations in this environment has been transformed. Construction has always prided itself in harnessing the powers of nature to create the needs of civilization … to produce the fabric of society: road, rail and airport transport infrastructure, places to live, work and places to learn, to be entertained, places of culture, places for our health and welfare, magistrates' courts, and police stations and prisons for law and order, supermarkets for shopping. If the industry is producing the very fabric of society, so its place in society has to be recognized as a pillar in that society.

Whereas the construction industry simply delivered this infrastructure and fabric in the past, today it delivers and owns and maintains that same infrastructure and fabric (through PFI/PPP) and so its remit to deliver greater public relations is paramount: strategic, tactical and essential.

The construction industry today is a major stakeholder (or owner) of roads, bridges, hospitals, schools, colleges, law courts, police headquarters, prisons, local authority office complexes and innumerable other 'public' services and facilities. The construction industry is a public service. As a major contributor and stakeholder of public services, the construction industry has to be the very best at public relations. Failure to provide this public relations function professionally and efficiently will inevitably lead to the failure of the organization itself. Reputation is survival in today's world of corporate ownership in the public sector. If the public relations function in the construction industry fails in the coming decade, then construction's foray into PFI/PPP will be doomed to failure. That is, today, the importance of public relations to the construction industry.

Inevitably, the more responsible attitudes towards whole life costs, sustainability, maintenance and environmental considerations brought to the contractor through the PFI/PPP process, is spreading to other, conventionally bid projects; thereby bringing improvements throughout the industry.

Corporate communications today

Reflecting the radical, not to say revolutionary, changes that have confronted the construction industry today, the corporate communications strategy, including public relations in its broadest sense, has had to evolve with equal rapidity and dynamism. But, rather like three-dimensional chess, it has also had to adopt the parallel revolution in electronic media, in the instant communications medium of the intranet and the Internet. Local is suddenly global.

Inevitably, the communications strategy of the modern construction giant is sophisticated. It is high-tech, employing the best resources for its website, its intranet and its e-mail e-newsletter services. But has it adopted the best processes, systems and fabric upon which to meet the needs of our new construction environment as described above?

The core objective of a public relations department should be to enhance and protect the reputation of the company, thereby supporting the business objectives of the organization. Involving all business units (construction, design, PFI projects, property development, FM and similar), the public relations function should cover all aspects of both internal and external communications, ensuring that they are all consistent, not contradictory, and co-ordinated. The aims surrounding the core objectives should, in simple terms, include the following elements:

● Maintain pro-active public relations and marketing communications activities in support of the corporate business development objectives and strategies
● Raise the profile of the organization within the technical, financial, commercial and technical press
● Influence policy development on construction-related issues at senior civil servant and ministerial level within government
● Encourage and assist the organization and its employees to become excellent corporate citizens in the communities within which they work
● Exhort participation of all staff in the promotion of their own organization at local level
● Enhance the organization's customer relations activities in order to nurture an environment for repeat business and to improve customer service
● Assist in the recruitment process to bring in the best personnel at all levels by developing the reputation of the organization as the best place for training and individual development
● Assist in the development of the best forms of communications to develop a culture of health and safety awareness throughout the organization.

The construction industry is evolving so rapidly that any corporate communications' plan has to be flexible, adaptable and constantly updateable. Having said that, the fundamental disciplines have to be laid out and adopted by the main board of directors as a commitment to a corporate communications strategy.

The first elements must establish the objectives of the communications plan, then the strategy for implementing that plan. The key messages need identifying for each audience: general; marketplace (clients/customers); safety; employees; recruitment; financial markets/ investment analysts; community/local audiences; supply chain.

Next is the implementation of that strategy and plan. This means identifying the tools and medium through which these messages are to be conveyed to those audiences identified. Typically this will include: publications (annual report and accounts, staff newspapers/magazines, corporate brochures, external client magazines, community relations guidance documents and the like); Press and media policies and strategies, including targeted publications in the construction and trade press; site-based safety communications initiatives; industry awards nominations; advertising and exhibitions campaigns; intranet development; internet website development; corporate sponsorship and charitable giving programmes; development of company videos or CD Roms presentations; directors' staff 'road-show' events; other (including, inevitably, promotional gifts – umbrellas, pens, diaries, mousemats, key rings, etc.).

Government relations is a key element of the public relations/corporate communications remit and, although not covered in any detail in this chapter, remains a core aspect of business development. In today's environment of PFI and PPP, a full understanding and appreciation of current government policies and thinking on key issues affecting the industry need to be identified, assessed and then considered in a business development environment. Today's government agenda on private sector investment in the railways, in the underground rail network, in investing in the country's health, education, law and order and other infrastructure facilities is critical to the future of our industry. Advanced warning or knowledge about debates surrounding such issues is one thing, but active involvement in the debating process at White Paper or even Committee stage is also of vital importance.

For those charged with delivering public services, from roads to hospitals and schools, there is a strategic need to know current government thinking and current cabinet intentions. Moreover, for those same deliverers of public services and those investing in building schools, hospitals and police stations, there is an equally vital need to have an influence upon the debating process for future plans and policies. Here, the construction industry and its public relations function needs to be fully involved in the legislative process ... both from a lobbying and a consultative process/point of view.

Corporate identity is another issue close to the heart of the public relations practitioner in the construction industry. Familiarity breeds content. As companies expand with sites spread across the country, in city centre developments, out-of-town retail areas or town bypasses, so their hoardings follow them. Signage up and down every motorway and monoflex plastered across the scaffolding of every building site screams corporate identity. And rightly so. It is a statement of possession, a statement of territory, a statement of achievement and, to many, a statement of the winner. We use corporate identity as a flag to wield whenever we can to goad the opposition, to become tribal in our defence of what is ours. Moreover, a strong corporate identity so overtly and powerfully used can be incredibly motivational for existing staff and a vital tool in the recruitment of new staff. Again, familiarity is a powerful tool in the public perception of an organization.

Crisis management is, or should be, a major element in any corporate communications plan locker. It is not rocket science. Nevertheless, it is essential to have a tool-kit in the plan that provides guidance and advice to anyone in the company confronting a site-based crisis or incident. Whether it be a guidance document or a manual, any crisis management plan needs to have the basic ingredients of a holding statement and points of contact for future developments. It also needs a co-ordination plan for the involvement of the legal, insurance and personnel departments to ensure that all have the same song sheet and all are totally co-ordinated in their approach to the parties concerned.

Finally, any communications plan and strategy needs to have a fully monitored and assessable out-turn delivery. Whether it be through the conventional press cutting monitoring services available or through more formal feedback reports is debateable, but some form of assessment is essential. Intranet and Internet 'hit' data can very quickly reveal success and failure in the electronic communications sector (though 'user profiles', or data on *who* is visiting the website, can be more important than pure volume of 'hits': i.e. quality vs. quantity) and simple incentivised questionnaires linked to both internal and external communications publications can also provide a good assessment of product delivery. If the need be, the services of such organizations as MORI can be very cost-effectively used mediums through which to assess customer/client satisfaction in this context.

Community relations – forget at your peril!

Community relations is, today, one of the most potent business development tools in the construction industry's tool-bag. As discussed above, the bigger the organization the more sensitive it is to the preservation of its reputation, but, at the same time, the more open it is to the impact of local situations that can quickly become global. Every single project is an open target to bring down an empire should the wrong message go out or the reaction to a given situation is not handled properly.

As we have discussed in the context of PFI/PPP situations, every single community hospital, school or college under the wing of a construction organization, albeit under the PFI projects banner or the FM company title, is a potential public relations time bomb. But it is not restricted to PFI/PPP. On the contrary, every construction project reflects in the public eye the reputation of the organizations involved in that construction. Most clients are increasingly aware of their contractors' behaviour on each and every individual location that is being developed. Their public is also the construction company's public. Upset that public and you upset the client.

Most successful construction organizations are acutely aware of this responsibility and most project managers and agents know how to behave and how their site team are expected to behave as representatives of their companies. However, the public relations function should be involved on an integral basis with the whole ethos and culture portrayed by every construction site. Typically, this expectation is impossible, given that the average public relations department in the construction industry is totally unresourced in terms of personnel and finance. Thus the greatest contribution of the public relations function in this context is to guide, encourage and foster best practice by giving strong central support and guidance documentation.

The main board has to be committed to community relations if the public relations function is to succeed in educating site personnel in best practice. That commitment needs to be spelt out in unequivocal terms: as individual citizens, as a company and as a partnership with clients, subcontractors and suppliers, the organization must be seen to genuinely care for the communities and environments within which they live and work.

It is clearly understood that our type of business, whether involving new construction or refurbishment, inevitably has some impact upon the environment and people surrounding our works – noise, dust, vibration, traffic disruption and similar inconvenience. However, with commitment from the top and guidance from the public relations department and regional directors, we can all do our utmost to reduce some of the negative impacts upon communities resulting from our construction works and to do our best to mitigate any temporary inconvenience brought to customers and the public. Therefore, it makes sense to produce a suitable guidance document that is specifically site based in terms of audience and usage, and is fully piloted by several operational sites to ensure that it is workable. If nothing else such a document will encourage consistency in a company's community relations activities across the country.

Undoubtedly we have to recognize that there is already tremendous pressure upon our construction teams to deliver projects in ever tighter timescales, with increased quality and safety requirements, in parallel to reduced costs. So it is important to point out that the need for responsible community relations is not intended as an additional burden upon construction site management, but is aimed at reducing complaints and distractions that unhappy neighbours can cause you. It is without doubt that a little time invested in the local community early on will pay long-term dividends in the overall construction process.

Good citizenship reflects a good company. It also makes good business sense. Our behaviour on site reflects upon our client.

Every project team involved in a construction project has direct responsibility for fostering excellent community relations among its neighbouring residents and businesses. From the start of a project the project team needs to establish an individual who is responsible for managing liaison with the public. A key role of this person is to instil upon all of those in the workforce, from operatives to senior site management, the need for a considerate and respectful attitude towards the public. They should also implement a formal complaints procedure that is fully logged and becomes an integral part of reporting procedures for the weekly Contract Progress Meetings with the client, consultant and/or architect.

Successful community relations is also dependent upon a close relationship with the relevant local public service officers: police, fire, environmental health and so on. It is often these officers who receive the first complaints from the public and they need to be kept fully informed at all times about any actions that may have the potential to impact upon the community or the environment.

Any community relations programme needs to include guidance on the production of site newsletters for public audiences, about dealing with the local press and about the holding of public or residents' meetings to explain activities surrounding a project. All of these activities are aimed at:

- Giving a broad understanding of the scheme under construction
- Introducing the site team as individuals
- Giving warning about the dangers of construction sites to the public, particularly children
- Explaining whatever planning restrictions or issues that are pertinent to the public
- Providing an opportunity for concerns and questions to be raised by neighbours
- Establishing points of contact and complaints procedures
- Committing the team publicly to minimize disruption that can be caused by site operations.

School liaison is an important aspect of local community relations. If there is a school in proximity to a project site, efforts should be made early on in the construction process to communicate with staff and pupils. Construction sites can be dangerous and so staff, parents and pupils need to be made aware of the potential dangers. Where possible, a representative of the site and or a safety advisor should arrange to visit the school to give talks to pertinent age groups.

Local media is also a vital part of the matrix. The local newspapers, radio and television have usually been involved in a significant project early on in the planning stage, so when a contractor arrives on site, this media interest is ripe for feeding positive messages. Therefore it is equally vital for the public relations department to give very clear guidance on dealing with local media and, where possible, takes direct control of on-going local media enquiries in conjunction with the client.

One of the best mediums for guidance and providing sites with the tools for successful community relations today in the intranet. Guidance documents on crisis management, dealing with local media and even templates for site newsletters can successfully be accessed from the intranet given suitable publicity from the public relations function.

Press relations – an extension to marketing communications

Other chapters in this book have gone into great details about press relations or media relations within the construction industry. Nevertheless, in the context of the topics covered by the title that includes 'public relations' it is worth making a few short remarks about handling the press.

The key to successful press relations often lies in open, honest and frank relationships between organizations and key journalists. We are all human beings and all our relationships depend upon trust and understanding. There is nothing different when it comes to dealing with the press.

We should not be defensive with the press. We should not be reactive. Nor should we be content with simply throwing out numerous press releases about contracts awarded. If we are proud of our profession, our industry and our company, then it makes sense to share that pride and tell people about it. Naturally, most of our enthusiasm may fall on deaf ears because every public relations executive is out there selling their wares, but keep plugging away at the successes you can demonstrate.

National press is always very difficult for the construction industry to penetrate. It's not exciting enough, it is generally not too controversial, it certainly does not boast unseemly profits in the market! Occasionally a real landmark project may hit the national press such as the Second Severn River Crossing bridge, the wobbly Millennium Bridge over the Thames and any high-profile Foster building that certain prominent individuals may choose to berate in public. On the other hand, if an angle can be found, whether it is associated with a particularly big infrastructural issue or linked to a specially significant architectural achievement, can attract national interest with some effort.

Local press is particularly important (as demonstrated in the previous section of this chapter) but is also particularly uncontrollable and unpredictable. What might seem to us as an irrelevant event can often balloon into a major issue in the local press. This in turn can quickly be picked up by local radio and television and, before you know it, you are national news. Handle local press with kid gloves and with the utmost respect. Patronizing attitudes to local journalist can quickly escalate out of control.

In the context of the construction press, relationships are important and a demonstration that your organization is keen to be involved in debating key issues confronting our industry – training, safety, skills shortages, insurance, subcontractors, etc. – will always engender a more open relationship. Gone are the days of the press conference in our industry and, unfortunately, gone are the days of the group press site visits when a crowd of five or six sector journalists would spend a day visiting a site and interviewing site managers, the client, the consultant and others in the team. These used to be good fun for one and all!

One-to-one interviews are the most enlightening for both the journal concerned and the executive being interviewed since the questions and the answers given can better reflect the particular audience of each niche publication. One may be more geared to the client readership while another might best be relevant to site-based staff – your own employees and those of rival organizations – where more detailed messages need to be communicated. Likewise, building, civil engineering, architecture, property, maritime engineering are all very different disciplines within the broad church of construction and one-to-one interviews are vital if you need to get across your message.

Of course the support and commitment of the board in general and chief executive in particular are paramount in this exercise. If they prefer anonymity and low profile, then the public relations function can only be defensive and reactive. You cannot in these circumstances do a great deal to raise the profile of your organization. The business development function will have to look elsewhere for such profile building. And the only alternative could be very expensive and very unquantifiable advertising expenditure.

And finally, CSR …

Corporate Social Responsibility has been embraced by all major retail and consumer organizations and today is one of the key benchmark elements in assessing a corporate body. Construction, in general terms, is one of the main industries not yet perceptively embracing CSR; with one or two notable exceptions. But what is CSR and how relevant is it to construction?

In simple terms, CSR is the impact of a business and the relationship between it and society, particularly those involved or affected by its activities. In a construction organization CSR encompasses a multitude of already existing company activities and policies, including, training and development of staff, in-company sports and social clubs, community relations, environmental policies, health and safety, sustainability, charitable giving and public relations. It is in fact a central core that should run through a company's very ethos and culture. It should embody what that company represents both to its external public and all its own staff and supply chain participants … as well as its clients. Indeed, CSR is a vital business development tool. However, a CSR policy must be proven and deliverable, through tangible, verifiable benchmarks that can be subjected to transparent third-party scrutiny and auditing.

Many larger, but especially those deemed as 'influential' companies, and those … particularly retailers and manufacturers … whose businesses and business processes have an immediate impact on society, were the first to recognize the significance of being socially responsible, often because it was evident that their social irresponsibility was having a detrimental effect upon their bottom line. Evolving social and business trends, as well as increasing awareness among consumers, has had a direct impact upon government thinking and its acknowledgement of the importance of social involvement by business.

CSR will very quickly become the benchmarks by which major clients will assess the reputation of their construction services providers. A result of a positive human rights record, investment in local communities and society impacted by their operations, policies and actions involving the environment and sustainability and the way employees are treated will have a direct impact upon an organization's corporate reputation. Likewise relationships within the whole supply chain from suppliers to subcontractors, as well as the diversity of the workforce, will also impact upon the company's competitiveness.

It is only a matter of time before all construction-related businesses will need to adopt a genuine CSR policy and strategy – and not just paying lip service to such aspirations. The nature of the construction industry means that the main characteristics of our responsibility to society embrace the broad elements of education and training, safety and health, environment and sustainability, regeneration through construction and refurbishment and genuinely positive and supportive community relations.

By their nature these topics embrace many departments within an organization, transcending any barriers between human resources, personnel and training, safety, environment and public relations. However, the public relations department has to take the lead as the end results impact chiefly upon the organization's reputation. It is imperative that the whole company embraces the CSR ambitions and all staff are exhorted to participate in its implementation.

On an holistic basis, the business of the construction industry is to provide the built environment and we create and nurture the essential facilities for community citizenship: hospitals, places of learning, law courts, offices, retail stores, industrial buildings, places for entertainment like theatres and cinemas, leisure centres and swimming pools. Our day-to-day activities involve investing in, building, operating and maintaining this very fabric of society. We need, as an industry to extend this into a positive social conscience.

On a concluding note, it is worth repeating the introduction paragraph of the HBG Construction Ltd official CSR policy issued some time ago:

> Social accountability is an increasingly important element in society today. The willingness to help others and a commitment to being socially tolerant and environmentally conscious are key values that encapsulate the term Corporate Citizenship. They are the values that, as part of a general obligation to society, characterise a company that aspires to having a Corporate Social Responsibility (CSR).

Conclusion

This brief skirmish into public relations within the construction industry is not meant to be definitive, but it is aimed at highlighting some of the recent issues that have moulded what is a completely new outlook and obligation within the public relations function for the construction industry today. We live in a dynamic industry today that is changing rapidly all the time. Trees confront us all the time as we try to look for the wood beyond. We hope to have given you a chance in this short chapter to look over the parapet and see where we have come from recently and where we have embarked upon for the future. This is not a definitive look at all the issues confronting the public relations function within the construction industry, but it is an honest attempt to put the public relations role of today into its proper context as a major contributor to the business development element of a construction business that has evolved so dramatically over the past few years.

Public relations is a fundamental cornerstone upon which business development in the construction industry depends. Business development has become increasingly sophisticated.

The Internet, the evolving dynamics of procurement and the change of relationships with clients and the full supply change have revolutionized the business development function. However, the public relations function has not been idle in each duty as pillar of the business development strategies. Public relations and what it delivers is not, and never has been, a service to business development. It is a most important and critical element to corporate integrity in its own right and only part of its activities are directly business development orientated. But those elements are, nevertheless, often critical to the success or failure of a business development programme.

We hope to have demonstrated here that, when thinking 'outside-the-box', the public relations function is often ahead of the game and can actually contribute enormously to an organization's business development strategies by addressing issues not normally associated with business development but which can rapidly become critical to the on-going success of a business active in the construction industry. At the end of the day it is a partnership between public relations and business development. One should not be subordinate to the other. Both should be encouraged to think independently and then to bring the best of those thought processes together to deliver what is best for the organization.

10

Change in context

Paul B. Smith*

Introduction: construction sector change in perspective

As a subset of industry in general and a key part of the production process the construction sector has not been immune to change both in terms of its production and marketing. The built environment (roads, housing, water and sewerage, manufacturing and healthcare facilities, etc.) is a crucial part of the economic production process. The pivotal role that it occupies demands that as a sector it is capable of producing an end product as efficiently and effectively as any other sector of the economy, by understanding and servicing customer needs.

Traditionally, this sector was perceived to lag behind the general body of industry in terms of world class manufacturing, production, people, marketing and management. It has been seen as a highly fragmented, low tech, low skills and commodity industry.

Attempts to address both the perception and reality of the situation came to a head in the late 1990s, due to the combined pressures of the economic recession of the early part of the decade, and a major change in the composition of the client base. Major changes were highlighted by the privatization of many substantial utilities that had a high construction component, such as the phone, water and gas industries and the advent of new procurement methods such as PFI.

These newly privatized industries were forced for the first time to compete in an open market, and in turn sought better value for money for their construction procurement and asset base (property and physical production assets).

These factors forced the industry to address issues that had been identified as early as the 1930s. No longer was it acceptable to pay lip service to issues that were again identified in a series of reports in the 1960s, most notably Banwell (1964) 'The Placing and Management of Contracts for Building and Civil Engineering Works' and Higgins and Jessop (1965) 'Communications in the Building Industry'. According to Stuart Lipton of Stanhope Properties and chairman for Architecture in the Built Environment (CABE) little has changed over this period:

> If Bossom were writing his book now in 1999 instead of 1934, he would be saying almost precisely the same things about the industry. Nothing seems to have improved over the last 70 years.
>
> (Ciria, 1999)

* University of Leeds

The pressure for change in the 1990s reached a peak as manifest by the production of the following series of key reports.

- NEDO (1991)
- Crine (1994)
- Latham (1994)
- Active (1994)
- Building Down Barriers (1997–2000)
- Egan (1998).

All these reports aimed at improving the poor performance and image of the industry. Most were consigned to history without making any lasting change. The driving forces of global industry change that initiated these reports and in particular their influence on construction and construction marketing are the subject of this chapter.

Global change in context

The last two decades have seen major political, economic, social, organizational and personal change. The impact of change is all around us. Yet the nature and impact of change, as judged by the proliferation of both academic (Van De Ven and Poole in their seminal 1995 paper, identified a million articles) and general publications, points both to a general acceptance of its existence and a probable lack of uniformity and understanding as to what it means.

Welcome to the revolution. The evocative title of Prof. Tom Cannons (1996) book sums up the magnitude and scale of the challenge that Business, Management, employees and society in general face as we enter the third industrial revolution. The core question postulated by Cannon is whether today's dominant groups can learn and adopt fast enough and deeply enough to succeed beyond the millennium. The challenge that the convergence of all these factors is to force.

> most companies not merely to adjust or adopt as they had in the past but to confront the need for transformational change
>
> (Ghoshal and Bartlett, 1998)

This will necessitate companies, managers and employees to change fundamentally in order to avoid the situation of a company that in the words of one of its managers

> was trying to implement third generation strategies through second generation organizations run by first generation managers
>
> (Ghoshal and Bartlett, 1998)

Ultimately time will tell how perceptive or otherwise writers such as Cannon and Ghoshal and Bartlett are, or were. But this is not really the issue. This section has not sought to correlate the collective wisdom of the worlds leading minds as to the nature of the future. Instead its principle objective is to establish beyond doubt, the rate of change, the uncertainties and opportunities that this will bring, and above all the absence of an agreed view of the future.

The key implication would appear to be that a linear projection of the past is no longer a guide to the future, as may have been the case up until the 1980s. According to Beckhard and Harris (1978) the change challenge to all is to

1 prevent it (intransigence)
2 let it happen (indifference)
3 help it happen (co-operation)
4 make it happen (execution).

The latter is critical in that it highlights the need for the corporation – at all levels not just at a 'mystical visionary CEO level' – to be aware of future trends and respond to the change event.

From this global awareness the corporation, at all levels, should be in a better position to develop and share a vision of the future which will help it to consciously manage a rapidly changing environment.

Change and renewal – a conceptual framework

The preceding section has established that change occurs whether organizations want it or not. This section seeks to establish the principle sources of change and the responses of organizations to the change phenomenon.

> However, the large and growing literature on change and its management focuses on its objective rather than subjective aspects. It assumes that most of the managerial problems created by change derive from its rate. This may be true, but it is apparent that we cannot deal with change effectively unless we understand its nature
>
> Ackoff (1981)

A major objective of this paper is to examine both the transition from change management as an 'event' to the injection of the customer requirement into the core of the business to achieve perpetual renewal. Therefore, to paraphrase the words of Ackoff we need to understand change and renewal before considering what should change, why it should change and how?

Waterman (1987) provides a clear conceptual framework. He argues that renewal is not change or change management but that change is the lubricant for renewal. He cites examples of changes that do not renew the company, ranging from acquisition executives betting money on businesses they do not really know, growth for growth sake, accumulation of debt, internal changes such as downsizing. His list is not meant to be definitive. What it does do, is highlight that many changes may not renew and in fact may have the opposite effect and leave the company less able to serve its customers. Beer *et al.* (1990) define renewal in similar terms as

> enhancing the abilities of, and contribution made by, managers, workers, and the organization as a whole to cope with an increasing competitive environment

The direction and purpose and long-term implications of change is a key differentiator between change for change sake and renewal. In Watermans (1987) view renewal is about builders. Builders range from the custodians of the status quo, manipulators of wealth (through deal making), entrepreneurs:

> But the majority of the builders are – and always will be a much larger and significant number – everyday corporate managers who simply find ways to renew and refresh their units, their departments, their companies. These are the leaders who generate excellence, the ones we need to study, to emulate, to understand

The focus of this chapter is the journey from change for change sake to the use of change as a lubricant for corporate renewal through the achievement of excellence (as defined by meeting customer needs and values) in all aspects and areas of the business. To achieve this objective an understanding of the source and process of change and the impact on the achievement of operational and service excellence, in order to satisfy customer needs, is required.

Levels of change

The all-encompassing and embracing nature of change both as a term and a phenomenon runs the risk of diluting the concept to a level that change means all things to all people. Robbins and Finley (1997) in their book 'Why Change Doesn't Work' provide a conceptual framework to evaluate change. They propose a three-stage framework:

- *Global change:* The big changes that happen to us no matter what we do, technological, global and social.
- *Organizational change:* Change initiatives undertaken to cope with bigger change, quality, restructuring, new philosophies.
- *Personal change:* The little things and micro-issues that diminish our flexibility to change in our job.

Global external change in context

Management writers, Philosophers, and Futurists, such as Cannon, Handy and earlier Toffler have explored the nature of the economic, social, technological and political changes that mark the last two decades of rapid change as revolutionary.

The last two decades have seen major political change with major economic impact. The end of the cold war triggered by the fall of the Berlin wall, fall of communism and the subsequent reunification of Germany. This has lead to the closer integration of Europe (the Euro), which in effect created the world's second biggest trading block after the USA.

Events like this coupled with the rise of new economies such as China and India and the emergence of third world economies will fundamentally alter the world we live in, leading to a massive reallocation of resources. (Both ABB and GE cut employment numbers in first world and increased them in New World.)

In the first world advances in technology ranging from the increase in power of microchip technology, Genetic engineering of food and the advancement in human medicines and genetic research raise infinite change opportunities. These developments also raise major questions as to the nature of society and the commercial organizations that will serve this new economic order.

They also mark the start of a new economic era marked by new technologies and organizational structures. Freeman and Perez (1988) in there seminal work on business cycles define a new cycle as 'Changes of techno-economic paradigm', which they define as major changes in an entire economic system. This is the apex of a four-stage change categorization system based on the concept of innovation as an indicator of change:

1 *Incremental innovation:* more or less continuous change as exemplified by learning by doing and learning by using.

2 *Radical innovation:* discontinuous innovation and change such as the development of an entirely new technology or material such as nuclear power and nylon. Developments, which are a marked departure from the previous industries of, coal mining and woollen sectors respectively.

3 *New technology systems:* combines both radical and incremental innovation to organizations and management to several (but not all) branches of the economy.

4 *Changes of techno-economic paradigm:* this represents a major influence on an entire economy such as the advent of the railways, electricity and the microchip.

Based on this hierarchy Freeman and Perez map out the major cycles experienced by society and which map the current changes as being at the start of a fundamentally different techno-economic paradigm (Table 10.1).

In his 1970s landmark publication 'Future Shock' Toffler (1970) sought to increase societies awareness of the overwhelming impact of change on industry and society and in particular the importance of adopting to change:

Among many there is an uneasy mood – a suspicion that change is out of control (1970).

Eleven years on (1981) Toffler again raises alarm bells by arguing that the world is changing at an ever-increasing rate and that many of our existing structures are not working. This theme was taken up by Naisbitt and Aburdene in 'Reinventing the Corporation'

Table 10.1 Sketch of main characteristics of long waves (modes of growth)

Phase	Years	Description	Key factor industries	Other sectors growing from base O	Org forms and forms of competition
1	1770>	Early mechanism	Cotton, pig iron	Steam engines, machinery	Individual entrepreneurs and partnerships
2	1840>	Steam power and railways	Coal, transport	Steel, electricity, gas, synthetic dyestuffs	As markets grow, high noon of small firms and the dev of limited liability joint stick companies
3	1890>	Electricity and heavy engineering	Steel	Automobiles, aircraft, telecommunications, radio, consumer durables	Emergence of giant firms, cartels, mergers regulation or state ownership of natural monopolies Emergence of specialist middle management
4	1940>	Fordist mass production	Energy (especially oil)	Computers, radar, machine tools, nuclear power, micro electronics	Oligopolistic competition Multi-national corporations. Increasing concentration, divisional and hierarchical control
5	1990>	Information and communication	Chips micro-electronics	Third generation biotechnology products, space activities, fine chemicals	'Networks' of large and small firms based increasingly on computer networks. Close cooperation in technology, quality, J.I.T., Internal Capital markets

Source: Freeman and Perez (1988).

(1985) where they argue that the time has come to transform our organizations. This concern was further developed in Naisbitts, 1994 publication 'Global Paradox'. He envisions a radical change in world order, the end of politics, as we know it, the power of the technological revolution, a new area of self-rule; the breakdown of economic and political power blocks. A twenty-first century of 1000 countries in cyberspace.

> A world with 1000 countries picture 1000 or 2000! – Andorra's, all connected to global computer networks, all co-operating and competing. Not the countries connecting, but individuals in the 1000 countries connecting. You have just had a glance of the 21st century.

A twenty-first century of individuals, not countries connected with traditional companies conspicuous by their absence.

Already we see multi-nationals such as ABB rewrite conventional business roles and rules. It now describes itself as a large number of small companies connected globally rather than a big company. They have rewrote and reversed the Hewlett Packard dictum of thinking globally act locally to think locally act globally. ABB'S CEO Percy Barnevik stated.

> 'We grow all the time, but we also shrink all the time' … 'We are not a global business … . We are a collection of local businesses with intense global co-ordination'
>
> (Naisbitt, 1994)

Whether Naisbitts vision of the twenty-first century materializes is not the issue. What is clear is that society in general and in turn business (both in terms of how it is transacted, manufactured, structured, etc.) will change. The challenge is whether this change will produce.

> the required shift in management thinking and assumptions about the best ways to produce results. Often the 'right way' seems to conflict with the old way … . The anguish expressed by many people and the variety of explanations for failure highlights the difficulties posed by change in this form and of this scale.
>
> (Cannon, 1996)

Sources of organizational change and renewal

Organizational change originates from:

> … departures from the status quo or from smooth trends. They are almost without exception the products of an energizing force. There are two such forces for change: the organizations top managers and the organization environment
>
> (Hubert and Glick, 1993)

In essence the two principle sources of change are:

1 Internal
2 External.

Other writers have adopted and developed this basic concept but have essentially not deviated from the basic principle. For example, Want (1995) proposes a three tier hierarchical order of change model, which in essence subdivided the sources of external change (Table 10.2).

Table 10.2 Hierarchical order of change

First order change	Second order change	Third order change
Markets	Industries	Workers
Scientific/technological, political, social, economic	Globalization, technology, regulation and deregulation, consolidation, etc.	Labour marker restructuring, new core capabilities dev
Macro ⟶		Micro

Source: Want (1995) modified.

Alternate conceptual models have been developed to expand and explain the internal and external sources of change. Kanter (1983) puts forward a model based on a combination of the following five major building blocks:

- Force A. Departure from tradition
- Force B. Crisis or galvanizing event
- Force C. Strategic decisions
- Force D. Individual 'prime movers'
- Force E. Action vehicles.

Tichy (1983) explained the change process as a three stranded approach which centred on the inter-relationship between the:

- political
- cultural
- technical.

Strands of an organization. He uses the metaphor of a rope and contends that in order to capitalize on the desired change:

strategic management is the task of keeping the rope from becoming unravelled in the face of technical, political, and cultural problems.

Drucker in his influential book 'Innovation and Entrepreneurship'(1985) focuses on the impact of these two elements on the change process:

and it is change that always provides the opportunity for the new and different. Systematic innovation therefore consists in the purposeful and organized search for changes, and in the systematic analysis of the opportunities such changes might offer for economic or social innovation

This in essence is a reiteration of his famous 1955 claim that there are only two functions of a business – *marketing and innovation.*

Drucker identifies seven sources for innovative opportunities.

Within the enterprise

1 The unexpected – the unexpected success, failure and outside events
2 The incongruity – between reality as it actually is and reality as it is assumed to be or as it 'ought to be'
3 Innovation based on process need
4 Changes in industry structure or market structure that catch everyone unawares.

Outside the enterprise or industry

5 Demographics

6 Changes in perception, mood and meaning

7 New knowledge, both scientific and non-scientific.

Beer and Nohria (2000) combine the internal and external aspects in their integrated change theory. They also advocate that

> it is imperative that executives understand the nature and process of corporate change much better. But even that is not enough. Leaders need to crack the code of change

They postulate that most change in business has been an either or proposition driven. Theory E is change based on economic value. Theory O is based on organizational capability. In order to improve on the 70 per cent failure rate associated with most change initiatives they propose an amalgamation of both theories based on their forty years of studying and consulting in the change arena (Table 10.3).

Van De Ven and Poole (1995) attempted in their landmark article to produce some order and insight from the vast range of literature on organizational change. Their methodology was based on an initial electronic search, which to their amazement produced more than a million articles on change ranging from disciplines such as psychology, sociology, education, business, economics as well as biology, medicine, meteorology and geography. From this initial search they reviewed 200,000 titles from which they reviewed 2000 abstracts and studied in depth 200 articles. Their basic approach was to understand different perspectives and insights without nullifying each other. The net result was that they identified twenty different process theories, which could be grouped into

Table 10.3 Cracking the code of change – comparing theories of change

Dimensions of change	Theory E	Theory O	Theories E and O combined
Goals	Maximize shareholder value	Develop organizational capabilities	Explicitly embrace the paradox between economic value and organizational capacity
Leadership	Manage change from the top down	Encourage participation from the bottom up	Set direction from the top and engage the people below
Focus	Emphasize structure and systems	Build-up corporate culture: employees' behaviour and attitudes	Focus simultaneously on the hard (structures and systems) and the soft (corporate culture)
Process	Plan and establish programmes	Experiment and evolve	Plan for spontaneity
Reward system	Motivate through financial incentives	Motivate through commitment – use pay as fair exchange	Use incentives to reinforce change but not to drive it
Use of consultants	Consultants analyse problems and shape solutions	Consultants support management in shaping their own solutions	Consultants are expert resources who empower employees

Source: Beer and Nohria (2000).

four basic schools:

1 life cycle
2 teleological
3 dialectical
4 evolutionary.

They mapped these theories against both the unit of change and modes of change to arrive at the following change thography. Each has a different events sequence and generative mechanisms, which they term as 'motors' (Figure 10.1).

A life cycle model depicts the process of change as progressing through a sequence, that an entity has a logic, programme or code that regulates the process such that an entity moves from a given point of departure towards a subsequent end. The methopor and concept of organic growth and decay is one of the more popular aspects of this theory.

A Teleological model is based on the philosophical doctrine that purpose or goal is the final course for guiding movement of an entity through a process of goal formulation, implementation, evaluation and modification based on what was learned by the entity.

In Dialectical model colliding events, forces, and values compete with each other for dominance and control. Change occurs when opposing values, forces or events gain sufficient power to confront and engage the status quo. Confrontation and conflict between forces generates the dialectical cycle.

Evolutionary theory is used in a more restrictive sense to focus on cumulative change in structural forms of community, organization, industry or society at large. Competition for

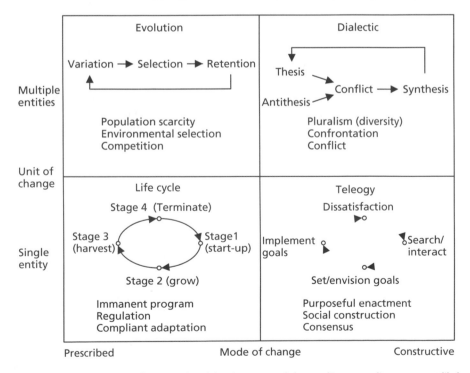

Figure 10.1 Process theories of organizational development and change. (Arrows on lines represent likely sequences among events, not causation between events.)

scarce environmental resources between entities inhabiting a population generates this evolutionary cycle. The most populist form of this theory is similar to Darwin's theory of evolution.

Unit of change is it a single organizational entity or interaction between two or more organizations?

Mode of change is defined as *either* a prescribed or constructive mode.

1 Prescribed mode channels the development of entities in a pre-specified direction. First order change within an existing organization.
2 Constructive mode involves novel often discontinuous and unpredictable departures from the past. Second order break with the past change.

Van De Ven and Poole (1995) make two fundamental points in respect of their model.

Theories seldom exist in their pure form. Most are more complicated than the ideal because of spatial dispersion of units and actors (people) coupled with time.The essence of change can be captured within their framework. In most change situations change can occur within different categories or by combining elements of the change model.

Types of change

Just as it is important to identify the source of change in order to manage it effectively it is equally important to understand the type of change involved. Is it a life threatening change that requires immediate and dramatic action or at the other end of the spectrum is it evolutionary change that can be planned and managed without massive disruption and change to daily business?

Nadler (1997) argues that change is not a 'hazy, mysterious force swirling through the corporate universe in random, indecipherable patterns. Instead he argues that the can to some extent be chartered and therefore managed. In support of his proposition he cites both his own work and the fundamental work of Tushman and his colleges at Columbia University.

Tushman and his team studied the evolutionary of hundreds of companies in a wide variety of industries at a macro level. Meanwhile Nadler and his colleagues studied a smaller sample but in more depth over a fifteen year period. Nadler combined his macro level work with Tushman's macro level analysis to arrive through analysis at the traditional S curve.

However, their analysis went further. They identified industry cycles of both equilibrium and dis-equilibrium and chartered these periods of great oscillations on the curve. The greater the oscillation, the more destabilizing the change. The results of their work led to a modified S curve known as the punctuated equilibrium theory as mapped below (Figure 10.2).

These distinctions as to the nature of change closely mirror work in the social sciences. In a much earlier work Watzlawick *et al*. (1974) developed a change categorization system from their work in the area of Psychotherapy and Group theory. They postulated that there are two basic types of change:

● *First order change:* one that occurs in a given system that itself remains unchanged.
● *Second order change:* one whose occurrence changes the system itself, a change to an altogether different state.

Abernathy and Clarke (1985) advance a four part model based on the twin axis of:

1 Market and customer linkages
2 Technology and production.

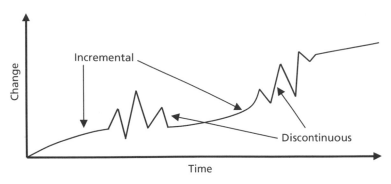

Figure 10.2 Types of change.

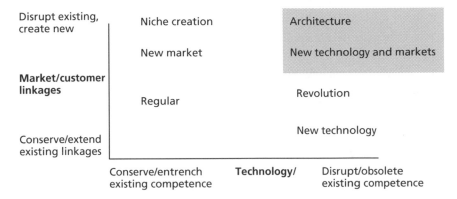

Figure 10.3 Mapping the impact of innovation (source: Abernathy and Clarke (1985, amended)).

Mapping these parameters produces a map of four distinct types of change (Figure 10.3). Stacey (1990) also derived a map of the change situation by mapping two key variables:

1 Volatility of the variable set – the factors constituting competitive capability.
2 The volatility of the parameters – customer requirements, competitive advantage, technological and cost structures.

By mapping these two key variables he derived the following three situations (Figure 10.4):

1 *Closed change:* the variables are clearly identified and constant and the parameters are constant.
2 *Contained change:* an additional set of variables and parameters connecting the variables to the desired state are not precisely known, but can be estimated using past experience with a reasonable level of probability.
3 *Open ended change:* both the variables and parameters are extremely volatile. Past experience is of little help due to the high number of variables and the outcomes are unknown.

Courtney *et al.* (1997) define four levels of uncertainty:

Level 1: a clear enough future.
Level 2: alternate futures – the future can be described as one of a few alternate outcomes.

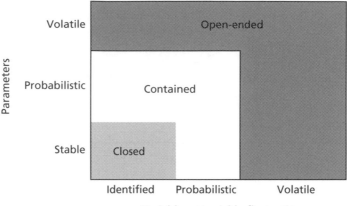

Figure 10.4 Change map (source: Stacey (1990)).

Level 3: a range of futures – the range is defined by a limited number of key variables but the actual outcome may lie anywhere along a continuum bounded by the range.

Level 4: true ambiguity – multiple dimensions of uncertainty interact to create an environment that is virtually impossible to predict.

A clear understanding of the purpose and type of change is fundamental to its success. This position is articulated by Pascale in 'Managing on the Edge'(1990).

> Incremental approach to change is effective when what you want is more of what you've already got

The central premise of his book is that the ultimate and largely ignored task of management is one of creating and breaking paradigms. The trouble in Pascale's view is that 99 per cent of management attention is devoted to the techniques that squeeze more out of the existing paradigm.

> Tools, techniques, and 'how to' recipes won't do the job without a higher order, or 'hyper' concept of management

Blanchard and Waghorn developed this distinction further in their book 'Mission Possible'(1998).

> … Operational improvements regardless of their magnitude are Evolutionary. Tinkering with the organizational structure is evolutionary. The re-engineering of core processes, and/or the outsourcing of non-core are evolutionary.
>   However, creatively phasing out the old organization structure while simultaneously creating a new one is revolutionary

Goodstein and Butz (1998) take this line of though a stage further by challenging the prevailing view held by most managers that organizational change is about efficiency and cost reduction. In their view:

> organizational efficiency is not a strategy; it is a necessary but not a sufficient condition for long term, sustainable success.

The acceptance of this paradigm injects the customer into the centre of all organizational decisions. Without the customer voice the change actions run the risk of focusing on cost and price to the exclusion of all the other factors that differentiate a product and service and move it for the position of a commodity product purchased on price alone.

The deceptively simple S curve chart based on empirical research and authors such as Pascale and Watzlawick map out clearly two distinct types of change:

1 Incremental change
2 Discontinuous or radical change.

Incremental change

In some instances the change process is not clearly noticeable. This form of unconscious change may in fact masquerade as a continuation of business as usual. The business is not consciously changing but the ebb and flow of daily business is changing the form of the business over time. In real time, the small incremental changes generated through normal business may seem so small as to not register but over time the cumulative effect is marked. This is a theme developed by Hinning and Greenwood (1998). They argue that whether an organization is changing or stable is largely a

> matter of the time span of examination ... position is that all organizations are changing but at different rates

This contrasts with clear and immediate change in response to specific threats. The analogy advanced by Connor (1998) is that of the 'Burning platform'. He advocates that no change is not an option. One either stays on the burning platform and faces certain extinction or jumps into the raging sea and fight for an uncertain future. In such a case the rate of change is quick.

For managers and businesses the fundamental question is whether they embrace change or cling on to the status quo. One of the most successful change managers of the 1980s John Harvey Jones (1988) believes that one of the fundamental roles of management is not the preservation of the status quo but the maintaining of the highest rate of change that the organization and the people within it can stand.

Harvey Jones is advocating a philosophy based on the recognition of the very fine boarder between order and chaos. This thinking has been developed into a concept known as Chaos theory. Stacey one of its chief advocates sums up the argument thus

> If the organization gives in to the pull of stability it fails because it becomes ossified and cannot change easily. If it gives in to instability it disintegrates. Success lies in sustaining an organization in the borders between stability and instability (Stacey, 1992)

Is this dividing line between stability and change something that can be managed as advocated by Harvey Jones or is the world so chaotic that managers are carried along by external momentum, powerless in an ever-changing world? The implications are at the heart of management and leadership in particular. Are companies like ships in the see being tossed around at the mercy of unexpected storms? Alternately can they be steered like GE under JackWelch?

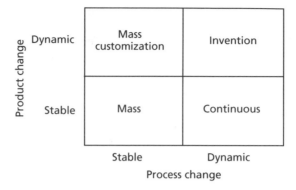

Figure 10.5 Product and process change (source: Webster (1994)).

Radical change

Only the Paranoid survive. Sooner or later something fundamental in your business world will change.

This strong and strident statement from Andy Groves (1996) CEO and Chairman of Intel succinctly highlights the nature of discontinuous change, and has impact and relevance way beyond the high technology world of computers. The Technology sector as described by Groves may be an extreme example, but it graphically summaries the impact of radical change on the product and/or process. Webster (1994) maps the impact of changes on product and process as shown in Figure 10.5.

It serves as an antidotes to considering change in isolation. The preoccupation with change as a subject – and in particular with subsets such as Quality and BPR – can create the impression that change is a discreet event that can almost be turned on and off at random. The preceding section sought to establish that this is not the case. Change is ever present and the challenge to management is to recognize the fundamental changes in the global environment and to actively manage the process. Management's challenge is no longer to manage growth. Now managers must cope with:

breakpoints or sudden shifts in the rules of the business game, may shape the course of an industry, or a company (Strebel 1992)

Conclusion: why wait for a change event

There are many arguments for and against change, but perhaps the most pressing and compelling argument is the avoidance of failure. Off the many studies carried out on the causes of failure 'The Icarus Paradox' a study by Miller (1990) as to the reasons why once great companies fail is particularly enlightening. His central thesis is that the factors that once made the firm successful are potentially the same ones that lead to its down fall because these once successful factors lead to a closed system of looking at the world or 'Group think' as coined by Irving L Janis. He defined it as

> a mode of thinking that people engage in when they are deeply involved in a cohesive in group, when the members striving for unanimity overrides their motivation to realistically appraise courses of action.

Examples include Pearl Harbour, North Korea, Bay of Pigs, and Vietnam. In business terms Miller defines the phenomenon thus 'unfortunately, it is very hard sometimes to distinguish between the focus, harmony and passionate dedication so necessary for outstanding performance, and the excesses and extremes that leads to decline' Miller identifies the symptoms as:

- Not merely a lack of awareness about the environment but a lack of self awareness
- Not a failure of rationality but a narrow rationality
- Not an inability to solve problems but an inability to recognize or define them
- Not just ignorance of the facts but disregard for them and
- Not a failure to meet standards but an adherence to the wrong standards.

These factors are principally internally driven and form a powerful checklist for managers as to how they view the world and in particular the need to introduce double loop learning in order to break out of the cycle of collective myopia. This has been defined as a situation in which members of a certain community or system are able to make sense of the context in which they live, but are not able to monitor the institution as a whole created by themselves. These are 'windows on the world and lenses that bring the world into focus' (Bolman and Deal, 1997).

Tadlow (Groves, 1996) advocates a market-orientated reason for company failure:

1 Because they leave their customers, i.e. they arbitrarily change a strategy that worked for them in the past (the obvious change)
2 Or because their customers leave them (the subtle one)
3 Or both happen simultaneously.

In 'Only the Paranoid Survive' Andy Groves (1996) of Intel demonstrates the danger of looking at the world and ones customers through a narrow mindset:

> no member of the old computer industry would have given a chance to a proposition that said that people would buy computers through the mail. It would simply have been seen as an unnatural act; just as dogs don't fly, people don't buy mail order computers. At least, they didn't in the Old World order.

Pickens and Dess (1998) refer to this situation where managers internal frame of reference are out of touch with the realities of the business, a state they term as 'Right Strategy-Wrong Problem'. The consequences of an invalid or inappropriate theory are a lack of customer and market focus resulting in a corresponding impact on performance.

Bibliography

Abernathy, W.J. and Clarke, K.B. (1985) Innovation: mapping the winds of creative destruction. *Research Policy* **14**, 3–22.

Ackoff, R.L. (1981) *Creating the Corporate Future* (New York: Wiley).

ACTIVE (1996) *Active Engineering Construction Initiative: The Action Plan* (London: ACTIVE).

Banwell, H. (1964) The Placing and Management of Contracts for Building and Civil Engineering Works (HMSO).

Beckhard, R. and Harris, H.T. (1977) *Organizational Transitions: Managing Complex Change* (Reading, Mass: Addison-Wesley).

Beer, M. and Nohria, N. (2000) Cracking the code of change. *Harvard Business Review*, May–June, P133–141.

Beer, M., Eisenstat, R.A. and Spector, B. (1990) *The Critical Path to Corporate Renewal* (Harvard Business School Press).

Blanchard, K. and Waghorn, T. (1998) *Mission Possible* (McGraw Hill).

Bolman, L.G. and Deal, T.E. (1997) *Reframing Organisations: Artistry, Choice and Leadership* (Jossey-Bass).

Cannon, T. (1996) *Welcome to the Revolution Managing Paradox in the 21st Century* (London: Pitman Publishing).

Connor, D.L. (1998) Leading at the Edge of Chaos: How to Create the Nimble Organisation (Wiley).

Courtney, H., Kirkland, J. and Viguerie, P. (1997). Strategy under uncertainty. *Harvard Business Review*, November–December, P67–79.

CRINE (1994) *Crine Report*. Institute of Petroleum, London.

Drucker, P. (1955) *The Practice of Management* (Heinmemann).

Drucker, P. (1985) *Innovation and Entrepreneurship* (Butterworth-Heinemann Ltd).

Egan, J. (1998) *Rethinking Construction*. Department of the Environment, UK.

Freeman, C. and Perez, C. (1988) Structural crisis of adjustment: business cycles and investment behaviour. In: Dosi, G., Freeman, C., Nelson, R., Silverberg, G. and Soete, L. (eds.) *Technical Change and Economic Theory* (Frances Printer).

Ghoshal, S. and Bartlett, C.A. (1998) *The Individual Corporation* (London: Heinman) .

Goodstein, L.D. and Butz, H.E. (1998) 'The Linchpin of organizational change. *Organizational Dynamics*, Summer 1998, 21–33.

Groves, A.S. (1996) *Only the Paranoid Survive* (Harper Collins Business).

Harvey Jones, J. (1988) *Making it Happen* (Collins).

Higgins, J. and Jessop, N. (1965) *Communications in the Building Industry* (London: Tavistock).

Hinnings, C.R. and Greenwood, R. (1989) *The Dynamics of Strategic Change* (Basil Blackwell Ltd).

Hubert, G.P. and Glick, W.H. (1993) *Organisational Change and Redesign* (Oxford University Press).

Kanter, R.M. (1983) *The Change Masters* (London: Routledge).

Latham, M. (1994) *Constructing the Team*. Department of the Environment, HMSO, UK.

Miller, D. (1990) The Icarus Paradox: How Exceptional Companies Bring About Their Own Downfall: New Lessons in the Dynamics of Corporate Success, Decline, and Renewal (Harper Business).

Nadler, D.A. and Nadler, M.B. (1997) *Champions of Change* (San Francisco: Jossey-Bass).

Naisbitt, J. (1982) *Megatrends* (New York: Warner Books).

Naisbitt, J. (1994) *Global Paradox* (BCA Books).

Naisbitt, J. and Aburdene, P. (1985) *Reinventing the Corporation*.

NEDO (1991) *Faster Building for Commerce* (London: HMSO).

Pascal, R.T. (1990) *Managing on the Edge* (London: Viking).

Pickens, J.C. and Dess, G.G. (1998) *Right Strategy – Wrong Problem. Organizational Dynamics*, Summer, 36.

Robbins, H. and Finley, M. (1997) *Why Change Doesn't Work* (Orion Business).

Stacey, R.D. (1990) *Dynamic Strategic Management for the 1990's* (London: Keogan Page).

Stacey, R. (1992) *Managing Chaos: Dynamic Business Strategy in an Unpredictable World* (London: Kogan Page).

Stacey, R. (1993) *Strategic Management and Organisational Dynamics* (London: Pitman).

Strebel, P. (1992) *Breakpoints: How Managers Exploit Radical Business Change* (Harvard Business School Press).

Strebel, P. (1998). The change pact. *Financial Times* (Pitman Publishing).

Tichy, N.M. (1982). *Managing Strategic Change, Technical, Political and Cultural Dynamics* (Wiley).

Toffler, A. (1970) *Future Shock* (New York, USA: Random House).

Van De Ven, A. and Poole, M. (1995) Explaining development and change in organizations. *Academy of Management Review*, **20** (3), 510–540.

Want, J.H. (1995). *Managing Radical Change* (John Wiley).

Waterman, R.H. (1988). *The Renewal Factor* (Bantam Press).

Watzlawick, P., Weakland, J.P. and Fish, R. (1974) *Change; Principles of Problem Formation and Problem Resolution* (New York: Norton).

Webster, F.E. (1994). *Market-driven Management: Using the New Marketing Concept to Create a Customer Orientated Company* (John Wiley).

PART 3

Challenges of a new age

e-Business development

David Bentley* and John Butler†

The Internet in context

Introduction

A new technology that would enable us all to explore the world and beyond without taking a single step – the Internet was coming alive.

Every so often a groundbreaking development or invention changes the world in profound and irrevocable ways. We can argue about the definition of 'progress', or if something is a 'good' or a 'bad' thing. But you cannot dispute the tremendous impact of such changes, which affect all aspects of our private and working lives, and have helped to ensure the continued dominance of commerce, trade and industry across the globe.

Since the industrial revolution that took place in Britain between 1730 and 1850 a series of technological developments have fundamentally changed the way society operates. The industrial revolution – with the help of our colonial activities – made Britain the richest country in the world. Great strides forward in science and engineering followed. Steam power led to the birth of the railways in 1825 following George Stephenson's invention of the Rocket, the first true steam locomotive. By 1840 there were 1500 miles of track in operation in the UK, rising to 6000 miles by 1850 and approaching 15000 miles by the mid-1870s. So too with the motor car. Rudolf Diesel's invention of the internal combustion engine in 1893 led to the proliferation of motorized transport. In 1900 the UK boasted 500 motor vehicles, by 1904 there were 18000, by 1914 the number had reached 250000 and now we have a staggering 25m vehicles on our roads.

You can plot similar growth patterns in other technologies. By 1903, brothers Wilbur and Orville Wright had built a 'flyer', which actually flew. The electromagnetic telephone was invented in 1876 by Alexander Graham Bell. In 1926, John Logie Baird transmitted moving pictures of human faces over a short distance, with the BBC beginning televised broadcasts in 1930. By 1969, our insatiable thirst for knowledge and exploration had taken us

* NetConstruct, Leeds
† Edinburgh University

thousands of miles through space to land on the moon. A giant leap indeed by astronaut Neil Armstrong – but few knew at that time that a small group of pioneering computer scientists were already working on a new technology that would once again totally change the way we live, work and communicate. A new technology that would enable us all to explore the world and beyond without taking a single step – the Internet was coming alive.

A brief history

Companies began to recognize the Internet's potential to improve not only how a business communicates, but more fundamentally, how it operates.

The idea of a set of globally interconnected computers through which information, data and programs could be quickly accessed from any site was probably first described by J.C.R. Licklider of the Massachusetts Institute of Technology in 1962. He referred to it as his 'Galactic Network' concept.

Licklider was the first head of the computer research programme at the US Defense Advanced Research Projects Agency (DARPA), originally called the Advanced Research Projects Agency (ARPA). He convinced his successors to pursue the idea of a 'Galactic Network'.

By the end of 1969 four host computers – three in California and one in Utah – were connected together to form a research sharing tool, the 'Arpanet', primarily for the use of closed communities of scholars. This was the precursor to the Internet. The Arpanet was first demonstrated to the public in 1972, and in the same year, e-mail technology was developed to support its use. By the mid-1970s, the new technology was being widely used by bodies such as the US Department of Defence; the US Department of Energy and NASA. As an anti-missile control network devolved across the US in the then cold war, multiple connected centres could maintain defence integrity even if some locations had become inoperable due to attack.

The term 'Internet' became increasingly accepted from the 1980s onwards, when America's National Science Foundation was developing its high-speed NSFNet backbone linking a collection of regional networks to serve the entire US higher education community. The Arpanet itself was finally decommissioned in 1990.

The Internet and the World Wide Web

It would also be useful here to briefly explain the development of the World Wide Web, which is often wrongly used as a synonym for the Internet. In 1989, Tim Berners-Lee, the so-called Father of the Web, came up with the concept of an online repository for information available to anyone across the globe. By the early 1990s the World Wide Web – an application running on top of the Internet – was starting to be widely used.

So why the sudden explosion in the use of the Internet and the World Wide Web in the mid-1990s? For the answer, we need to stand back and consider the differences between computing power in three distinct user groups – academia, business and the general public. Compared with other walks of life, back in the 1970s when the academic community was first developing the Internet, they already had vast computing power and capacity enabling them to link up and start 'networking'. This was certainly not the case for the business community at the time, while a home computer would have been a rarity. It was not until the early 1990s that low-cost local area networks (LANs) began to proliferate, with the use of personal computers becoming commonplace by the mid-1990s. Hardware and software costs tumbled, fuelling extraordinary growth in the market.

Then, almost simultaneously – and nearly 20 years after academia adopted electronic networking – business and the public woke up to the opportunities the Internet could offer. The transmission medium PSTN (the commonplace public service telephone network) was already installed at most business and domestic premises, which made for easy take-up. A raft of supporting industries quickly sprang up to meet a demand that rivalled anything the motor car, railways and other such technologies had created before. Businesses now found it worthwhile to exploit their greatly increased computing power to communicate via e-mail and to start providing Web-based services. Compared with publishing and sending printed material through the post, e-mail and the Web offered great savings in cost and time. Soon, companies began to recognize the Internet's potential to improve not only how a business communicates, but more fundamentally, how it operates – a central issue I will return to later in this chapter.

The revolution that had begun seven years before humans landed on the moon was now accelerating rapidly and continues to do so. The construction industry, traditionally a conservative beast, probably has a little catching up to do.

Changing the business model

Future success will still be governed by enduring generic business principles, but the business model through which the success is delivered needs to be under constant review. And nothing has had a more far-reaching effect on the business model than the Internet.

Before looking at the construction industry specifically, it is worth asking why the Internet is of such significance. The starting point is not to be found in the bits and bites of technology, but in the company boardroom. At the end of the day, company performance is mainly dictated by a limited number of criteria – improving product, better service, expanding markets, speeding up delivery, cutting costs, increasing skills and so on. If a new technology comes along that can improve company performance, directors will want to know about it. They may not always understand how it works, but they are usually pretty good at evaluating benefits and, where relevant, deciding how the new technology should be applied.

Everyone at board level has some responsibility for addressing the commercial challenges of their organization, and if you are looking for guidance on the thought processes that should be going on in the boardroom, you will find it in abundance throughout the chapters of this book. You should also consider generic business management issues, and make yourself familiar with works such as Dr Michael Porter's celebrated 'Competitive Strategy, Techniques for Analysing Industries and Competitors' (The Free Press). Despite being published in the 1980s, its incisive examination of the fundamentals of success shows how the principles of good management he describes remain equally valid today. For example, what is the nature of competition? How can you use cost leadership, differentiation and focus to survive and grow within a given industry structure? How do you maximize the returns of your company's various offerings as they move through their natural lifecycles? Can you be more in control of your surrounding commercial environment?

Dr Porter's book demonstrates why some individuals achieve the seemingly impossible and succeed not only in one business sector, but in several. It is because they have realized that in most cases, if you distil situations back to core fundamentals – whether in the public or private sectors, whether in products or services – you will find common solutions at work. A knowledge of these common solutions is invaluable in the commercial world and for the construction marketeer. If you can think like your client and understand what your client is trying to achieve, you will spot the new approaches and technologies from which you will both benefit.

The business model under review

Future success will still be governed by the enduring generic business principles mentioned above, but the business model through which the success is delivered needs to be under constant review. And nothing has had a more far-reaching effect on the business model than the Internet.

When, in the mid-1990s, boards of directors and their senior managers started to look at the opportunities offered by e-mail and the World Wide Web, they found themselves presented with a new set of business tools that had a significance to equal the great inventions of former years – the motor car, the railways, the telephone and more. Initially, they saw e-mail and the Web as tools to move text and images rapidly, globally and at dramatically reduced cost. Soon, however, they realized the impact of the Internet could be even greater if used to improve the way standard business routines are handled between organizations and individuals. As a result, the opportunities to create a new business model began to unfold, aided and abetted by providers of special software and hardware solutions that claimed to do things better, faster, cheaper and more easily than ever before.

The global adoption of Internet technologies took place at a staggering speed. In the four years from 1998 to 2002, it penetrated to the heart of almost every business operation and, at the same time, to over half the UK's households. Of course, as with any emerging concept, progress is littered with dramatic failures. Many brave but ill-conceived innovations fell by the wayside, particularly in the 'dotcom' crashes of 2000 and 2001. However, the reality is that they are dwarfed by the numerous Internet successes.

In generic terms therefore, the new business model had well and truly arrived – 'e-business'. For those who embrace e-business, the challenge for the future will be to what extent they are prepared to exploit the Internet. For those who turn their backs on e-business, the future is hard to imagine.

The curiosity of the construction marketeer

As e-business creates radically new ways to work more closely with everyone up and down the supply chain for mutual benefit, the e-thinking construction marketeer should be taking some very large strides up the organizational ladder.

What separates human beings from other creatures inhabiting this planet is a faculty for sustained curiosity. Since the days of Adam and Eve, the human race has been continually asking questions and coming up with new ideas.

It is not surprising therefore that the construction industry, charged by society with meeting many of its physical needs, has an inherent reputation for solving problems.

A less formal version of the Institution of Civil Engineers' motto 'Scientia et Ingenio' is 'Harnessing the forces of nature for the benefit of mankind' or, as some put it, 'doing the best you can with what you have got'. Many in the construction industry will relate to that.

After reading so far, the curious construction marketeer should by now have a lot of questions about e-business. Not least, how do you harness the power of the Internet? If the Internet is so important – and if competitive advantage is the prize for those who make the right moves – what is the way forward?

e-Business applications designed to increase competitiveness are numerous and continually evolving, but they do not come with an 'increase competitiveness' label on them. Instead, the Internet has taken every discipline within an organization – be it client handling, design, planning, estimating, buying, recruitment, project management, cost control, construction, maintenance, or support services – into a period of turbulent change which is set to last for a decade or more. Once the people in a particular discipline have accepted the possibility of a new e-business way of working, and are prepared to listen to possible solutions, they will have entered a period of constant evaluation and implementation. This radically changes the role of the construction marketeer too.

Instead of being super-efficient in a vertical silo of traditional marketing activity, the effective construction marketeer should be an instrument through which the e-business enabled organization repositions itself within the marketplace. The outward-going messages still have an element of 'what we do', but are now reinforced by 'how we do it'.

To look at this further, let us consider the constant plea throughout the construction supply chain for more collaboration. What this really means is often unclear, but it can have something to do with a recognition that, in construction, few organizations can maximize their performance on their own. We all rely on minimum standards of performance by our clients, our suppliers and others who are in some way involved including, at times, even the general public itself. The better they perform, the better chance we have for success. So how can the Internet help collaborative working?

The Internet in action – the online 'project room'

An easy example is the project extranet, or 'online project room', which is now a well used Internet application in construction. The aim of the project extranet is to provide an area on the Internet through which all documents, project programmes, drawings, correspondence, communications and even payments can pass on individual and multiple contracts. Entry to the extranet is restricted to those involved, with some people having access to everything (e.g. the client and the project manager) and others having access to only those parts which affect them (e.g. materials suppliers and contractors). In particular, with only one 'master set' of drawings in circulation, held on the project extranet central server, revisions can easily be made and checked by all involved.

As you would expect, the benefits are well documented by the suppliers of extranet software, with reductions in contract administration and faster decision-making being two that are top of the list. The project extranet can reduce the development process by some months which, when you think about the time-related costs of all the various people involved, can generate considerable savings. It is not surprising therefore to find clients leading the demand that their major contracts are undertaken using project extranets – the client has the most to gain!

And where does this leave the contractor or supplier? The financial advantages to the client are so great that your own price can be less of an issue. If you are pitching for the work and can demonstrate your competence in working with project extranets, you are probably well placed compared with opponents who are less familiar with this e-business model, no matter how low their quotations.

Creating competitive advantage

For the construction marketeer therefore, showing how your company works – particularly how it works in e-business terms – can create significant competitive advantage. It is not just about the use of the technology per se. e-Business should enable the effective construction marketeer to move into a much wider role. After all, the construction marketeer is one of the organization's main relationship managers – knowing what clients are doing, wanting and needing. As e-business creates radically new ways to work more closely with everyone up and down the supply chain for mutual benefit, the e-thinking construction marketeer should be taking some very large strides up the organizational ladder. In future, without strong marketing representation at board level, any construction organization will be at risk. That place must be earned however, and involves far more than deciding the colour of the next promotional item or how to spend the hospitality budget.

And if that sounds tough, it is. The construction marketeer must understand every aspect of every part of the construction process. What is achievable and what is not. How people work together. Where pressure points exist, some of which may be the legacy of the past. Change cannot always be instantaneous, so compromises are inevitable.

As well as being good at information gathering and analysis, the construction marketeer must be able to get inside the minds of the client, suppliers, colleagues and everyone else who could influence business success. Then, by careful interpretation of needs and skilful consultation, the construction marketeer can help bring together the organization's portfolio of e-business use in ways that provide maximum support to the marketing objectives and position the organization as a leader in future markets.

The Internet as a solution

How can the Internet and e-business so fundamentally change and improve how construction works? What must the construction marketeer actually be doing in practice on a day-to-day basis?

Any business working in the construction industry has underlying problems to face. Although a design or contracting organization will often be inexpensive to start up, the nature of payment terms and the technical guarantees that have to be given mean it is an expensive industry to leave.

Competition is cut throat. There is continued pressure to cut costs and provide value for money, while still needing to employ the right quality personnel to help improve productivity and reduce defects.

The key question is how can your construction business differentiate itself from thousands of others? What will set it apart and ensure it a place on any tender list? My answer, as I suggested earlier, is that this will increasingly depend on the *way* your company does business and the quality and range of services it offers. And this is where the Internet is so important.

The online construction project

How can the Internet and e-business so fundamentally change and improve how construction works? It sounds great in theory, but what must the construction marketeer actually be doing in practice on a day-to-day basis?

To illustrate this I will look at the main elements of a construction project, and explain in outline how e-business can be used to transform individual parts of the construction process and individual relationships with those involved. If you have adopted an e-business approach already, some of this should be familiar and already engrained in your business culture.

To give the project some shape, let us think of it as a new £20m edge-of-town leisure centre that will be owned and operated by BigTime plc, an expanding group wanting to gain a reputation for progressive developments that appeal to high spenders. You can modify the examples of Internet use to suit your own situation.

The germ of an idea

Someone at BigTime has a germ of an idea, which triggers off the need for more information. This includes research for use in their feasibility study into the viability of the project, for sourcing the right advisers and for finding suppliers that could meet their requirements. What better resource for the BigTime exec team to turn to than the Internet? BigTime will:

- need to know where land is available, and will probably register with Web-based property databanks as well as enquiring through normal agents
- find out how online property finding services can help its search, and register on selected sites
- research the consumer demographics, trends and spending statistics for potential locations by downloading data from websites such as the government's www.statistics.gov.uk.

As you can see, for the construction marketeer, several opportunities are already opening up for sponsoring or advertising on these Web-based sources of information.

The next step

Having completed the feasibility study and land option successfully, the next step for BigTime is to translate the leisure centre concept into something more tangible prior to the planning application. And this means finding a good architect. The BigTime team is not convinced the architect from its last development has sufficient skill, so it is off to the Web again where it finds GreatArch, an up-and-coming practice. GreatArch has just gone live with its new website covering all its core architectural disciplines, including some award-winning developments in the leisure industry.

Architects often shy away from overt marketing, but it is just as important for professional service providers as for everyone else. A well designed website, which loads quickly, has clear navigation and plenty of good case studies, should be a priority for any architect nowadays. And if properly coded and promoted by the web developer, the site should achieve a high search engine listing. So, when BigTime types 'architects for leisure centres' into the search engine, up comes the GreatArch site – hopefully on page one – and BigTime immediately sees the practice as a strong contender for the project.

Sourcing suppliers

GreatArch is appointed and its design team swings into action. Plans need preparing, materials chosen, planning approval secured and potential tenderers shortlisted. For the construction marketeer, this is a crucial time. GreatArch has been receiving regular e-newscasts from several suppliers of technically advanced materials that would be just right for a job like this. The e-newscasts were very low cost for the companies to produce, and much more acceptable than old fashioned newsletters. They now prove their worth as the GreatArch team is already familiar with what these companies offer, and for some materials, it does not bother to hunt out further suppliers.

GreatArch particularly likes two companies who have drawn attention to their online knowledge banks, which are full of standard specification details and CAD drawings which can be inserted straight into the design – saving GreatArch a lot of effort and cost. These suppliers really are using the Internet well, thinking about the specifier's problems and trying to position themselves as 'partners'. They are certainly positioning themselves well with GreatArch.

GreatArch has to find suitable contractors too. The team uses the construction industry directories to see what contractors are doing – in some cases quite literally.They notice that some contractors have installed webcam to provide live pictures of what is happening on projects which can be viewed via their company website – either on open access or in a password protected area. This is an excellent marketing tool, and will also be of considerable help to GreatArch and BigTime. It would mean they can see what is happening on the project without always having to travel to the site, saving money and time, especially for busy executives. Webcam images can be automatically archived, which means there is always a contemporary photographic record to fall back on to reduce disputes.

A few other good uses of the Web, plus a check on the level of expertise offered in this type of work, soon convinces GreatArch that the contractors and suppliers who have adopted an e-business approach will give good value for money on the BigTime job and justify their recommendation. Short lists are drawn up accordingly.

Tendering

Tendering for the project is all carried out online, with no paperwork exchanged. One contractor falls by the wayside at this stage. It claimed to know all about the e-business approach, but its capability is eventually found to be skin deep. It has a good website and good marketing, but is let down by some of its operational people and inadequate internal (back office) electronic systems. It has not spent enough time thinking the processes through, and has ended up with two cultures – e-business and 'the old way'. Perfectly understandable. Nobody said e-business adoption would be easy. At least it was trying.

Training

When making decisions on plant, materials and equipment, an interesting factor emerges – use and maintenance. BigTime is worried about its responsibilities for staff training in these areas and knows that increasingly, training will be a health and safety issue. Inadequate training could lead to legal action either from the public or from BigTime's own staff which, in the leisure market, has quite a high turnover rate. But training in specialist plant, materials and equipment is expensive. Here, e-learning swings the balance. Several suppliers have designed special Web-based training courses for installers and end-users of their products.

e-Training courses are quite different from normal courses where a tutor is present. The courses are shorter but more numerous and are often accompanied by an automatically marked test which can produce a certificate or qualification straight away. Contractors can use the courses to find out how to fix the products and, once the centre is opened, BigTime's staff can train and retrain on their use and maintenance whenever they wish. Learning can be delivered in all Web-based formats with sound, video, animation and interactivity all helping to make learning more effective.

GreatArch sees this as a major contribution to safety and to the whole-life objectives of the scheme and BigTime agrees. A computer training area is added to the construction site offices, for use by all personnel, and a similar permanent facility is put into the leisure centre. From now on, any supplier marketing e-learning as part of its support package for products has a clear advantage.

Handling public relations

As soon as site excavation gets underway, a problem arises which could be disruptive if not handled well by the on-site team. Despite a painstaking environmental impact assessment and widespread local consultation, the project finds itself the subject of pressure group action. GreatArch and the contractor work together to run a project-specific website for use as a communications channel to the public and, especially, to the media, for whom regular online press packs are provided.

So often, poor external communication can undo much good technical work. However, on this occasion, by giving people the facts about what is happening and what to expect, the initiative stays with the project team. Expensive and time-consuming disruption is avoided and, just as important, BigTime's Board of Directors appreciates the effective contribution of technology in avoiding bad publicity – this is good marketing for the next BigTime project, for architect and contractor alike.

Using application software

One of the areas where e-business can transform the construction process is in application software. You do not have to continue to buy software in the conventional and costly way. Software can be provided online by product and service suppliers, for example to help with the design of a special part of the project, or it can be shared with a number of other users on a remote server, as with market research or questionnaire systems.

One use for the BigTime leisure complex, and an outcome of the pressure group problem, is an online quarterly feedback questionnaire to 500 nearby residents to assess their real feelings about the project. These turn out to be reassuringly positive. An application form with e-commerce payment facility is added offering discounted rates for early subscribers to BigTime's membership scheme. This is good public relations for BigTime, and a number of residents sign up.

Another example of commercially available application software used by BigTime is a project extranet like the one described earlier in this chapter. It has the added advantage of alerting key members of the team to project changes requiring their decision by texting them on their mobile phones anywhere worldwide and giving them a set time to respond.

This highlights the Internet's use in cross-platform integration, which can extend to bring various communication devices together whether connected by landline or operating over remote links such as satellite.

With almost all the project's data now Web based, the project extranet and common e-business culture of the various organizations involved make it much easier to manage the project reporting. By the time the centre is complete, the project extranet is credited with saving six weeks on the construction time and over £600k in costs.

Legal checks

A factor not overlooked by BigTime's legal eagles is the regulatory controls needed for Internet activity, which is slightly different to standard legislation. Terms, disclaimers and privacy statements should be in place for all Internet uses, especially websites. This particularly applies to suppliers and their products. With websites being visible worldwide, the construction marketeer in a product company should, among other things, check whether there are any countries in which the products are not legal, for example due to their materials, packaging, or recommended use. BigTime's lawyers provide useful guidelines and confirm that CyberInsurance, giving cover for such eventualities as e-mail libel, is in place for the project.

Ongoing marketing and communications

Towards the end of the project, the main contractor draws up a directory of e-mail addresses for every individual involved. This will be invaluable during the maintenance period. Contractors' people move so often that tracking them down to answer a small but important defects question can be difficult. An e-mail address can be the only static link to an individual once they leave the project. As an aside, the product and plant hire suppliers are keen to get hold of this list too, as it is an excellent database for their next e-newscasts and marketing campaigns.

Conclusion

The review of the BigTime project could go on, but we will leave it there. By now, you can probably see how things are panning out. Every part of the construction process offers an opportunity for the construction marketeer to use e-business to gain competitive advantage to win orders and improve relationships. e-Business can be used to challenge the way every activity in construction is carried out, making the process better, faster and more time and cost efficient. In some cases, e-business creates opportunities that were just not feasible before. The trick for the construction marketeer is to bring all this into play as components of a winning bid and, as most marketing people will readily agree, it is very satisfying to win without having necessarily to be the lowest tenderer.

Remember that, wherever possible, e-business systems should be compatible between organizations which, while seeming obvious, is not always the case. Talk with your IT people for an insight into system compatibility, and you will find a marketing issue in its own right. Also, any marketeer who can reach the point whereby the client is (willingly) relying on part or all of the supplier's own systems will be making real progress. In the past, such an outcome would be rare. Now however with a greater appreciation of the value of collaboration to client and supplier alike, single supplier and partnership working are becoming more common.

Key questions for the e-marketeer

Although not an exhaustive list, here are some of the questions you should be asking your-self or your colleagues.

Internal

What is the information workflow from start of marketing, through estimating and con-struction to completion of maintenance and settlement of account? Who needs what infor-mation, when and where (especially important in a multi-location and often transient business like construction)? What security and technology constraints are there on data access and why? Do the right personnel have the tools to interrogate data themselves and, if not, why? Who do we share information with, and how? Could external collaboration improve internal processes? Are internal processes restricting market potential?

Clients and specifiers

How do clients and specifiers work? What are their business objectives and to whom are they accountable (often overlooked)? What do they want from the contractor or its sup-pliers? How can new e-business initiatives improve the performance of the client or spec-ifier? Can a situation be envisaged in which the combination of e-business and existing offerings removes all competition?

Suppliers and partners

Despite the value of their products or services, are the benefits of working with them diminished by their lack of e-business skills? What could be done to create improvement? Is this why clients are now taking the lead in insisting on the types of e-business used on some projects? How can the cost and management of contractual arrangements be made more efficient? Should future development of systems within supply chain organizations be carried out with greater collaboration?

The public in all its forms

What does the public look for in the contractor? How influential is the public in business success? What can be done through e-business to manage and improve public relation-ships? What are the potential benefits? How this may affect other related organizations?

Technology

How well informed is the construction marketeer on current and emerging e-business tech-nology? What channels are in place for gaining e-business knowledge? Bearing in mind that progressive change becomes difficult for the construction marketeer without under-standing and cooperation, are relationships good with internal influencers and decision-makers in the relevant e-business disciplines?

The influence of the IT industry

This amazingly powerful tool has opened doors we did not even know were there.

The great challenge for the construction industry this decade must be to find new ways to exploit the opportunities offered by this rapidly evolving technology. But, just as construction clients commission the industry to deliver its bricks and mortar solutions, so the IT industry is behind every e-business development used by construction.

The IT industry itself is a major driver for change. It is always looking for new ways to make money, and is therefore constantly coming up with new ideas and applications. The construction industry must respond by firstly keeping up to date with what is happening in the online world, and secondly, by ensuring it then exploits these new developments to the full. If you do not, your rivals somewhere else in the construction industry will – you can be sure of it.

One invention – multiple repercussions

The development of these new 'e-business' methods presents numerous opportunities for the construction industry. The comparison with the invention of rail transport is instructive here. The advent of the railways affected the way we live and work in profound and often unforeseen ways. It led to the introduction of standard time across the country, enabled working people in urban areas to take holidays in the countryside or the coast for the first time, and opened up new business opportunities, which previously would have been impossible or uneconomic. One invention is multiple repercussions. And so it is with the Internet.

The Internet is itself a vehicle or mode of transport, not for goods, but for information as the saying goes, we have moved from bricks and mortar to clicks and mortar. The Internet's brief history has further parallels with the railways. The rail industry underwent a 'boom and bust' cycle, as, it could be argued, did the Internet with a spate of 'dotcom' failures following huge growth in e-business start-ups. This may have given comfort to the complacent – particularly in traditional industries such as construction which can be wedded to old ways of working – but a percentage of new businesses will always founder and the dotcom failures were a necessary adjustment experienced by all new technologies from the railways in the 1840s through to radio in the 1920s.

The lesson here is that the old ways are not the best. And certainly do not represent 'doing the best with what you have'. Because what we have is the Internet and we ignore it at our peril. If properly used and exploited it can help us speed up production, improve business performance, cut costs and time, remove the barriers of distance, and work more efficiently having a direct, and often dramatic, effect on the bottom line.

This amazingly powerful tool has opened doors we did not even know were there.

The technology

What was impossible yesterday is not only possible today, but is already being improved on for tomorrow – the construction marketeer must stay up to date.

I think I have already made it clear that the Internet and related technologies are constantly developing and changing. Moore's law – developed by semiconductor engineer Gordon Moore in 1964 – states that the amount of information storable on a given amount of silicon has roughly doubled every year since the technology was invented. This held true until the late 1970s, when the doubling period became about 18 months – still a phenomenal rate of expansion.

As computer processing power grows exponentially, increasingly sophisticated software applications are being written to take advantage of this. What was impossible yesterday is not only possible today, but is already being improved on for tomorrow. This means the construction marketeer must stay up to date.

My advice is to be constantly looking ahead. If you are thinking strategically about your business five or ten years into the future you must also be aware of current research and developments in computing technologies. Find out what is happening in the electronic research laboratories at Universities, and in manufacturers' own research establishments. Make it your business to know what applications are becoming available and what new technologies are being worked on. Consider those early days of Internet research when the first e-mails began to be exchanged by universities, providing a clear indication of what was coming down the track. If you had spotted the trend then – and it was there to be seen – well, I will leave that to your imagination.

The construction marketeer should not be merely trying to deliver the workload the business needs to pay the current wage bill and, where relevant, shareholders. It is vital to look ahead and consider the shape of the construction industry in the future, and how the most successful companies will be taking their business forward. The Internet plays a key role in this and if exploited to the full will give you a leading edge and competitive advantage. And not only will you be improving the efficiency of the way your own business works, you will also gain the double advantage of improving the efficiency of the clients and suppliers you deal with.

Conclusion

No longer *a* way for the construction industry to do business – it is *the* way to do business.

A week may be a long time in politics, but it is even longer when it comes to the Internet. The Internet has revolutionized the way we do business, and will continue to do so at breathtaking speed. I strongly argue that construction companies who remain immersed in traditional ways of working will increasingly struggle against their more forward thinking and Internet literate competitors. And if your business is not working online my bet is that in the years to come it will not be working at all. The Internet is an exciting, dynamic and constantly evolving business tool. However, the term 'e-business' gives the dangerous impression that doing business electronically is an 'optional extra', somehow bolted on to a construction company's 'main' activities and perhaps seen as a minor distraction, or even irritant. But the Internet is no longer *a* way for the construction industry to do business – it is *the* way to do business. Ignoring this is not an option.

And finally ...

It is always useful in marketing to be able to look over the horizon and get an early view of what is coming soon. That way you can adapt the principles to your own situation, and influence the business plans for your department, your company and even your client.

To help us do that, John Butler of the Division of Informatics at Edinburgh University, has put down a few thoughts about changing technology and the likely effect on our e-business lives. John has been involved in the development of networks and now business systems for over 20 years, so is well placed to shed some cautious light on the future.

Whither e-business? – John Butler

We are very early in the process of applying technology to businesses. Commerce has existed since at least the time of the Phoenicians and managed businesses as we know them have been around for may be a century. Leo 1, arguably the first business computer, went live in Britain in 1951 and the Web has been a business tool for less than ten years. The only thing one can guarantee about making predictions is that they will be wrong. What follows is a small selection of topics illustrating some ways in which people imagine we may be going.

XML: exchanging meaning

Although this is a book on marketing, introducing the concept of the Extensible Markup Language or XML here is unavoidable. Behind the scenes XML is being used by programmers to change how we will work in future and, as you will see further on, it is significant.

Conventional Web searches accept simple queries and return sequences of words – it is up to the human browser to be selective and make sense of them. XML provides mechanisms (sets of rules) for tagging information so that structured information can be represented and the meaning extracted automatically.

The effect of this can be seen if we consider a *procurement hub*, which is becoming more accepted in construction. A purchaser posts a description of an item he wishes to purchase on a central exchange – quantity, quality, material, tolerances, target cost, time-to-delivery and so on. Suppliers post their product catalogues similarly indexed and the procurement hub can in principle match supply and demand and broker the whole tendering process. Of course it is not as simple as this and for all except the simplest procurement the parties selectively reveal additional information about their requirements and capabilities in subsequent rounds of negotiation. This in turn involves the exchange of meaningful information.

Getting this right and achieving (in this case) the ultimate goal of fully automatic tendering for materials or projects is a complex interplay of technology, business practice and law. The payoff is a huge saving in costs, something not lost on, for example the motor industry, which is engaged in setting up exactly this kind of hub for streamlining component procurement (General Motors and DaimlerChrysler). The process raises new questions of security and the meaning of contract – the tendering process takes place in stages in many locations – at what point and under whose law is the deal finally struck? XML is an enabling technology, which is being applied to movement of information as diverse as photo collections or shopping lists, contracts or house descriptions.

Grid computing and the virtual organization

Eventually, users will be unaware they are using any computer but the one on their desk, because it will have the capabilities to reach out across the (inter-) national network and obtain whatever computational resources are necessary

(Larry Smarr and Charles Catlett, 1992)

The latest and most systematic attempt to develop a new generation of computing infrastructure is the *Grid*. Like the Web, the Grid concept originated at CERN and embodies several fundamental principles. CERN has the particular problem of handling truly stupendous quantities of data in a controlled manner among the scientific community but what is learned there has relevance in business.

The Grid allows computing power to be bought-in dynamically on a problem-by-problem basis. A problem is described in XML and then put out to tender – the facility best able to solve it is engaged through a rapid tendering process and the solution delivered back to the customer.

The Grid allows exchange of information in a structured fashion on a 'need-to-know' basis. Again, going outside the construction industry, many companies might contribute to the design of a new aircraft. The company designing the fuselage will be conducting continuous simulations; a different company may be designing the control surfaces and needs to know the aerodynamics of the fuselage. The economics required of the finished aircraft in turn places constraints on the fuselage. In all cases there will be sensitive information, which must *not* be divulged to another party.

The Grid will deliver dependable, pervasive and uniform access to the computing *fabric* (computing servers, information storage, sensors, networks), *solutions* (knowledge) and *people*. Building on this is the concept of the *virtual organization* where people and resources come together through a process of automated resource discovery and procurement, define a problem, provide a solution or service, then disband.

The smart network

The common factor behind both of these examples is the shift of intelligence from the desktop PC into the network it is attached to. The names will change and fashions will come and go but the underlying long-term trend is the creation of markets for knowledge. Well, today at least.

Reference

General Motors and DaimlerChrysler. www.covisint.com, servicing Ford.

12

Knowledge management

Christopher Preece* and Krisen Moodley*

Introduction

Knowledge has always been important. Through the history of mankind victory has gone to those at the cutting edge of knowledge. Those parts of our society that have learnt and developed their thought processes have constantly held the advantage over time. Knowledge is now more important than ever. As information becomes more important, the role of knowledge takes on a more important role. Convergence in broad strategic goals and production capability means that new ways of gaining strategic advantage must be found. Knowledge and its management has become the new arena for competitive advantage and differentiation. Businesses of all types can no longer escape the importance of knowledge in their development. Commentators commonly refer to a new era of business activity based in a knowledge economy. It is clear that knowledge has a role to play in business development.

Classifying knowledge?

Knowledge is information combined with experience, context, interpretation and reflection (Davenport, 1998). Knowledge is more than just data and information; it implies a deeper and more considered understanding of a subject, issues or facts. Knowledge comes in a variety of forms. It can be broadly classified as explicit or implicit. Explicit knowledge is more familiar and is tangible and identifiable, and consists of details that can be recorded, catalogued, stored and transmitted relatively easily. As a consequence, it can be incorporated in an organization's strategy relatively easily, particularly through the use of information and communications technology.

Implicit or tacit knowledge is difficult to identify, quantify, record and store, as it is personal and resides in the minds of individuals guiding their values, behaviour and actions. It is hard to articulate with formal language and it is embedded in personal experiences and involves intangible factors, such as personal beliefs, perspectives and value systems, (Nonaka

* School of Civil Engineering, University of Leeds

and Takeuchi, 1995). It is what enables them to be productive and react quickly and effectively to emergencies. Nonaka and Konno (1998) argue that there are two dimensions to tacit knowledge. The first is the technical dimension, which encompasses the kind of informal personal skills or crafts often referred to as 'know-how'. The second is the cognitive dimension. It consists of beliefs, ideals, values, schemata and mental models which are deeply ingrained in us and which we often take for granted. While difficult to articulate, this cognitive dimension of tacit knowledge shapes the way we perceive the world. Both types of knowledge are complementary, as explicit knowledge without the tacit insight quickly loses meaning. This relationship between tacit and explicit knowledge is further enhanced by Polanyi (1966) when he states that tacit thought forms an indispensable part of all knowledge. Even if knowledge has been articulated in words or mathematical formulae, this explicit knowledge must rely on being tacitly understood and applied.

The essential characteristics of these definitions is that knowledge is an intangible, something more like a process and definitely not an object or a thing that we can manage in the same way that we can manage data, information or cash flow. It is this essential distinction that makes any system of aggregation and management of knowledge problematic. It is an unfortunate aspect of the term 'Knowledge Management' (KM), because the term itself presupposes knowledge as a thing rather than as something, which is '...a fluid mix of framed experience, values, contextual information and expert insight that provides a framework for evaluating and incorporating new experiences and information.' (Davenport, 2000).

The knowledge economy

Knowledge and information differ from cash, machines and labour. Knowledge can be used without being consumed in the traditional sense. Acquisition of knowledge does not preclude others from obtaining it or using it. It is not consumed in the traditional sense. Knowledge is created in vast abundance but can be as time sensitive as physical assets as it may be superseded. In almost every activity we undertake and we create more information than is consumed. In every construction project more knowledge is created than is used. In an economic environment driven by knowledge the danger is ignorance.

The process of adding value is the application of knowledge to the product, service or technology. Knowledge industries have to consider different strategies for competition. Collaboration is widely used in knowledge industries. Alliances that exchange knowledge have lower information costs are able to use complementary skills more effectively. Cooperative strategies also offer better options to defending market leadership. Learning is an integral part of knowledge development. A company that can learn has the capability to create advantage. The knowledge economy is a fast dynamic environment that requires organization to leverage their knowledge to the maximum benefit of the organization. Organizations that fail to cope with the knowledge economy will struggle.

How is knowledge created?

Despite the presence of knowledge assets within an organization, it has to continue its relentless pursuit for knowledge to maintain a competitive edge. While knowledge does not wear out, as do most physical assets, it is frequently exposed to rapid depreciation because of the creation of new knowledge (Nonaka and Teece 2001). Davenport and Prusak (1998) suggest that organizations generate knowledge by various means:

- Acquisition
- Dedicated resources
- Fusion
- Adaptation
- Knowledge networking.

The knowledge acquisition comes through the hiring of people with certain knowledge that is strategically important, or buying of other entities, which add valuable knowledge to complement existing assets. Knowledge, the writers add, can also be leased. Research and development is a form of dedicated resources. The aim is to conduct research toward gathering knowledge for specific areas of business to achieve and maintain competitive edge.

Fusion lies in synergy where different skills are put together to come up with a solution for a problem. The diversity of values and skills can generate creative solutions, which Nonaka and Takeuchi (1995) call 'creative chaos'.

The environment surrounding the organization is dynamic and is in constant change. New products, technologies and social and economic changes force responses by organizations to adapt to the changing conditions. Communities of practice are also a source of knowledge as they form knowledge networks.

Nonaka and Takeuchi (1995) however view that knowledge in an organization is created in an interaction between tacit and explicit knowledge in the form of conversation. They define knowledge as the capability of a company to create new knowledge, disseminate it through the organization, and embody it in products, services and systems.

Nonaka and Takeuchi (1995) contend that within the process of conversion between tacit and explicit, knowledge is created. They further explain that the implications for recognizing tacit knowledge are the view of the organization as a living organism rather than an information-processing machine (Nonaka *et al.*, 2001).

Defining knowledge management

There are many definitions of KM. A common definition is 'the collection of processes that govern the creation, dissemination and leveraging of knowledge to fulfil organizational objectives. Knowledge management refers to the organizational processes that seek the combination of data and information-processing capacity with the creative potential of people. It is concerned with the management of knowledge processes, interaction with individuals and teams and means through which they acquire and exploit knowledge (Preece *et al.*, 1999). Malhotra (2002) defines that KM caters to the critical issues of organizational adaptation, survival and competence in face of increasingly discontinuous environmental

Figure 12.1 Competitive advantage. Adapted from Nonaka and Takeuchi (1995), the knowledge creating company.

change. Essentially, it embodies organizational processes that seek synergistic combination of data and information-processing capacity of information technologies, and the creative and innovative capacity of human beings.

Gurteen (1999) defines KM as a business philosophy. It is an emerging set of principles, processes, organizational structures and technology applications that help people share and leverage their knowledge to meet their business objectives. This puts focus and responsibility on the individual, the knowledge worker and on the holistic nature of KM. Also critically it is about meeting business objectives. Knowledge management is not an end in its self. It is also fundamentally about sharing knowledge and putting that knowledge to use, Gurteen adds, a distinction also has to be made between individual knowledge and organizational knowledge. The latter is quantitatively and qualitatively different from the former in that organizational knowledge is inherently in a constant state of flux as individuals leave or join the organization, and as knowledge bases change and grow. Individual knowledge is ever changing. Organizational knowledge is also changing, but at a greater rate than that for each individual employee.

Knowledge management strategy

In the knowledge economy, the challenge for the organization is a formidable task to build, combine and integrate the knowledge assets of many individuals (Nonaka and Teece, 2001). All organizations have to excel not just in managing, but also creating, applying and exploiting knowledge to the full. To realize its value, they must combine distinctive, renewable sources of know-how with complementary skills and assets. Since knowledge can be an extremely valuable organizational asset, there should be a strategic framework within which it is generated or captured, represented or codified, transferred and assimilated. Jones (2000) explains that knowledge strategy as aligning organizational knowledge to a defined business strategy.

Wiig (2000) argues that a few advanced enterprises pursue a central strategic thrust with four tactical foci. However, most tailor KM practices to their needs and environments and have narrower perspectives. Of these, some focus on knowledge sharing among individuals or on building elaborate educational and knowledge distribution capabilities. Some emphasize the use of technology to capture, manipulate, and locate knowledge and initially, many focus on knowledge-related information management rather than KM. Others focus on knowledge utilization to improve the enterprise's operational and overall effectiveness. Still others pursue building and exploiting intellectual capital (IC) to enhance the enterprise's economic value. Some exceptional enterprises have created knowledge vigilant to focus constant, widespread attention on ensuring competitive IC to sustain long-term success and viability. The presumption is that competitive IC, properly utilized and exploited, is central behind effective behaviour.

Tierney (1999) indicates that a company's KM strategy should reflect its competitive strategy with a focus on creating value for customers, turning a profit and managing people. Zack (1999) on the other contends that, 'the most important context for guiding knowledge management is the firm's strategy. Knowledge is the fundamental basis of competition. Competing successfully on knowledge requires either aligning strategy to what the organization knows, or developing the knowledge and capabilities needed to support a desired strategy'.

Dunn (2002) maintains that the greatest organizational challenge lie in how KM organizational assets should be leveraged to maximize their contribution in wealth creation or organizational optimization of resource management. He suggests that there are five strategies depending on the organization type and sector:

- Knowledge replication
- Knowledge diffusion/leverageability
- Knowledge innovation
- Knowledge giveaway
- Knowledge commercialization.

Replication is often used by fast food companies and retailers, where an original formula is used regardless of the prevailing conditions, with very minor local changes. Operations are conducted in precisely the same way wherever they are located. Diffusion is about organizations knowing what they know and using it. This, Dunn (2002) maintains, seems to be the key strategy in KM endeavours as most organizations seek to surface the knowledge of their employees and associates and to make it available throughout the organization for the benefit of decision-makers and organizational learning. Innovation is employing innovative ideas like the Internet-based business or through new product and technology development

The giveaway knowledge is where an organization adopts a strategy of making its knowledge available for others free of charge. The commercialization strategy is where an enterprise builds and knowledge base and recognizes a market need (or a business opportunity) for it outside the enterprise. British Gas, for example, sell their expertise to other organizations in need of it. Commercialization of knowledge is where knowledge activities, objects or ideas are developed for revenue generation. The simple explanation of commercialization would be a patent which could then be used to generate revenue either as a product or included in other products.

Organizational culture and knowledge transfer

David Gurteen (1999) states that organizational culture can be thought of as a relatively rigid tacit infrastructure of ideas that shape not only our thinking but also our behaviour and perception of our business environment. It effectively establishes a set of guidelines by which members of an organization work and how those organizations are structured. It is rigid mainly due to our paradigms – we do not recognize why we do so much of what we do and we tend to resist change rather than embrace it.

The creation and application of new knowledge is essential to the survival of almost all businesses. Comprehensive and organization-wide knowledge sharing tends to emerge when an organization recognizes its knowledge assets to be business critical, and where knowledge is high and where it operates globally (KLICON 2001). The importance of sharing as a concept and practice stems from many reasons relating to the individuals and the organization. Gurteen summarizes them in the following.

Intangible products – ideas, processes, information are taking a growing share of global trade from the traditional, tangible goods of the manufacturing economy. Increasingly the only sustainable competitive advantage is continuous innovation. In other words, the application of new knowledge. People don't take a job for life any more. When someone leaves an organization their knowledge walks out of the door with them.

'Our problem as an organization is that we do not know what we know'. Large global or even small geographically dispersed organizations do not know what they know. Expertise learnt and applied in one part of the organization is not leveraged in another. As things change so does our knowledge base erode, in some businesses, as much of 50% of what you knew five years ago is probably obsolete today.

Moving the organization into practicing a knowledge-sharing culture requires the continuous encouragement of people to work together more effectively, employing the philosophy of collaboration and sharing and ultimately making the organizational knowledge more productive. Sharing of knowledge helps organizations meet their business objectives, but it is a change in culture, which is often very tough.

The old paradigm is that knowledge is power; the new culture should advocate the concept that sharing knowledge is power. Gurteen believes that removing disincentives to sharing rather than introducing rewards is the key factor to promoting the culture change. He further argues that the real answer is to help people see for themselves that knowledge sharing is in their personal interest. If people understand that sharing their knowledge helps them do their jobs more effectively; helps them retain their jobs; helps them in their personal development and career progression; rewards them for getting things done (not for blind sharing) and brings more personal recognition, then knowledge sharing will become a reality.

People rarely give a way possession, including knowledge, without expecting something in return, Davenport and Prusak (1998). People are encouraged to share their knowledge if they can develop a behaviour that hinges on a number of cultural concepts.

Sharing knowledge results in gain. A famous saying in the Arabic culture is that money diminishes by spending, but knowledge grows by giving. Sharing knowledge is a synergistic process whereby one gets more out than he or she puts in.

Knowledge is perishable and short lived, it soon looses its value if not used. Another fact is that knowledge soon becomes obsolete if not used. Furthermore, if a member does not share his idea, someone else in the same organization will most certainly do. Collaborative working is a key approach to getting things done in an organization; the tendency to work alone will more likely result in failure.

For an organization to implement a KM strategy, it has to engender a knowledge culture. Sharing information and being part of a team are both important in creating a culture in which the organization is able to learn (KLICON, 2001). Modack *et al.* (1999) goes along the same lines by saying that leveraging knowledge is possible only when people value building on each other's ideas and sharing their own insights. Much of this is shaped by the culture of the organization.

To create a knowledge-sharing culture, it is essential to make a visible connection between sharing knowledge and practical business goals, problems or results, Modack *et al.* (1999) and McDermott (2001). Davenport and Prusak (1998) and Nonaka and Takeuchi (1995) refer to the same concept when they stress the need for employees to share an awareness of the organization's goals and strategies. Such commitment to common aims encourages individuals to direct their own work toward cooperative goals.

Drivers for knowledge management in construction

A great deal of construction activity is project based although many construction companies are trying to change this situation. It is also unique in that the delivery of projects takes place in a multi-party environment, thus making it rather difficult to capture and disseminate knowledge that is critical for the improvement of the industry. This is further exacerbated by the fact that project delivery teams are temporary in nature. The Egan report, 'Rethinking Construction' (1998), states that 'The repeated selection of new teams in our view inhibits learning, innovation and the development of skilled and experienced teams. Critically, it has prevented the industry from developing products and an identity – or brand – that can be understood by its clients'.

There are many drivers for KM, including the need to learn from past experience, the need to retain key staff and their skills and the need to become more efficient at delivering value to the client or end-user. The construction industry is concerned with the delivery of service to its customers. As such, there is a need for a shift in its culture, from being motivated by the product to being driven by customer satisfaction. The Egan report, 'Rethinking Construction' (1998), notes that 'the construction industry tends not to think about the customer (either the client or the consumer) but more about the next employer in the contractual chain. Companies undertake little systematic research on what the end-user actually wants, nor do they seek to raise customers' aspirations and educate them to become more discerning'. Holt *et al.* (2000) maintain that 'Most construction organizations function in a strategic mode that is inflexible and unresponsive to changes in customer demands'. Holt also suggest that to maintain competitive advantage an organization must do three things more effectively than its competitors:

● It must quickly recognize changes in demand that could have an adverse impact on its operations
● It must be flexible enough to respond to changes in customer needs and demands; and it must understand its own capabilities relative to demand.

A continuous system of knowledge generated in the business development arena is needed to meet these requirements. The knowledge generated through individual projects needs to be fed back into the business development activities such that the organization responds better to the future.

The 1990s have seen sustained initiatives to improve the performance of the construction industry. Both the Latham and Egan initiatives preached the benefits of adopting modern manufacturing management practices, Latham by largely concentrating on reducing the adversarial nature of the industry as it then was, Egan largely by preaching the benefits of greater standardization. The combined impact of the enormous and sustained energy that these initiatives unleashed have undoubtedly created much change for the better. Both the Egan and Latham report have to be seen in the context of changing environments. The government was a major sponsor for both initiatives and the Egan agenda was very much led by large-scale clients. The groups wanted a more modern and efficient industry with better performance from construction. The industry has to become more customer focussed and understand the need for a knowledge-based environment. In an increasingly competitive market, construction firms, consultants and clients recognize that the reuse of their know-how is now essential to grow business and increase their operational efficiency.

Trends in approaches to knowledge management in the construction industry

The construction industry has adopted many different initiatives to improve its performance, including partnering, supply chain management, risk and value management, electronic document management, to name but a few. Many of these initiatives have been directed at the 'technological' side of a construction business (the contracts, procedures, standards, etc). This is confirmed in work by Preece *et al.* (2000) and Moodley *et al.* (2001). In their research, Liston *et al.* (2001) also have shown a tendency to portray KM as being technology dependent. Egbu (2000) argues that KM that focuses on creating network structures to transfer explicit knowledge will be severely limited in terms of its contribution to innovation. Preece *et al.* (2000) go further to explain that '... technology should be designed to promote, and not to hinder, collaboration, conversation, connection and communication to ensure full corporate knowledge is easily accessible and packaged in a format for direct application'. It is possible to conclude that technical and explicit knowledge transfer exists within construction.

Knowledge management issues in construction

It seems that research has identified a number of issues that are relevant to the construction industry and that need careful consideration. Professor Paul Quintas of the Open University Business School, Management of Knowledge and Innovation Research Unit, maintains that the effective management of an organization's knowledge assets and capabilities (e.g. capabilities to create new knowledge) is vital for improving organizational competitiveness. There are few empirical studies of KM in the construction industry, and the limited numbers of studies that have been conducted focus heavily or solely on explicit knowledge and the role of information technologies.

In their study of a number of firms, Davenport *et al.* (1998) identified four basic types of knowledge systems:

● Systems that involved some kind of repository. The objective was to take some form of knowledge that had been extracted from human brains, and store it in a technical system for later access. Another form of knowledge was less structured, consisting of the insights and observations of employees. These repositories might be called 'discussion databases' or 'lessons-learned' systems.
● The second system is the knowledge transfer, which is achieved either through technology or more human means. The final type of repository holds not knowledge itself but pointers to those who have knowledge.
● Systems that measure value. These are supplemental project components which are used to measure the value of a repository.
● The final type of knowledge project did not address any specific knowledge domain, but rather tried to improve the overall knowledge environment.

Earlier sections concluded that KM needs to address both explicit and tacit knowledge and that tacit knowledge greatly contributes to organizational innovation and competitiveness, and is difficult to communicate, transfer, share, audit and imitate. Quintas (2002) further suggests that the importance of tacit knowledge is particularly relevant in the context of the construction industry where manual skills and other forms of accumulated knowledge acquired through experiential learning retain their importance.

The important question for a construction organization is, what use is the knowledge gained during a project if it cannot be used by those who did not work on it?. Egbu (2000) remarks that ' ... architecture, engineering and construction are knowledge intensive. The ability to learn from others, from the organization around oneself and from one's own past, is critical in making progress … knowledge needed for innovation is increasingly distributed within organizations … For innovating firms, this poses challenges in terms of creation, sharing and the management of expertise'. Egbu (2000) further maintains that in construction organizations, the culture and climate and the mechanisms in place should allow for the possibility for knowledge to be readily shared and transferred from project to project and across project teams. Egbu (2000) notes that there are certain characteristics associated with culture that are seen to be favourable to innovation and knowledge management, these characteristics are:

- A culture of openness and willingness to share
- Support from top management
- Presence of a knowledge champion
- Feeling of ownership (empowerment)
- No blame culture and risk tolerant climate.

McNamara (2002) also advocate similar issues for successful change to occur in organizations. He states that successful change must involve top management, including the board and chief executive. Usually, there is a champion who initially instigates the change by being visionary, persuasive and consistent. A change agent role is usually responsible to translate the vision to a realistic plan and carry out the plan. Change is usually best carried out as a team-wide effort. Communications about the change should be frequent and with all organization members. To sustain change, the structures of the organization itself should be modified, including strategic plans, policies and procedures.

Research conducted by Preece *et al.* (2000) also concluded that leadership is a crucial element for the implementation of knowledge management. A clear recognition by management of the need to champion knowledge management is evident, they add. Egbu (2000) also stated that if the construction industry is to build and maintain capability, it has to change its adversarial culture to a sharing culture. It also has to learn from each project and transfer knowledge from project to organizational base. The industry will also need to invest in long-term relationship.

Al-Ghassani (2001) remarks that in construction, KM aims to manage the knowledge (lessons learned, best practices, etc) that is gained from individual projects, during their lifecycle, to make it more widely available through the organization. He further advocates that KM helps to improve performance and increase productivity within organizations by:

- Avoiding work duplication
- Preventing the repetition of mistakes
- Aiding problem solving
- Supporting decision making
- Retaining tacit knowledge
- Facilitating staff training
- Managing and improving work practices and processes
- Generating competitive advantage so as to lead market (due to increased chances of innovation)
- Improving business performance.

Egbu's work indicates that there are a number of factors that inhibit knowledge development. (Table 12.1). These ideas suggest that knowledge sharing has a number of barriers to overcome.

Table 12.1 Factors promoting or inhibiting knowledge sharing

Factors promoting knowledge sharing	Factors inhibiting knowledge sharing
Link to economic performance and strategy and coherent knowledge vision	Incoherent knowledge vision lack of ownership of the knowledge vision
Senior management support	Lack of appreciation of knowledge as an important asset
Use of technology infrastructure	Inappropriate tools for measuring knowledge
Proper organizational structure (teams, relationships, networks)	Rigid organizational structure
Standard, flexible knowledge structures	Inadequate standardized process
Knowledge friendly culture	Lack of information-sharing culture
Clear purpose and shared meaning of KM	Lack of clear purpose
Change in motivational practice	Fear of the use of IT
Multiple channels of knowledge transfer (with departments, clients, customers)	'Knowledge is power' syndrome
Formal education and training	Time constraints and pressure on staff

Knowledge sharing in construction

Previous sections discussed, in some details, the issue of knowledge sharing. The literature reviewed suggests that this is one of the most important aspects for organizations to promote if they were to have successful knowledge systems.

Preece *et al.* (2000) and Moodley *et al.* (2001) both identified problems in sharing knowledge in the case studies they conducted. The cultural barrier to KM and transfer is likely to be significant within the construction industry (Preece *et al.* 2000). This issue takes another, more complex dimension when considered across organizations, as is the case in the project environment. Relationships between organizations in a project environment are generally adversarial (Elhag *et al.*, 2000). This is more so in many developing countries, where the collaborative approach to project delivery is not necessarily materialized. Organizations often consider their own interests. Malhotra (2001) contends that the effectiveness of information flow across the boundaries of the multitude of organizations in a project environment is reduced by the competitive nature of these enterprises.

Collaboration and partnering in construction is one fundamental practice that leads to better learning and sharing of information. The Egan report (1998) highlights that 'alliances offer the co-operation and continuity needed to enable the team to learn and take a stake in improving the product. A team that does not stay together has no learning capability and no chance of making the incremental improvements that improve efficiency over the long term'. Holt *et al.* (2000) remark that strategic alliances are becoming an important means of survival for managing construction organizations. Such alliances are a compromise between organizations doing business in isolation and in mutual partnership with another organization(s). The key to competitive advantage and improving customer satisfaction lies in the ability of organizations to form learning alliances; these being strategic partnerships based on a business environment that encourages mutual (and reflective) learning between partners. Well-designed, successful alliances enhance co-operation and a high level of trust and commitment.

Knowledge management and business development

What is the role of KM in business development? Knowledge in developing a business is lifeblood for success. The process of developing a business from the understanding of the business model to the engagement of clients and providing customer service, all require intense levels of knowledge. The issues of projectized construction practice have already been highlighted and the problems with knowledge recovery are well documented. Much of the business development knowledge may be vested in the individual. The question is how does the organization tap into that knowledge and improve performance throughout the organization. For example, a manager developing retail construction clients may have extensive knowledge of stakeholder interaction and customer service and care issue. This remains within a particular domain. The same company may be developing its healthcare service markets and there might be considerable overlap in strategies that can be adapted for consumers of healthcare services. Integrating possible knowledge objects across the organization is where business development will benefit a great deal from.

Knowledge management implementation also requires a change in culture. There has to be a culture of sharing to create learning communities. Engineering organizations have professionals that require learning communities to facilitate their professional and personal development. Having information systems is not good enough, there has to be a culture of learning and knowledge transfer for KM implementation to work. Knowledge transfer cannot be restricted to technical activity and projects, it has to be part of the business development activities of the organization. To initiate cultural and organization change, KM should become part of the business objectives of the organization. Knowledge management offers the opportunity of developing shared values within the organization. As knowledge is disseminated and learning develops, it is possible to develop an organizational ethos that shared by all. Creating common values is part of creating good companies.

In an economy where the only certainty is uncertainty, the one lasting competitive advantage is knowledge. Few senior managers understand the true nature of a knowledge creating company yet these organizations contain highly educated, highly motivated and dynamic individuals with immense potential. The challenge is how to develop an organization that harnesses the knowledge and intellectual capital of the people within them. A well thought out KM strategy may be the starting point to open the intellectual capital treasure chest and creating additional value for the firm.

Recommendations

It is recommended that construction organizations give greater consideration for the importance of KM. Such consideration can be manifested in the following actions or policies as implications for organizations:

- Develop a vision for KM as a strategic choice
- Structure the organization to consider KM as a widespread and comprehensive function
- Develop an understanding of knowledge assets and their types (explicit and tacit) which should reflect on the approach to knowledge systems
- Shift focus to organizational culture that promotes knowledge sharing, encourage communities of practice and interpersonal networks and create a shared sense of purpose

- Build reward and motivational systems within the corporate policy for knowledge use and sharing
- Promote a culture that transcends the individual circle of interest to encompass organizational interests through co-operation, openness and willingness to share
- Clarify responsibility for KM and initiate and support the role of a Knowledge Officer to drive change and align practices with strategies
- Further the sophistication of initiatives to include knowledge creation in the organization, not just knowledge sharing. 'Second-generation' KM reflects a blend of supply and demand perception of KM
- Develop a clear understanding of knowledge life cycle which needs to be a continued process to achieve value in the organization
- Adopt a conceptualization that considers and manages projects as behavioural systems rather than technical systems resulting in mechanistic approaches
- Make KM an integral part of business development.

References

Elhag, T.M.S., Deason, P.M., Morris, P.W.G. and Patel, M.B. (2000) *Development of a Knowledge System for a Construction Contractor*, Centre for Research in the Management of Projects, UMIST, Manchester, UK.

Davenport, T.H. and Laurence Prusak (1998) *Working Knowledge: How Organizations Manage What They Know* (Boston: Harvard Business School Press).

Davenport, T.H., Long, D.W.D. and Beers, M.C. (1998). Successful knowledge management projects, *Sloan Management Review* (Winter), 43–57.

Davenport, T.H. and Smith, D.E. (2002) Managing knowledge in professional service firms. In: Cortada, J.W. and Woods J.A. (eds) *The Knowledge Management Yearbook* (Boston: Butterworth-Heinemann), pp. 284–299.

Dunn, D. (2002) Business strategies through knowledge management. In: *Proceedings of Business Information Technology Management Conference*, Ecuador, June.

Egbu, C.O. (2000) The role of tacit and explicit knowledge in improving organisational innovations in architecture, engineering and construction. In: *Proceedings of the Joint Meeting of the CIOB Working Commissions W55 and W65 and Task Groups TG23, TG31 and TG35*, UK (Department of Construction Management and Engineering, The University of Reading), September 13–15, pp. 4.

Egan, J. (1998) Rethinking Construction. Department of Environment, Transport and the Regions. HMSO.

Finneran, T. (2002) *A Component-Based Knowledge Management System*, The Data Administration Newsletter (Online). Available http://www.tdan.com/i009hy04.htm [Accessed 17th June 2002].

Gurteen, D. (1999) Creating a Knowledge Sharing Culture, *Knowledge Management Magazine*, 2 (5).

Holt, G.D., Love, P.E.D. and Li Heng (2000) The learning organisation: toward a paradigm for mutually beneficial strategic construction alliances. *International Journal of Project Management*, 18, 415–421

Jones, P.H. (2000) Developing a Knowledge Strategy. *KMWorld 2000 Conference & Exhibition*, [Online] Available http://www.kmworld.com/00/ [Accessed 5th May 2002].

KLICON (Knowledge Learning In Construction) *The Role of Information Technology in Knowledge Management within the Construction Industry*, UMIST (Online). Available http://www.umist.ac.uk/civilandconstruction/research/management/klicon/ [Accessed 5th January 2002].

Liston, K.F.M. and Winograd, T. Focused sharing of information for multi-disciplinary decision making by project teams, *Electronic Journal of Information Technology in Construction* website (Online). Available http://www.itcon.org/2001/6/paper.pdf [Accessed 25th July 2002].

Malhotra, Y. (2002) *Knowledge Management for the New World of Business* (Online). Available http://www.brint.com/km/whatis.htm [Accessed February 2002].

McNamara (2002) *Basic Context for Organizational Change* (Online). Available http://www. mapnp.org/library/mgmnt/orgchnge.htm [Accessed 6th August 2002].

McDermott, R. (2001) Overcoming cultural barriers to sharing knowledge. *Journal of Knowledge Management*, **5** (1), 2001.

Moodley, K., Preece, C. and Kyprianou, R. (2001) An examination of knowledge management implementation within civil engineering consulting firms. In: *ARCOM 17th Annual Conference Proceedings* (University of Salford), pp. 587–596.

Nonaka, I. and Takeuchi I. (1995) *The Knowledge Creating Company* (New York: Oxford University Press).

Nonaka, I. and Konno, N. (1998) The concept of 'Ba': building a foundation for knowledge creation, *California Management Review*, **40** (3), pp. 40.

Nonaka, I., Tayama, R. and Konno, N. (2001) 'SECI, Ba and leadership: a unified model of dynamic knowledge creation. In: Nonaka and Teece (eds) *Managing Industrial Knowledge* (SAGE Publication), p. 14–44.

Polanyi, M. (1966) *The Tacit Dimension* (London: Routledge and Kegan Paul).

Preece, C., Moodley, K. and Hyde J. (2000) Knowledge management strategies to improve construction business development processes – a preliminary case study In: *ARCOM 16th Annual Conference Proceedings*, Glasgow Caledonian University, pp. 325–334.

Tierney, T. (1999). What's your strategy for managing knowledge? *Harvard Business Review*, March–April.

Wiig, Karl, M. (2000) Knowledge management: an emerging discipline rooted in a long history. In: Charles, D. and Daniel C. (eds) *Knowledge Horizons* (Butterworth Heinmann), pp. 4.

Zack, M.H. (1999) Developing a knowledge strategy, *California Management Review* (Spring), **41** (3), pp. 125–145.

13

Business development and collaborative working

Paul Wilkinson*

Introduction

'Collaborative working' is not exactly a new concept to the UK construction industry. The notion of working more co-operatively, in a team atmosphere of mutual trust, co-operation and openness, with the client, fellow consultants, contractors and suppliers, has been widely discussed since at least the mid-1990s when the buzz-word was 'partnering'. To the industry's credit, it has begun to tackle some of the deep-rooted problems that prompted the landmark reports by Sir Michael Latham and Sir John Egan calling for wide ranging and sustained reform across the industry, but there was never going to be a 'quick fix'. This is, after all, a conservative, risk-averse industry in which projects frequently take months, even years, to move from inception to completion. Clients have traditionally employed a complex, fragmented, multidisciplinary, geographically dispersed and relatively temporary group of professionals to deliver projects using sometimes antiquated and bureaucratic processes. And the industry's problems were so wide ranging that real progress would only be achieved if the complex mesh of people, processes and technology could be effectively reformed.

Influential clients such as Sainsbury's and BAA have played a key role in driving the change, demanding new approaches to delivering construction projects, and many contractors, consultants and suppliers have responded positively to the challenges. Attitudes and processes have changed, and, after some false starts, the industry has also begun to tackle some of the technology issues.

This chapter briefly reviews the background to the concept of 'collaborative working' and its gradual adoption by some within the industry. Progress has been hampered by both cultural and technological barriers. If organizations are to adopt more collaborative approaches (some, of course, may not wish to, but they risk a desperate race to catch up if collaboration becomes the norm rather than the exception), they will need to change their internal culture and develop new ways of working with other organizations. This will prompt changes to business development activities to reflect the growing importance of

* Head of corporate communications, BIW Technologies Ltd, London

long-term relationships, both up and down the supply chain (could 'alliance competence' become a new area of market differentiation?). As collaborative working is built on a combination of people, processes and technology, the lack of an infrastructure to support new approaches has also hampered progress, though the advent of new collaboration technology could hasten the necessary supply chain integration and provide further potential for businesses to develop competitive advantages.

Managing reputation in a poorly regarded industry

For those tasked with driving a company's business development activities, particularly to new clients of the industry, the reputation of the UK construction industry has not exactly helped. As an industry, it is seen as fragmented, unprofitable, low tech and prone to cultural inertia. Almost regardless of their individual merits, many construction enterprises will be tarred with the same brush – characterized as inefficient, confrontational, unreliable, unsafe, short term in outlook, lacking innovation, with a record of delivering projects late, over-budget and of poor quality, working to low margins that generate poor profits with lowest price often the most important factor.

Certainly, overhauling the industry is not going to be achieved by a single 'magic bullet', but the industry has begun to review its core combinations of people, processes and technologies, and to identify areas for reform. As part of this review, the idea of building collaborative working relationships up and down the supply chain has been widely discussed in the industry since at least 1994, when the influential Latham Report, 'Constructing the Team', was published. Since then, early converts within the industry have also tested the concept and improved understanding through their efforts with partnering charters, alliances, framework agreements, prime contracting and the like. And the 1998 Egan report and related initiatives have also helped maintain some kind of momentum.

From partnering to collaborative working

Sir Michael Latham made numerous recommendations to change industry practices, to increase efficiency and to replace the bureaucratic, wasteful, adversarial atmosphere prevalent in most construction projects with one characterized by openness, co-operation, trust, honesty, commitment and mutual understanding among team members. A year later, he wrote the foreword to the Reading Construction Forum's best practice guide to partnering in construction, called 'Trusting the Team' (Bennett and Jayes, 1995). This defined partnering as:

> a management approach used by two or more organisations to achieve specific business objectives by maximising the effectiveness of each participant's resources. The approach is based on mutual objectives, an agreed method of problem resolution and an active search for continuous measurable improvements. (p. 2)

> † also emphasized that partnering was not all about cost cutting:

> In addition to reducing costs partnering can also improve service quality, deliver better designs, make construction safer, meet earlier completion deadlines and provide everyone involved with bigger profits. (p. iii)

Within a notoriously conservative industry, some contractors and consultants enthusiastically embraced the concept, recognizing the value of establishing long-term relationships with customers and other members of the supply chain (why, after all, should the construction industry be any different from other sectors, where relationship marketing was already a familiar concept?), and the RCF and others strongly advocated moving beyond project partnering to 'strategic partnering' or 'alliancing' to cover just such an eventuality. Such relationships had to be preferable, they argued, to the continued reliance on business relationships that were frequently complex, geographically dispersed and relatively short lived. Why assemble a large, expensive, virtual organization including the client, architects, engineers, contractors, suppliers, construction managers and other professionals only to disband it once the project is handed over?

Clients too could see the advantages. Innovative organizations such as BAA and Sainsbury's could justify building more long-lasting, strategic relationships on the grounds that they were also capturing information, experience and best practice. They realized that information created during project delivery was a valuable 'whole life' asset that could be used to enable better planning, continuous performance improvement and risk reduction across their current and future property portfolios.

Many other businesses – particularly subcontractors, suppliers and manufacturers – remained sceptical, but the industry did start to move forward. The pan-industry Construction Industry Board (CIB) was established in 1995 to drive forward Latham's change agenda. The Construction Best Practice Programme (and its sister organization, the IT Best Practice Programme) was created to provide guidance and advice, enabling UK construction and client organizations to gain the knowledge and skills required to implement change. And the Design Build Foundation (DBF)[†] was launched in 1997 as a catalyst for change, drawing together forward-thinking construction industry customers, designers, contractors, consultants, specialists and manufacturers, representing the whole construction supply chain.

Latham and the ensuing industry initiatives also sparked government action. In October 1997, the Deputy Prime Minister John Prescott commissioned the Construction Task Force, chaired by Sir John Egan, to advise on opportunities to improve the efficiency and quality of the UK construction industry's service and products and to make the industry more responsive to the needs of its customers. Informed by experiences in other industries (notably manufacturing), the Task Force report 'Rethinking Construction' (1998) – the Egan Report – endorsed much of the progressive thinking already under way. 'Rethinking Construction' acknowledged that its foundation was the Latham Report, which the CIB had helped implement by promoting a focus on client value, partnering and standardization. It sought to achieve a further step change in performance through eliminating waste or non-value-adding activities from the construction process, and identified five key drivers of change: committed leadership, a focus on the customer, integrated processes and teams, a quality driven agenda, and commitment to people. Having put the client's needs at the very heart of the process, it advocated an integrated project process based around four key elements: product development, project implementation, *partnering* the supply chain and production of components. Existing industry bodies such as the CIB, CBPP and the DBF enthusiastically incorporated the Egan agenda into their activities, and were augmented by organizations such as the Movement for Innovation (M4I), the Housing Forum, the Local Government Task Force and the Government Client Construction Panel.

Also within the government sector, the 'Building Down Barriers' initiative was established in January 1997, funded by the then Department of the Environment, Transport and the Regions and by Defence Estates within the Ministry of Defence. This had three over-all objectives:

1 To develop a new approach to construction procurement, called Prime Contracting, based on supply chain integration.
2 To demonstrate the benefits of the new approach, in terms of improved value for the client and profitability for the supply chain, through running two Pilot Projects ....
3 To assess the relevance of the new approach to the wider UK construction industry.

The initiative yielded a new procurement process and a 'tool-kit' to support it, largely cap-tured in a Handbook of Supply Chain Management (Holti *et al.*, 2000). The work was being taken forward by the Warwick Manufacturing Group, who have examined best prac-tice in other industries and are working with major companies to implement the principles in construction, in conjunction with the DBF, though the term 'Building Down Barriers' had by then been replaced by 'collaborative working'.

In 2002, the Strategic Forum for Construction – successor to the Construction Task Force, and also chaired by Sir John Egan – produced a follow-up to '*Rethinking Construction*'. '*Accelerating Change*' (Egan, 2002) underlined the importance of collaborative working, stressing the need for greater integration:

A key to ... transformation is the integration of the team undertaking the construction process, including design. Integration allows pre-planning and through this the indus-try can drive out inefficiencies, waste, cost, poor working practices and accidents. (p. 8)

Collaborative commerce: c-commerce

The emergence of the phrase 'collaborative working' during the late 1990s/early 2000s more or less coincided with the arrival in the UK construction market of new Internet-based collaboration – or c-commerce – technologies (widely touted by as a major growth sector by IT analysts such as Gartner and by the business process re-engineering gurus Michael Hammer (2001) and James Champy (2002)).

A key aspect of the inefficiency that had provoked Latham and Egan was its reliance on slow, paper-based processes to share project information: documents, drawings and corres-pondence, with all the on-going amendments, many out-of-date before they reached recip-ients by conventional means of delivery. During the design and construction processes of even the most modest projects, project teams traditionally created, copied, distributed and stored huge volumes of information. In any information-dependent industry, sharing accu-rate, up-to-date information is critical for all participants. Wasted time and cost can almost always be traced back to poor co-ordination caused by inaccurate, inadequate or inconsis-tent information – sometimes a combination of all three (indeed, back in 1994 Latham recommended: 'use of co-ordinated project information should be a contractual require-ment'). Moreover, when the facility is handed over to the new owner or operator and the team members go their separate ways, that accumulated information or knowledge gradu-ally dissipates until it is effectively lost.

By the late 1990s, almost all construction professionals had become computer users, particularly for word-processing, spreadsheet work and CAD, with high rates of e-mail and Internet access. Yet, as a Building Centre Trust Survey (1999) suggested, for many users, the technology was not yet used to its full potential and capacity, with training, lack of investment and a preference for paper cited by the research as users' key concerns.

A tiny minority of construction projects had experimented with expensive electronic document management systems (EDMS) commonly used in manufacturing and process industries, but these rarely proved suitable in a geographically dispersed team setting. Fortunately, however, the rapid development of web-based technology had created a new breed of business applications. With websites, e-mail and intranets becoming more common, e-business systems were already improving internal communications; the challenge was to extend those benefits to improve communications up and down the supply chain – a challenge taken up by both established names and new start-up businesses. For example, some US-based EDMS vendors (e.g. Documentum, OpenText) adapted their technology to try and get a foothold in the UK construction market (targeted as the AEC – architecture, engineering and construction – sector); established industry names such as UK contractor Bovis and multidisciplinary practice Arup created their own project document handling systems (Hummingbird and Integration, respectively – the latter was acquired by Causeway Technologies in 2001). Newly formed businesses began to focus specifically on the UK AEC market, including US-backed Cephren (now part of Citadon) and Buzzsaw (now part of Autodesk), and UK-based BIW Technologies (BIW) and Cadweb. The products or services differed greatly in their technical structure and capabilities (some were EDMS based, some simply replicated existing, often inefficient, project processes electronically), but most of the providers began to market them as web-delivered project 'collaboration systems'.

Broadly, what are they? Taking advantage of new Internet technology, such services – sometimes referred to as 'project extranets' – are usually accessed through a standard computer browser. No matter where they were located or when they use the system, authorized users could have immediate access to a central repository of project data that grew as the building, road, bridge, etc. developed. Feasibility studies, budgets, sketches, drawings, approvals, schedules, minutes, photographs, specifications, standards, procedures, virtual reality models could all be viewed; team members could add comments or requests, make amendments or issue new documents. Everyone worked on the most up-to-date, accurate and relevant information, backed by all the archive material. Importantly, particularly for smaller suppliers and other project participants, use of a web-based extranet normally demands no major investment in new technology.

The partnering objectives of trust, openness and co-operation are, of course, promoted through use of such extranet technology. In such a transparent environment, everyone knows who did what and when. It is easy to see who is responsible for a delay or problem; this encourages team members to work harder to achieve targets and settle disputes before they became causes for litigation. Better information flow means that design changes have less impact, decision-making is quicker, resulting in less delay, fewer attendant costs and more chance of a project completed on-time and on-budget. As Sir Michael Latham said (in Smith (2002)): 'Apart from the obvious advantages of avoiding confusion, duplication of effort and waste, improved communication also lies at the heart of the modern trend away from the adversarial system, towards partnering and collaborative working.'

Perhaps a side issue, but Latham's suggestion that such systems are a move towards collaborative working is worth noting, as he draws a distinction between new ways of working and traditional systems. For example, Schrage (1990) defines collaboration as:

> the process of *shared creation*: two or more individuals with complementary skills interacting to create a shared understanding that none had previously possessed or could have come to on their own.

As this definition suggests, collaboration is a process of value creation that cannot be achieved through traditional communication and teamwork structures. The key requirement is an environment to which a community of authorized collaborators have equal access, and which they can use to interact in real time towards the achievement of an agreed objective. Whether face to face or virtual, such a community creates belonging, trust, passion, learning and relationships – all of which fuel performance, motivation and ingenuity. Importantly, they can encourage a shared sense of identity and purpose that often breaks down organizational or corporate barriers and creates synergies. The outputs from an online community, from genuine collaboration, therefore, are often *greater* than the sum of all individuals' expertise and knowledge inputs.

While the various extranet providers may like to describe their systems as collaboration services, some of them may not, in fact, enable collaboration at all. Instead, they electronically enable existing project processes. There will still be benefits in terms of faster communication, easier access to a central repository, reduced paperwork costs, etc., but more substantial savings of the kind envisaged by Latham and Egan will come from rethinking and changing the processes. In short, a collaboration system will need to be flexible enough to adapt to new more integrated ways of working in teams.

dot.boom or dot.bomb?

Some client organizations were already adopting partnering approaches and so 'collaboration technology' was the logical next step. For example, in 1999, Sainsbury's one of the UK's largest building clients adopted BIW Information Channel as its corporate system, heralding a dramatic increase in the use of collaboration technology by its supply chain and others. Sainsbury's example helped persuade other client organizations about the virtues of online collaboration, and 'early adopters' included Asda, Manchester Airport, Marks & Spencer, Capital One Bank, Defence Estates, the Wellcome Trust and Stanhope. From 850 users in 170 companies at the end of 1999, usage grew to 3400 from 570 at the end of 2000, and then accelerated to 11,000 users from 1600 companies a year later. Similarly, BAA built on its earlier framework agreement experiences by using extranet services to manage team communications, and by early 2002 was using BIW, Bidcom and 4Projects systems; it had also added its name to the host of other clients backing Asite (launched in October 2000 and describing itself as 'a community of like-minded organizations who want to get construction right – designed right, built right and used right. Asite's approach is a partnering approach which encourages the sharing of benefits across the whole supply chain.').

Collaboration technology emerged during a period of frenetic dot.com hysteria, to which the construction industry was not immune. Dot.com start-ups had exploded onto the AEC scene in a blaze of venture-capital funded publicity; some existing companies tried to reinvent themselves as e-businesses; and several companies and consortia aimed to establish transaction hubs or portals for whole communities of construction enterprises.

However, the 'dot.com bubble' burst in 2000 and many of these businesses eventually merged or disappeared. For instance, some of Asite's predecessors, including the Arrideo, AECventure and Mercadium portal initiatives – some heavily backed by industry organizations – all disappeared, partly reflecting a view held by many suppliers that such construction e-marketplaces posed a threat to existing, and often mutually beneficial, supplier relationships (Forrester, 2001). BuildOnline quietly switched focus from being an online trading exchange to delivering extranet services, while some extranet providers also merged or folded (e.g. Citadon emerged from the merger of Cephren (formerly Blueline Online) and Bidcom; I-Scraper folded in early 2001, its UK operations being taken over by BIW and its German operations going to BuildOnline).

The dot.com implosion fuelled uncertainty about some e-businesses' financial backing, stability and long-term prospects – providing a convenient excuse for some to delay decisions about using them (alongside sometimes spurious issues such as legal admissibility of electronic documents, lack of awareness, absence of industry standards, and security concerns). But, perhaps because it had already begun to achieve credibility with a few leading clients, online collaboration started to become an accepted part of AEC life. Analysed in terms of the traditional product life cycle, the technology had successfully negotiated the 'introduction' and 'growth' phases; awareness and interest had been stimulated by 'innovator' clients; 'early adopter' clients had then started to join in. 'Innovator' clients', themselves, also encouraged acceptance: e.g. BAA's Martin Ong told a London conference in March 2002 that some marketplace consolidation among the service providers was already taking place, limiting the chances of new clients making the wrong choice ('e.g. opting for Betamax instead of the VHS standard', to use his video recorder analogy).

Clients were increasingly adopting extranet technology for all significant construction projects. A July 2001 e-business survey (www.constructionconfederation.co.uk/ebus/index.html) by the Construction Confederation revealed that 4 per cent of all respondents used online project tools, with a further 10 per cent planning to do so after 2002. The results were significantly higher for larger firms, with 43 per cent of contractors with over 1000 employees managing some projects online. Research by the Business Advantage Group in December 2001 (www.business-advantage.co.uk/Spaghetti/project_hosting.htm) estimated that one in five UK construction sites were operating a web-based project hosting service. By then, leading industry figures were already suggesting the scale of adoption would grow. Sir John Egan, now chairman of Asite and of the government-initiated Strategic Forum for Construction, continued to preach the need for a disciplined supply chain (e.g. *Building*, 10 August 2001); engineer Mark Whitby, President of the Institution of Civil Engineers, told the Construction Industry Computing Association in September 2001 that project extranets would soon become the norm rather than the exception.

Browsing through the websites of the various extranet technology providers, the benefits to both team members and organizations seem clear:

- earlier/more timely involvement in key decisions (design, specification, fabrication, installation, maintenance, repair, replacement, etc.)
- faster communications (supplier-specific decisions communicated more quickly and completely; reduced time spent processing requests for information, etc.)
- less time spent searching for already existing information
- more open discussion of design issues, leading to ...
- improved understanding (better design, less duplication and rework, fewer delays)

- fewer drawing revisions
- increased scope for innovation (e.g. for manufacturers online collaboration can yield ideas for product innovations that may lead to further differentiation)
- cost savings in document printing, reproduction, distribution, storage and management; also reduced need for on-site meetings (lower travel costs, etc.)
- a more transparent audit trail encouraging adherence to programme, cutting scope for disputes and claims (peer pressure replaces blame shifting as an incentive to faster turn-around)
- greater reuse of information (less 're-inventing the wheel', more WORM – write once, read many)
- product information becoming part of knowledge base for future projects (or repeat aspects of the same project)
- product information forms part of operation and maintenance and health and safety files (linking suppliers to the asset's future repair, replacement and maintenance regimes; providing feedback on their products' (real not theoretical) whole life performance – assuming, of course, that the client uses the knowledge bank accumulated during the asset's prebuild and build phases)
- faster projects (resulting in lower on-site costs and earlier revenues to owner/developers through use, rental, lease, etc.).

Towards a collaborative business development culture

In an AEC industry where a growing number of client organizations are looking to develop more long-term relationships with their supply chain, the ability of contractors, consultants and suppliers to demonstrate understanding of, and commitment to, collaborative working could well prove a key marketing differentiator – contrasting with others persevering with more traditional, adversarial methods of project participation. Clients will, of course, be wary of businesses who 'talk the talk' but are culturally unable to work in a more integrated, collaborative way.

While the practical benefits of using extranet technologies (above) may be clear, collaborative working means more than passively using a particular technology system. Assuming that it even allows value-adding collaboration of the kind envisaged by Schrage (1990, *op. cit.*), the new technology – on its own – will not deliver significant benefits (US economist Paul Strassman argues that there is no link between technology investment and productivity – it is all down to good management, and good managers are better able to exploit technology). Organizations also need to understand and develop new skills and abilities among their own people, and to devise suitable structures and processes, which will allow them to take advantage of new technical capabilities. It is at least partly for this reason, because the people and process issues have not always kept track with the pace of technology change, that the UK AEC sector has yet to fully embrace real collaborative working.

C-commerce experience in other industries (e.g. IT, retail, manufacturing) suggests that failure to understand and adapt human behaviour, rather than technology, is the biggest single impediment to successful collaborative working. Businesses have traditionally been resistant to the notion that they should share information, both externally and internally. Key functions – sales, IT, procurement, HR, accounts, etc. – have all sat in 'silos', with their own agendas, own systems, and varying degrees of influence over corporate strategy.

Arguably, in a more slow-changing – even change-resistant – industry like construction, culture, people or psychology issues are even more important. In construction firms, individual advancement has frequently depended upon gaining time-consuming qualifications followed by years of project experience. It is therefore perhaps even more difficult to persuade individuals that they need to adopt a different kind of mindset and behave differently. Organizations will need to promote a different style of leadership and alter their internal management processes if they are to succeed at working collaboratively. For example: senior management should be seen to preach and embrace collaborative working (or there will be little or no incentive for anyone else to work in this way), and managers should emphasize team working and de-emphasize individual achievement – instead collaboration should be both encouraged and rewarded, motivating employees to change their attitudes and behaviours.

Organizations must resolve any internal issues they have about collaboration before they start considering committed, collaborative relationships or alliances with external clients, partners or suppliers ('Enterprises that have learned to collaborate internally are the most successful in creating collaborative relationships outside the enterprise,' said AMR Research analyst John Fontanella – quoted in *Infoconomy Collaborate Newsletter*, April 2002). Once these intra-organization issues are eradicated, focus can switch to breaking down inter-organizational fear and mistrust that often exists. Traditionally, project participants in the UK AEC industry have established external trading relationships based on short-term commercial outcomes relating only to the immediate project. Essentially, the approach was adversarial, focused on cutting costs/maximizing profits from the transaction, while minimizing defects and delivering the project on time, with onerous contracts to manage participants' risks.

In a collaborative working environment, however, it is important to examine issues relating to the people and culture within each organization. For example, staff on both sides in a potential long-term relationship will need to display 'alliance competence' (Spekman and Isabella, 2000), enabling each organization to understand and to align their expectations and responsibilities (when establishing strategic partnering relationships, Bennett and Jayes (1995, p. 50) say partners should: 'analyse each others' goals, philosophies and cultures'). Assuming both sides are able to commit to a more mutual and more long-term relationship, time/cost/quality outcomes will remain important, but participants' will aim to maximize profits over a series of projects while achieving and sustaining improvements in design, service quality, health and safety performance, innovation, etc. They will also assess the success of the arrangement on more qualitative 'relationship' people/process factors such as improved co-operation, fewer disputes or claims, better communication, etc. Clearly, establishing a collaborative working framework can be complex and time consuming, but in 1999 the DBF launched a registration scheme to 'help companies and partnerships to confirm they have reached recognized levels of performance. The higher standards required may mean completely different relationships, tools and methods of working.'

It would all be very simple if each contractor, consultant or supplier dealt with only one client, but in reality construction businesses work for many different clients, most of whom will employ different processes, requiring teams to be flexible and multiskilled to adapt. The post-Egan agenda, therefore, should perhaps extend beyond improvements to how organizations collaborate internally and with other like-minded organizations to the development of more standard pan-industry processes.

Differentiation based on collaboration technical know-how

Having suggested that extranet technology alone will not make a significant difference, it perhaps follows that once an organization is culturally committed to collaborative working it is better able to take advantage of the technology (again, assuming it enables collaboration). However, managerial and process adaptations will also need to be made if the AEC sector is to integrate IT into its normal operations. In 2001, a Building Centre Trust report on IT and construction deliberately avoided discussion of the technology: 'It is our belief that the technical barriers are far less significant than the organizational and managerial issues which have to be addressed' (p. 7). Focusing more specifically on collaboration technology, Zara Lamont (2002), chief executive of the Confederation of Construction Clients, wrote:

> e-business can only support business processes. If they are the wrong processes, it will mean we are doing the wrong thing more efficiently. … We need teams, chains and clusters who are prepared to work together over time in an open and honest way to develop the right business processes. When that's done, those processes can be IT-enabled. … the more you put into getting the processes right and changing the culture, the quicker the payback.

Lamont clearly believes that people and processes have to be aligned correctly before collaboration technology can become truly effective. And once this alignment is achieved, it is vital that the technology is unanimously adopted: there is little point if some employees bypass the technology and continue with old communications methods and ways of doing things.

Once these issues have been addressed, IT capabilities can potentially become the crucial difference when it comes to be securing a project appointment. More specifically, if US experience is anything to go by, such capabilities should now include expertise with web technologies – by 1998, major American building owners and clients (e.g. Nations Bank and 3Com Corporation) were already demanding that their consultants and contractors become Internet-literate just to remain qualified to bid for projects.

Anticipating that UK clients would follow suit, some consultants, contractors and suppliers began to work with the various extranet technology providers. Bidcom's UK operation, for example, received investment backing from contractors Carillion and Wates and consultant EC Harris, and these backers began to use Bidcom's ProjectNet for some of their clients' projects.

Some construction businesses have moved beyond being IT- and Internet-literate to set up operations that are focused specifically on offering a complete solution. For example, many clients' main source of construction advice is a professional, perhaps an architect, project or construction manager or consulting engineer; alternatively, design-and-build contractors may offer clients a complete turnkey package. Some professionals, particularly those with responsibility for delivery of the scheme on behalf of their client (e.g. construction managers) are now combining their traditional strengths with expertise in implementing and supporting extranet technology. Construction manager PCM, for example, set up Knowledge Online in early 2000, offering IT services from BIW, BuildOnline, Cadweb and Causeway Technologies, among others.

Such businesses (e.g. BIW refers to consultants Gleeds and Citex, and contractors Kajima and ISG, as 'solution partners') add to their value propositions, being able to offer

IT audits, consultancy, training and other web related skills that complement their core services. Moreover, by advocating collaborative technology, they achieve other marketing advantages:

- positioning as innovators, championing the Latham and Egan principles of partnering, lean construction and integration
- use of collaboration technology can help improve the solution partner's own processes, internally and in relation to management of the project and the client's supply chain
- by considering the cost savings that can arise from using the technology, the consult-ant/contractor can also price its services much more competitively.

The gradual cultural shift of the UK construction industry towards partnering-type approaches has generally proceeded in parallel with the development of, and equally grad-ual adoption by the industry of, new IT capabilities. However, these movements have now plainly begun to converge and become intertwined. '*Accelerating Change*' (Egan, 2002) puts integration of both the entire team and its IT at the heart of its vision, envisaging an industry characterised by: 'Integrated teams, created at the optimal time in the process and using an integrated IT approach, that fully release the contribution each can make and equitably share risk and reward in a non-adversarial way' (p. 10). In short, collaboration technology and collaborative working are now irrevocably intertwined.

Building collaborative alliances

Once an organization can genuinely demonstrate that it is has the right combination of people, processes and technology, it is then in a position to become a more permanent and integral part of a client's delivery process for whole series of projects. This may be a pre-cursor to more fundamental changes both across and within supply chains.

For example, post-Egan moves towards a more integrated supply chain could lead to a reduction in the fragmentation of the UK construction industry. While Egan recognized that such fragmentation provided flexibility to deal with highly variable workloads, he said the extensive use of subcontracting prevented the continuity that is essential to efficient work-ing. If the industry moves towards his recommendation of greater standardization and pre-fabrication, there are opportunities for supply chain members to form temporary consortia or joint ventures or to merge their operations permanently, pooling their resources so that they can collectively respond more efficiently and effectively to their customers' demands.

While, on their own, many small contractors, subcontractors and consultants may be unable to provide the required level of service, by combining with other enterprises with complementary skills and/or resources, they could become valuable members of the clients' team. Moreover, these combinations may prove beneficial when it comes to bid-ding for work from other clients, leading eventually to friendly merger or acquisition activ-ity as temporary tactical alliances become more strategic and permanent.

Of course, businesses have often pooled their resources to compete for clients' work which they could not have won on their own, but the shift in recent years towards combin-ing finance, design, build and operation activities – through, e.g. Private Finance Initiative (PFI) and Public Private Partnership (PPP) projects – is adding new areas of responsibility to the project team. Instead of focusing just on design and build activities, the project team – and therefore the collaboration challenge – has been enlarged to include organizations responsible for raising funding for the project and others who will be responsible for operating and maintaining the completed facility through a concession period which may last twenty-five or thirty years. Responsibility goes hand-in-hand with risk, and the groups that successfully bid for most PFI/PPP projects have to manage higher levels of risk, often way beyond the levels they encountered in more traditional schemes. The rewards can, of course, also be significantly greater, and bidder organizations are looking to re-engineer themselves, to innovate, so that they increase their chances of success.

Evolving technology

In 2002, PFI/PPP teams were already using extranet systems to manage the vast array of documents and drawings required to support a successful bid. With a project's whole-life costs increasingly important, both PFI/PPP consortia and traditional clients have started to look to their extranet systems to manage information *beyond* the design and construction phases, throughout the life cycle of their facilities. And as design, construction and operation factors cease to be differentiators, the creative nature of collaboration may help consortia develop new ideas that give them a marketing edge (similarly, an individual member of a consortium may also find that collaboration generates innovations – e.g. new materials, new product designs, new service combinations – that it can profit from).

Whether the collaborative outputs are project or programme specific, or are simply good ideas that deserve to be more widely exploited, given the pace of change within the IT field, it is vital that information does not become 'trapped' inside an extranet. Some providers are aiming to 'future-proof' their technology by making it interoperable (interoperability is the ability of a system or application to work with other systems or applications without special effort on the part of the user).

Another area of particular interest – and one with potentially profound implications for manufacturers and suppliers of construction products – has been object-based technology.

This allows projects to be designed using 'intelligent' components whose dimensions are augmented by data about their specification, performance characteristics, manufacture, relationships with other components, maintenance needs, etc. Such technology will allow suppliers to create information-rich components that can be shared between applications, up and down the supply chain. (Faced with two similar products – one intelligent, the other dumb – which do you expect a designer or specifier will opt for?)

Conclusion

This chapter has necessarily had to present a snapshot of the situation in the early part of the first years of the 21st century. To recap briefly, partnering/collaborative working and its supporting technology have begun to change the ground rules for business development within the construction industry.

Latham and Egan underlined the need for radical changes to the processes through which the industry delivered its projects, insisting that these processes should be explicit and transparent to the industry and its clients. There needed to be substantial changes in the industry's culture and structure, they said, with competitive tendering replaced by a focus on long-term relationships. While experience had shown that businesses might achieve some short-term improvements by using new communications technologies, sustained performance improvements demand more deep-rooted change. People within the industry needed to adopt a culture of openness, trust and co-operation; they needed to develop flexible new structures and processes which encouraged such attitudes while improving efficiency of project delivery; and collaboration technology, so long as it was capable of supporting these processes and structures, provided a convenient platform to help them achieve this change.

Historically, this industry has been slow to adopt new work practices, but there is pressure to achieve change. First, the Latham/Egan agenda has created a platform for forward-thinking organizations representing both clients and the industry's supply side to promote collaborative working, and this is beginning to reach down the supply chain to those involved in manufacturing and supplying construction components. Second, pioneering clients and their supply chains are experimenting with, and then adopting, online project extranet technologies, giving themselves marketing advantages that will encourage others to follow suit. Third, responding to the demands made upon them by their users, the vendors of online technologies are constantly improving the functionality of their systems.

Having learned the lessons of the 'dot.com bomb', we will perhaps see more measured progress towards a more streamlined, efficient and complete supply chain, where the design outputs from project collaboration are used to drive online procurement of materials direct from distributors and manufacturers.

[†] Note added at print stage: The Reading Construction Forum and the Design Build Foundation merged in October 2002 to form Collaborating for the Built Environment (know as BE).

Bibliography

Bennett, J. and Jayes, S. (1995) *Trusting the Team. Centre for Strategic Studies in Construction*, The University of Reading, with the partnering task force of the Reading Construction Forum, UK.

Building Centre Trust (1999) *IT Usage in the Construction Team*, London.

Building Centre Trust (2001) *Effective integration of IT in construction: final report*, London.

Champy, J. (2002) *X-Engineering the Corporation* (London: Hodder & Stoughton).

Egan, J. (1998) *Rethinking Construction* (London: HMSO).

Egan, J. (2002) *Accelerating Change* (London: HMSO).

Forrester Research (2001) *The Construction e-Marketplace Fallout* (Amsterdam: Forrester Research).

Hammer, M. (2001) *The Agenda* (New York: Random House).

Holti, R., Nicolini, D. and Smalley, M. (2000) *The Handbook of Supply Chain Management* (London: CIRIA).

Lamont, Z. (2002) 'IT is not the answer'. *Building*, 19 April 2002, p. 33.

Latham, M. (1994) *Constructing the Team* (London: HMSO).

Schrage, M. (1990) *Shared Minds: the New Technologies of Collaboration* (New York: Random House).

Smith, C. (2002) 'Collaborative Working'. *Public Sector and Local Government*, January 2002.

Spekman, R.E. and Isabella, L.A. (2000) *Alliance Competence: Maximizing the Value of Your Partnerships* (New York: John Wiley).

14

The business development manager as hero!

Mark Lench*

Introduction

The role of the business development manager in the construction industry is largely undervalued, especially when considering the business development manager's role as the pivotal character in a series of commercial, technical and management processes that result in achieving the primary objective of any company – to win profitable new business.

Construction business development is all about market and customer knowledge, strategy and tactics, relationships, teamwork, marketing, proposal preparation, commercial acumen, contract terms and conditions, risk assessment and analysis, technical know-how, time management, project experience, networking, listening ... and more. It is a demanding, but ultimately rewarding role.

This chapter explores the role and responsibilities of the business development manager. More accurately, it paints a picture of the possibility for the role and highlights the opportunities for the business development manager to excel. The existence of such individuals, particularly in construction, is rare. Indeed the all-encompassing role in its purest form often does not exist within the organizational structure of many companies. Those individuals that exhibit such qualities are highly regarded and sought after.

The business development manager has the opportunity to be a strategist, an account executive, a champion of change, a winner, a leader – and, ultimately, a hero.

The business development manager as ... strategist

Strategic planning drives the process of identifying target customers, projects, prospects and opportunities to deliver a portfolio mix that contributes to achieving specific business and financial goals. The business development manager's role in strategic planning is fundamental.

Early identification of profitable business opportunities is one of the primary roles of the business development manager. If the first knowledge of a particular prospect is when

* Mark Lench Marketing

the invitation to tender arrives unexpectedly in the post, then the chances of success will be severely limited. It is highly likely that a competitor is already on the case!

The business development process in construction markets can often be ineffective, leading to low success rates and high bid costs. There are several common causes:

- a lack of disciplined focus on critical prospects
- a lack of integration between business development and project operations
- limited understanding of what it takes to win
- too much focus on getting the price right as opposed to developing a winning strategy.

A key 'tool' in the business development process is an individual job strategy, or Win Plan.

By assuming responsibility for the creation and development of a strategic Win Plan for each targeted project, prospect and opportunity, the business development manager creates the framework for an integrated series of actions aimed at gaining competitive advantage.

Creating a Win Plan instils discipline into the information and knowledge gathering process and provides a central focus for data collection. The Win Plan forces early responses to many fundamental questions, such as why the project is important, what it will take to win, whether the project is aligned with the company's strategy and what specific actions can be taken to position for winning.

A typical Win Plan should include essential project data (Table 14.1), a statement of strategic intent, a competitive evaluation, a superior value proposition, an outline commercial and technical strategy, a vulnerability assessment and a diary of significant actions and events.

Project data

The opening section of the Win Plan provides valuable background data and information about the project. Particular attention should be paid to the quality of data and information provided. Indeed, one of the traits of the engineering and construction industry is the lack of attention to detail, particularly when developing data and information about a specific project, prospect or opportunity. This is particularly true when inputting data and information to marketing databases. To avoid inconsistencies and misunderstandings that may arise later, the customer's terminology should always be used.

When dealing with large customers that may have several operating entities, it is important to identify the correct contracting entity, together with full contact details.

It is always a good idea to provide an outline of the scope of work to be performed, which helps to focus on the customer's specific needs. It also acts as an early prompt of the need to identify suitable joint venture or alliance partners to offer a comprehensive solution to the customer's needs.

The source and availability of funds for the project should be identified, and an estimate of the total installed cost (TIC) of the project included. The attractiveness of the project will be driven by potential revenue and profit forecasts. Estimates of potential returns, even at an early stage, will greatly assist the bid/no-bid decision process.

Early contractual information will assist the legal, insurance and commercial team members in their preparation. Typical information to be provided includes details of contract type, payment terms, form of agreement, bid currency and exchange rate (for international projects), contract issues and identification of potential risks.

Table 14.1 Typical Win Plan contents

Customer name
Project title
Project location

Contents
Project data
Strategic intent
Knowing the game
Competitive evaluation
Superior value proposition
Vulnerability assessment
Diary

Project data
Job title
Client
Project location
Project description
Work scope
Revenue
Profit
Schedule
Bid information
Contract type
Payment terms
Form of agreement
Performing entity
Risks
Contractual issues
Client key decision makers
Criteria for selection
Competition
Bidding costs
Probability of winning
Return on investment (ROI) (profit/bid costs)
Key nominees for project
Key proposal team members

Strategic intent
Why do we want to win this project?
Why is it important to us?
Does it meet our strategic intent (plan, technology, market, customer)

Knowing the game
Do we 'know the game' for this project?
What is the client's strategic intent/objective?
What key issues does the client face?
What are the client's needs?
What problems does the client face?
What will influence the client?
Do we know and understand the buying habits of our client?
Do we know the target price and have a plan to get there?
What is the competitive price range?
What can we do prior to tender receipt to position ourselves for the win?
What is our relationship with the client?
Who has the best relationship with the client? Are they involved?
What are the barriers to winning this project?

Competitive evaluation
An analysis of the competition, indicating their strengths and weaknesses
Do we hold a preferential position?

(*continued*)

Table 14.1 (*continued*)

Does any of our competition?
Do we have any negatives to overcome?

Superior value proposition
What proposal format and theme will get the winning message across to the client?
Emphasize differentiators and develop strategy for highlighting strengths
Review relevant experience and expertise

Vulnerability assessment
Assess any weaknesses in reputation, approach and price that may put up obstacles to selection by the client
and provide areas that can be exploited by the competition
Evaluate opportunities for influencing selection criteria
Fully understand the selection criteria and reinforce strengths when meeting client personnel/decision makers
Develop strategy for diminishing competitor strengths and elevating their weaknesses
Develop strategy for mitigating and reducing the importance of perceived weaknesses, e.g. price (cost/benefit
sharing), people (interviews), technology (innovation) and complexity (site visits)
Develop a Closing Plan
Incorporate information gained about competitors' offerings and new information gained from the client

Identifying the customer's key decision makers supports the need to develop influential communication strategies. By also identifying key selection for criteria, messages to be communicated can be tailored to suit.

Many customer decisions are made based on the quality of the nominated project team. Significant competitive advantage can be achieved by planning well ahead and identifying nominees for the project team and their likely availability. Similarly, the quality of the proposal effort may depend on the availability of key members of the proposal team.

Strategic intent

Many companies fall into the trap of responding reactively or speculatively to invitations to tender. In such instances, there is often little chance of success. The 'strategic intent' section of the Win Plan helps to validate the decision to pursue a particular prospect or opportunity.

The company business plan and/or marketing plan should define key targets – markets, customers, projects, prospects and opportunities. In the absence of such documents, the bid/no-bid process can become extremely difficult. If such documents exist, answering the following questions should not present too much of a challenge:

- Why do we want to win this project?
- Why is it important to us?
- Does it meet our strategic intent (plan, technology, market, customer)?

Knowing the game

To be successful, an understanding of how 'the game' is played in whatever market, industry or location is essential. This is particularly important in international markets. Parameters might include ethics, local politics or customs, technology, financing and currency issues. This is a critical part of business development expertise and is a fundamental expectation of the business development manager.

The business development manager must also be able to think and act like the customer. To be able to offer a winning solution, the business development manager must have a comprehensive knowledge and understanding of the customer's strategic intent and object-ives, and an understanding of the key issues that the customer faces. There may be spe-cific barriers to overcome, so early positioning allows time to identify critical issues and to develop strategies to address such issues.

Harnessing the customer relationships that exist throughout the company also helps to gather essential information, knowledge and intelligence. It is important to involve other individuals who have close working relationships with the customer in gathering such data.

Every customer is unique, adopting different methods of evaluation and selection. The business development manager needs to know and understand the buying habits of the customer, the customer's target price and the competitive price range. Once identified, the process of developing a winning commercial strategy can begin.

All of these activities help to position for the win prior to the receipt of bid documents.

Competitive evaluation

A competitive evaluation will determine where the company stands relative to its com-petitors based on the initial identification of the prospect. This evaluation also reviews rele-vant project experience and expertise of key personnel.

The business development manager's knowledge of the company's project experience pro-vides another opportunity to gain competitive advantage. Customers are genuinely interested in similar projects, and, in particular, client references. A client representative who can vouch for the company's performance on a particular project is an invaluable ally. Many customers do ask for a significant amount of detail on project experience. It is worth going the extra mile to provide this information, not only to the level of detail requested, but also in the required format to allow it be evaluated alongside competitors.

As more information becomes available, the competitive analysis can be continually reviewed to assess the company's overall position relative to its competitors' strengths and weaknesses.

Superior value to the customer proposition

There is no question that a well presented, fully responsive proposal contributes favourably to the customer's decision-making process.

During the planning phases, it is useful to consider what format and theme of the pro-posal will communicate the winning messages to the customer. It is good practice to draft an Executive Summary, highlighting key features and benefits of the company's proposed solution.

A review of the ROI and portfolio fit

Bidding can be an expensive process, so a realistic budget for pursuing a particular opportun-ity, including pre-bid and post-bid activities, should be determined. The bid/no-bid decision should be part of a formalized process, based on the strategic importance of the prospect.

The decision to bid or pursue a specific opportunity needs to be revisited at regular intervals to determine whether conditions have changed that make the project more or less attractive, particularly for long lead-time projects.

The bid/no-bid decision process should also take into account the probability of winning and the potential ROI expressed as a function of gross margin versus bid costs. Proposals should be considered as investments. On that basis, the expected return the company will achieve by investing in the opportunity can be measured.

Vulnerability assessment

The vulnerability assessment is an essential part of the planning process in preparing for customer interaction – telephone calls, meetings, presentations and interviews.

The purpose of the assessment is to be prepared for the customer's questions. It includes an assessment of any weaknesses in the company's reputation, approach or price that may put up obstacles to selection and areas that can be exploited by the competition.

It includes an evaluation of opportunities for influencing the selection criteria and reinforcing company strengths when dealing with or meeting customer decision makers.

It provides the opportunity to develop strategies for diminishing competitor strengths and elevating their weaknesses, neutralizing their strengths, raising their weaknesses indirectly and exposing generic weaknesses.

It provides a framework to develop strategies for mitigating and reducing the importance of perceived weaknesses – for example, price (cost/benefit sharing), people (interviews), technology (innovation) and complexity (site visits).

Initial closing plan

Another undervalued function that is integral to the business development process is proposal preparation, a process fundamental to winning. The business development manager needs to be intimately involved in this process, providing leadership and direction to a committed team of key individuals, each a specialist in their particular field of expertise and each focused on winning.

After submitting a proposal, most proposal teams are relieved to see the document leave the building! However, this is the stage of the process where a company needs to do everything possible to optimize its chances of winning.

How often does the proposal team emit a huge sigh of relief when the proposal document, which may have taken weeks or even months to produce and may comprise several volumes, finally leaves the building? Consider the analogy of a 400-meter track. When the proposal is delivered, only half the distance, 200 meters, has been covered! In addition to the Win Plan, therefore, there is a need for a Closing Plan to effectively close the deal.

The business development manager must assume responsibility as 'closing leader'. In this role, responsibilities include:

● developing a closing strategy
● re-examining the vulnerability assessment
● gaining management commitment to the closing strategy (particularly for pricing)
● co-ordinating contractual and legal reviews

- knowing where the company stands in competitive pricing
- overseeing all negotiations
- managing the budget for the closing activities.

The Closing Plan is a formal document that establishes the implementation plan for closing the deal. Its critical role is to raise the level of urgency and importance following proposal submittal and it publicizes and enforces the business development manager's responsibility and accountability for the win.

A Closing Plan typically:

- identifies strategies, tactics and actions for senior management review and approval, along with required budgets
- communicates to senior management and others who need to know, any new strategies and tactics to win or close the deal
- incorporates information gained about competitors' offerings, new information gained from the customer, any changes in local politics and late-breaking flashes on post-proposal innovation
- provides a risk assessment that specifically evaluates any assumptions about the prospect that may affect the company's ability to proceed
- reiterates the importance of the prospect throughout the company.

The business development manager as ... account executive

Probably the most important virtue of the business development manager is the ability to build enduring relationships with a wide network of stakeholders. This requires a range of business and social skills, including an ability to listen, to probe, to network, to communicate, to present, to write and to negotiate.

Such relationships need to be developed across a wide spectrum of stakeholders – those individuals that have an interest in a particular project. Stakeholders may include developers, architects, consultants, specialist contractors, government bodies, local authorities, pressure groups and the media.

Clearly, customer relationships are the most important. However, there are often many other third-party influencers and decision makers involved in the selection process. The business development manager's role is to penetrate this 'inner circle' of influence, building trust and laying the foundations for the continual development of relationships.

In sales-orientated companies, the business development manager is recognized as the principal custodian of the customer relationship. Implementing and co-ordinating a successful, efficient key account or relationship management programme is a major challenge for many organizations. It can be a potential 'mine-field'. The main issue is one of sharing information. Human nature often dictates that 'information is power' and as a result, sharing knowledge and information does not come easy to many individuals. The success of any customer database, for example, relies on openness and an ability to share key information.

The reality of the situation is that the relationship that a business development manager enjoys with a customer will almost certainly not suffer as a result of any internal company politics or claims to ownership.

The most crucial aspect is that business development managers spend enough time in front of their customers. In internally focused companies, internal meetings, bureaucracy and procedures occupy far too much time for a business development manager. The more sales-orientated a company becomes, the more it does to openly encourage and measure 'face time' and to remove the burden of internal requirements. Such orientation needs to become an accepted part of the company's culture, again changing internal perceptions of the role and recognizing the critical importance of the business development manager.

Another important factor is striking the right balance of 'account load' – the number of customers any business development manager is responsible for on an ongoing basis. The optimum number is between one and ten, depending on the size and complexity of the accounts. A business development manager managing a strategically important customer with significant opportunity potential may focus on that account exclusively. However, the average business development manager has three or four primary customer accounts to manage, and five or six secondary customers. Beyond such a load it becomes difficult to sustain sufficient contact with key people to make a difference in building relationships.

One of the most common sources of frustration amongst business development managers is the failure of senior managers and executives to communicate their interaction with customers. When others, including senior managers and executives, plan to meet with a specific customer, they should, as a minimum, alert the business development manager who 'owns' that relationship of their intent to do so. The responsibility then lies with the business development manager to provide a comprehensive 'briefing pack' of the status of the relationship, ongoing projects, target prospects and opportunities, issues for discussion and topics to avoid. If the business development manager is not invited to attend, then details and feedback from the meeting must be passed on afterwards.

There are clearly practical issues to be addressed in the flow of information, but sales-orientated companies place great value of the role of the account executive and significant efforts are made to co-ordinate customer contacts with or through that individual.

Conversely, it must be recognized that overly protective account executives can hurt overall relationships with customers and the issues of openness and trust comes into play, as well as the competence of the account holder.

Most customers prefer to be supported by a helpful, well co-ordinated series of relationships rather than an apparently unconnected series of random contacts from various individuals throughout the company.

No matter how strong operational customer relationships become, they should never overshadow the responsibility of the business development manager to manage the account.

One of the world's leading engineering and construction companies, Bechtel, operates a system it calls 'zippering'. The 'zippering' of customer contacts means keeping track of meetings and communications with a specific customer from the chief executive and senior management through to various company functions, such as engineering, procurement and construction as well as sales, marketing and business development.

The business development manager, in the role of account executive, manages this 'zippering' process, keeping track of contacts and initiating and arranging meetings at strategic points, as necessary. As the repository of information and knowledge, fed back by company representatives in the form of a Contact Report (which often only needs to be a brief e-mail), the business development manager becomes a true expert on the customer's needs.

Even when very senior management are meeting with a customer, the business development manager should be present – to validate their role and importance in the customer relationship and to keep them informed of information and commitments made to the customer.

The business development manager should lead negotiations and open and close presentations, particularly following proposal submission. Again, this validates their role and importance in the customer's eyes where the perception is one where the business development manager has the necessary power and accountability to be able to resolve any issues.

A business development manager must listen to customers and understand their perceptions, expectations, needs and wants. Opportunities to listen must be continuously sought out and captured. Thinking from the customer's point of view is a developed skill.

Customers value knowledge and understanding of global and industry trends that could affect them. The combination of listening and adding value through feedback is an important feature of building relationships.

The business development manager as ... champion of change

Historically, construction companies have tended to be operations-orientated. Many have now recognized the need to become more marketing and sales orientated but without losing sight of the operational and project management excellence that have become hallmarks of their success.

Much has been written about cultural change, particularly within large organizations. Quite simply, cultural change is all about individual and collective changes in mind-set, behaviour and attitude. In the context of business development, it is all about creating an environment that recognizes, and rewards, the critical importance of the role.

In sales-orientated companies, the customer's interests always come first. Customers define value – a simple proposition that has been redefining the scope and focus of business firms around the world. It is not a new idea. Peter Drucker was suggesting in 1950 that 'the purpose of business is to create and keep a customer.' The reward is profit. The concept is easy to understand, but not easy to deliver.

The most successful companies are those that understand that customer orientation requires a total organizational commitment, one that is pervasive throughout the culture and business development process and is not just the responsibility of the business development manager or a few members of the sales team.

In sales-oriented companies, business development has high visibility in the management infrastructure. This means that the business development manager enjoys equal status with high-level operations managers. When senior management conduct business meetings, business development needs to be treated at least equally with project management and financial control.

Business development needs to be considered as an integral part of company operations. Business development people need to be included in strategic planning, quality initiatives, financial analysis and other aspects of the company's operations. This characteristic relies on credibility, both from the customer's perspective and in the eyes of the operations team. Clearly, the business development manager must have excellent knowledge of their industry, clients, competitors and their own firm. Business development managers with this knowledge base should be capable of providing value to their firm and to their customers and should be an integral part of the management and operating team.

The function is essential and needs to be recognized as a valued aspect of a company's operations.

The business development manager as ... winner

Business development managers should take responsibility for their own effectiveness and in the measurement of their performance and success. There are several ways that this can be done.

Most organizations use a combination of qualitative and quantitative measures to determine how well their customer and business development efforts are working.

Qualitative measures are more subjective but can indicate effectiveness in certain areas that cannot be quantified, such as how well one knows the customer. An excellent business development manager (or account manager) should have no problem answering questions such as:

- What is the customer's business?
- What problems does the customer typically encounter that we can provide solutions to?
- What is the customer's proposed annual spend for our type of products or services, now and in the future?
- Who are the key people we must know and influence and do we know them?
- Who are the most active competitors with this customer and what competitive advantage do they have?
- What are the significant upcoming opportunities with this customer over the next five years?

These kinds of questions will determine how well a business development manager knows the customer. The role, therefore, is critical in determining how well the firm is positioned for future significant opportunities with a particular customer.

Typical quantitative measures include proposal-hit rate, sole source percentages, forecast accuracy and moving averages. Proposal-hit rate measures how effective a firm's proposals are and is typically measured as a ratio of projects won versus projects bid. A more accurate evaluation compares the revenue or projected profit of projects won versus bid costs. Although not an exact science, this method provides a good measure of the effectiveness of a firm's bidding efforts.

The ultimate goal for any business development manager is to secure profitable, sole source work with a satisfied customer. Sole source percentages measure the volume of sole source work relative to the customer's total contracts and can be measured in numbers of contracts or volume. It is an indicator of the firm's positioning with its customers.

Forecast accuracy is a measure of how accurate sales forecasts are and may include predicted annual volume of work with a customer and predicted gross margins. The accuracy of forecasts is an indicator of how knowledgeable business development managers are of their market, their customers and economic trends.

Moving averages measure how much revenue is generated per customer account on a historical basis and determine how well a firm is doing with a particular customer over time – typically five years. It is a good measure of the effectiveness of a business development manager.

Another key measure, and one that is often overlooked, is customer 'face time' – time spent in front of customer. This is a key activity in developing customer perceptions that a company is responsive and orientated towards understanding and serving its specific needs. Companies can demonstrate their commitment to customers by conducting customer satisfaction surveys, hosting customer panel discussions and problem-solving workshops, and seeking customer feedback on re-engineering efforts and other initiatives that could ultimately benefit the customer.

The business development manager as ... leader

Effective leadership is a rare quality in the construction profession. Leadership is the process of giving purpose – meaningful direction, focus and vision – to the collective efforts of others, and energizing and enabling them to achieve that purpose. Leaders create a vision, they set strategy, they motivate, they coach and mentor, they empower and most important of all, they get results. But in today's highly competitive world, a new kind of leadership is required – leaders who focus on their customers, build teams, empower their colleagues and implement best practice.

Effective leaders focus their team's full attention on adding value to clients, inspiring a sense of shared ownership. They develop trust through integrity and personal example. They demonstrate high standards of performance and accomplishment and motivate others to adopt such standards.

Leadership in business development is achieved through a combination of individual attributes, skills, competencies and processes. The individual attributes of a business development manager required for effective leadership are:

- integrity
- management, commercial and technical competence
- self-esteem
- self-confidence
- self-discipline
- tolerance of ambiguity and uncertainty
- resilience
- commitment
- a willingness to take risks
- persistence
- self-motivation
- respect for others.

In any company, winning profitable new business is a team effort. High performance teams run on trust. As a leader, the business development manager has the opportunity to apply the following skills and competencies to develop such teams:

- coaching
- communication
- empowerment
- motivation
- development of colleagues
- problem-solving
- decision-making

- planning and organizing
- mentoring.

To coach the team means to facilitate performance, taking a personal interest in the development of each team member. It also means communicating clear expectations to members of the team and delegating appropriately.

Effective communication is essential to enable people to work well together. A leader who communicates well shares information openly and keeps people informed of relevant issues.

The business development manager empowers others by asking and enabling people to do what they are capable of doing and causing them to assume responsibility and account-ability. By helping to shape and develop the careers of young people and emphasizing self-development, the business development manager can become an effective role model.

Effective leaders identify potential problems early. Problem solving requires leaders to weigh up the risks, costs and benefits of alternative solutions, as well as gaining the necessary support of people who will be involved in implementing the chosen solution.

Decisions are made in a timely manner, demonstrating sound judgement.

Planning and organizing are critical activities that involve working closely with cus-tomers and suppliers to define expectations and responsibilities.

Mentoring skills involve teaching and advising and empowering others, sharing expert-ise, guiding professional development and taking a genuine interest in other people's career enhancement.

The issue of career path and progression is an important one in encouraging people into the role. Promotion to senior executive or management positions tends to come from a project operations or financial background. Companies need to redress the balance and create opportunities for business development people to excel at higher levels within the overall management structure.

In encouraging younger people into the role, the best companies will route high poten-tial candidates through the marketing and proposals functions where they gain invaluable experience of co-ordinating proposals and presentations. They learn about the complex-ities of producing winning proposals. They learn how deals come together, what customers are looking for, what it takes to win, what commercial terms and conditions are all about, and how the company is differentiated from its competitors.

This 'apprenticeship' is a vital part of the learning process for young, aspiring business development managers. They learn the importance of teamwork and internal relationships where gaining the respect of certain individuals is key to ensuring that when support or information is required, it is provided in a timely and co-operative manner. Such a career path provides a firm grasp of business development and an understanding of its critical importance in the overall scheme of things.

The business development manager as ... hero

Highly effective business development managers are among the company's heroes. There is an uncanny reluctance throughout the industry to communicate and share success. In sales-orientated companies, stories about winning and deal making are told and shared. Many stories become legend and the dealmakers become legendary. When large projects are won, how often is credit given to the principal dealmaker? The person who has engaged and enroled the customer in the first instance is invariably the business development manager. Therefore, recognition and celebration of success is key.

Highly effective business development managers can become the company's heroes.

Summary

The roles and responsibilities of a business development manager are to:

- Develop and manage new business opportunities
- Develop, build and maintain customer relationships
- Develop alliances, joint ventures, partnerships and teaming arrangements
- Develop business strategies, Win Plans and Closing Plans for target prospects
- Assist in strategic planning and analysis of target markets, customers, prospects and opportunities
- Co-ordinate and manage all internal prospect and bid approval requirements
- Lead commercial and technical proposal preparation
- Manage assigned customer accounts
- Prepare management information, presentations and briefing materials
- Provide input to management information systems and business reports
- Provide after sales support to customers.

In summary, business development managers need to be professional, knowledgeable, experienced, resourceful, flexible, adaptable, persistent, competitive, honest and trustworthy.

Chapter end material

Bartlett, R.E. (1997) *Preparing International Proposals* (Telford).

DETR and Local Government Association (2001) *Delivering Better Services for Citizens* (DTLR.).

Groak, S. (1996) Chapter: project related research and development. In: Dunster, D. (ed.) *Arups on Engineering* (Ernst & Sohn).

Kumaraswamy, M.M. and Dissanyaka, S.M. (1998) Linking procurement systems to project priorities *Building Research and Innovation*, **26** (4), 223–38.

KPMG (1998) *Bidding to Win* (KPMG). Quote in full or extract from (this is extract).

Bartlett, R.E. (1997) *Preparing International Proposals* (Telford), pp. 78–81.

Construction Industry Board (1996) *Selecting Consultants for the Team: Balancing Quality and Price* (Telford).

Ng, T. *et al.* (1999) Decision-makes perceptions in the formulation of prequalification criteria. *Engineering, Construction and Architectural Management,* **6** (2), 155–63.

Martin, J. (1997) Winning the bid. *Project Manager Today*, (April).

DETR (1998) *Report of the Construction Task Force (Egan Report) Rethinking Construction* (DETR).

Crowley, L.G. and Hancher, D.E. (1995) Evaluation of competitive bids. *ASCE Journal of Construction Engineering and Management*, **121** (2), 238–45.

Merna, A. (1998) Financial risk in the procurement of capital and infrastructure projects. *International Journal of Project and Business Risk Management*, **2** (3), (Autumn), 257–70.

National Audit Office (2001) *Modernising Construction. HC 87 Session 2000–2001* (Stationery Office).

Kennedy, C. and O'Connor, M. (1999) *Winning Major Bids ... the Critical Success Factors* (Policy Publications).

Sant, T. (1992) *Persuasive Business Proposals* (Katz & Associates)AQ5.

Kantin, R. (2001) www.salesproposals.comhttp://www.salesproposals.com/default.htm.

http://www.salesproposals.com/article2.htm

Further reading

Holtz, H. (1990) The consultants guide to proposal writing, 2nd Ed. (Wiley).

Hoxley, M. (1998) Value for money: the impact of competitive fee tendering on construction professional service quality (RICS Research).

Joseph, A. (1989) Put it in writing! (McGraw-Hill).

Lewis, H. (1992) The consultants complete proposal manual (PTRC).

Porter-Roth, B. (1998) Proposal development, 3rd Ed. (Oasis Press).

Walker, K. *et al.* (1998) Creating new clients: marketing and selling professional services. (Cassell).

Chapman, C.B. *et al.* (2000) Incorporating uncertainty in competitive bidding. *International Journal of Project Management*, **19**, 337–47.

Griffiths, F.H. (1992) Bidding strategy: winning over key competitors. *ASCE Journal of Construction Engineering and Management*, **118** (1), 151–65.

Herbsman, Z. and Ellis, R. (1992) Multiparameter bidding system – innovation in contract administration. *ASCE Journal of Construction Engineering and Management,* **118** (1), 142–50.

Lo, W. *et al.* (1999) Effects of high prequalification requirements. *Construction Management and Economics*, **17**, 603–12.

Index

accelerating change 170, 177
account
    executive 4, 180, 187
    manager 189
approaches 1, 8, 14, 41, 47, 48, 87, 112,
    125, 130, 142, 167, 168, 172, 175, 183,
    185
    client 44
    client care 85
    collaborative 4, 163, 167
    construction organization 1
    customer care 84
    e-business 145, 146
    management 168
    market 27
    marketing 2, 33, 45, 47, 51, 54, 65
    sales 51
    stakeholder 10
    public relations 109
Association of Consulting Engineers (ACE)
    41, 43, 44, 46, 47, 52, 54, 56, 58,
    59–61, 63, 64
    Client Guide 46, 59, 63
additional
    indicators 58, 59, 61, 63, 64
    investment 41
    resources 14
advertising 2, 18, 26, 28, 33, 55–58, 62, 65,
    107, 112, 145
    expenditure 116
    material 45
    recruitment 56
Alexander Graham Bell 139
architecture, engineering and construction
    (AEC) 171–176
Arpanet 140

American National Science Foundation 140
Asda stores 108, 172
audit
    internal 31, 32
    external 2, 31, 32

bar charts 23
barriers 47, 117, 120, 150, 162, 172, 176,
    182, 184
    corporate 172
    cultural 4, 56, 163, 167
    customer care 84
    technological 4, 167, 176,
basic schools:
    dialectical model 127
    evolutionary theory 127
    life cycle model 127
    teleological model 127
bid 3, 37, 39, 46, 50, 52, 53, 58, 61, 62, 66,
    90, 95–98, 101, 102, 178, 182, 184, 185
    approval requirement 192
    budget 52, 95
    cost 92, 102, 181, 182, 185, 189
    count 63
    decision-making process 93
    investment 92
    leader 97
    performance 59, 64, 66
    process 97
    project 111, 176, 189
    team 99, 101, 102
bidder 100, 101
    and client 94
    organization 178
bidding 42, 58, 65, 90, 94, 97, 99, 102
    performance 58

bidding (*continued*)
  process 52, 63, 91–93
  strategy 3, 92
  success 65
bid/no-bid 91, 96, 102
  criteria 92
  decision 96, 184
  decision process 181, 185
  process 183
BigTime 145–148
BIW 173, 176
  information channel 172
  technologies 167, 171
Boston Consulting Group (BCG) 26, 27
BPR 3, 132
brand 14, 20, 37, 41, 45, 50, 77–79, 87, 160
British Airways 108
British Gas 158
Bodget & Scram Ltd 106, 107
Building Down Barriers 120, 169, 170
burning platform 131
business concept innovation 11, 13
business development 2–4, 7–12, 15, 29,
    30, 63, 74, 78, 91, 102, 105, 106,
    109–113, 116–118, 154, 160,
    164, 165, 167, 168, 174, 178, 180,
    181, 183–191
  activities 10, 15
  culture 174
  function 3, 106, 118
  manager 3, 4, 15, 180, 181, 183–191
  strategies 1, 118
  strategies and techniques 1
  vital ingredient 105
business excellence model 60
business model 1, 7, 11–15, 96, 141, 142,
    144, 164
  Margretta's view 15
business to business markets 75

CAD 146, 170
c-commerce 170, 174
Ceteris paribus 26
challenges 9, 45, 46, 120, 121, 124, 162,
    167, 171, 183
  commercial 141
  construction industry 149
  e-business 142, 148
  in collaborative working 4

management 132
organizational 157, 158, 164
champion 162
  excellence 97
  knowledge 162, 177
  of change 4, 180, 188
changes of techno-economic paradigm 122,
    123
changing corporate culture 35
'classical' marketing methodology 2, 31
classifying knowledge 154
client
  account 29
  care 35, 37, 82, 83, 85, 87–90
  group focus 14
  policy 34
  programme 2
  relations 109, 110
closing plan 183, 185, 186, 192
collaborative
  commerce 170
  working 4, 143, 159, 167, 168, 170, 171,
    174–177, 179
Columbia University 128
communications with tenants 87
community relations 3, 106, 108,
    112–117
competitor analysis 28, 55, 58
components of business model
  customer model 14
  business model 13
  financial model 13
  pricing model 13
  revenue model 13
computer industry 133
concept of management 130
constructing the team 168
Construction Best Practice Programme
    (CBPP) 58, 107, 110, 169
construction forecasting research 22
construction industry 1–3, 7, 10, 14, 15–18,
    21, 22, 29, 40, 41, 43–45, 47, 57–60,
    71, 73, 78, 82, 89, 94, 99, 100, 103,
    105–107, 109–113, 115, 117, 118,
    141–144, 146, 149, 150, 151, 153,
    160–163, 167–178, 180, 181
Construction Industry Board (CIB) 45, 58,
    94, 103, 169
Construction Industry Council 44, 59, 103

construction marketeer 142–146, 148, 149–151
construction marketing 29, 30, 41, 45–47, 120
construction sector 14, 119, 171
contact report 187
contract progress meetings 114
corporate
  communications 111, 112, 167
  events 36
  objectives 28, 30
  social responsibility 106, 116, 117
corporate social responsibility (CSR) 106, 116, 117
culture 2, 3, 19, 60, 77, 78, 82, 105, 107, 110, 113, 116, 146, 162, 164, 179
  business 89, 145, 174
  corporate 35, 126
  internal 4, 88, 167
  marketing 28, 34, 40
  organization 158, 159, 164
customer relationship management (CRM) 2, 41, 42, 71–79
  forum 73
  industry 73
  programmes 73, 76
  software market 72
customer care 74, 81–84
  philosophy 81, 83
  process 85
  programmes 83, 84
customer confidence 83
customer oriented
  company 83
  strategy 2
customer relationship management 2, 71, 73, 76

database 35, 37, 42, 72, 74, 148, 186
decision-making process 2, 18,10, 27, 77, 93
Design Build Foundation (DBF) 169, 170, 175, 179
dialectical model 127
discontinuous or radical change 131
drawings 21, 86, 100, 143, 146, 169–171, 178
  CAD 146

Early preparation 101
e-business 139, 142–152, 171, 173, 176
  application 3, 143
  development 139, 150
  model 127, 144
  on construction 3
  survey 173
e-commerce 41, 147
economic production process 119
eCRM 74, 75, 79
electronic document management systems (EDMS) 171
e-marketeer 149
e-newscasts 146, 148
e-newsletter services 111
enterprise 15, 40, 71, 77, 86, 88, 125, 126, 157, 158, 163, 175, 177
  commercial 83
  in construction 2, 168, 172
environments
  external 8, 19–21, 42
  global 132
  internal 20, 21
European Union (EU) 8
evaluation 3, 58, 94, 95, 97, 127, 143, 181, 182, 184, 185, 189
evolutionary theory 127
extensible markup language (XML) 152, 153

facilities management (FM) 8, 106, 109, 111, 113
financial
  models 13, 14
  performance indicators 13
  projections 23, 27, 120
first-order change 125, 128
free bidding 52
Freeman's definition of stakeholders 10

Galactic network concept 140
Gartner group 72
Generic management tool 18
Geographical 19, 21, 22, 33, 61
George Stephenson 139
Glasgow 31
Global external change 122
Global paradox 124
GreatArch site 145, 146, 147
Group theory 128

Hewlett Packard 124
HM treasury 95

the Icarus Paradox 132
impact of innovation 129
implementation 3, 9, 17, 22, 26–28, 30, 34,
    40, 43, 50, 56, 65, 73, 75–78, 83, 89,
    97, 103, 112, 117, 127, 143, 162, 164,
    169, 186
    customer relationship management 2
    of business development 1
    strategic 9
incremental change 131
industry 4, 11, 20, 33, 37, 52, 56, 62,
    66, 72, 76, 88, 96, 113, 120, 123,
    125–128, 132, 133, 139, 146, 153,
    175, 183, 188, 191
    segments 22
Infoconomy Collaborative Newsletter
    175
information gathering 36, 144
insurance industry 76
intellectual capital (IC) 157
internal relationships 191
Internet 3, 62, 76, 94, 111–113, 118, 139,
    140, 144, 145
IT industry 149, 158

John Butler 139, 151, 152

key performance indicators (KPIs) 46, 53,
    58–61, 63–66
keystones of future business development
    110
KMLab 12
knowledge
    economy 4, 154, 155, 157
    networking 156
    officer 165
    transfer 158, 161, 163, 164
knowledge management (KM) 15, 99,
    154–157, 159–165
    strategy 15, 157

leader 4, 28, 97, 144, 180, 185, 190, 191
levels of change 122
Life cycle model 127
Local area networks 141
Local authority 10, 32, 36, 110

macro (strategic) level 3
managing on the edge 54
manager
    a champion of change 188
    a hero 191
    a leader 190
    a strategist 180
    a winner 189
    an account executive 186
marketing 1, 2, 4, 14, 17–24, 26–58, 60–66,
    71, 72, 74, 77, 78, 81–85, 87–89, 91,
    97, 103, 109, 111, 115, 119, 120, 125,
    143–149, 151, 152, 169, 174, 177–181,
    183, 187, 188, 191
    audit 19, 20, 23, 24
    culture 28, 34, 88
    objectives 2, 17, 18, 24, 26, 27, 29, 30,
        32, 33, 40, 144
    of the construction industry 40, 45
    orientation 40
    overview 23, 46, 71
    plan formulation 48
    plannning 2, 17–20, 22–24, 26–30, 32–34,
        40, 46–48, 52, 54, 78, 91, 103, 183
    positions 49, 50, 52
    strategies 2, 17, 18, 20, 26, 27, 30–33,
        40, 46, 47, 54, 55
    theory 47, 51, 72
market
    plan 2
    research 2, 32, 42, 47, 54, 56, 84, 147
    segment strategies 2
    segmentation 21, 50
    shares 20, 40, 74
McDonald approach 21–25
McNicholas CARES 88
Michael Porter's five forces model 20
micro (operational) level 3
millenium dome 13
mission possible 23
mission statement 22, 23, 30, 35
mode of change 127, 128
Moore's law 150
movement of innovation 58
mystical visionary CEO level 121

NASA 140
National Health Service (NHS) 83
New technology systems 123

North America 8
NSFNet backbone 140

OJEC notice 91
online construction project 145
organizational culture 158, 164
outcomes 3, 8, 9, 37, 129, 175

pan industry 94, 169, 175
Paranoid survive 132, 133
partnerships 28, 106, 110, 123, 163, 175
Pascale's view 130
passive marketing 33, 35
PEST factors 47
pie charts 23
post bid review 93
press relations 3, 106, 107, 115
primary stakeholders 10
private finance initiative (PFI) 41, 95, 98,
    106, 109, 110–113, 119, 177
  project banner 113
procurement hub 152
product and process change 132
product segment strategies 2
programmes 18, 28, 29, 46, 52, 86, 90, 91, 98
  BPR 3
  client care 2, 81–84, 86–90
  culture 3
  customer care 2, 81–84, 86
  marketing 48, 51, 58
  of visit 35, 37
  TQM 3, 84
progress 4, 17, 22, 28–30, 34, 114, 139,
    142, 148, 162, 167, 168, 179
project management 3, 13, 18, 29, 101,
    143, 188
project room 143
profit 2, 12, 14, 27, 28, 30–32, 37, 49–51,
    57–60, 66, 82, 92, 97, 157, 178, 181,
    182, 188, 189
promotional material 33–35, 56, 91
public private partnership (PPP) 98, 106,
    109, 110, 112, 177, 147
public relation (PR) 2, 3, 18, 28, 58,
    105–118, 147, 149
  functions 3, 106–107, 110, 112, 113,
    115–118
  practitioners 3, 76
public service telephone network (PSTN) 141

quality service 45, 52, 64, 65
quick fix 2, 77, 167

radical
  change 124, 131, 132
  innovation 123
rail industry 150
rain dance 3
repeat business 42, 49, 51, 53, 58, 59, 61,
    82, 87, 88, 108, 110, 111
retail industry 76
rethinking construction 160, 169, 170
return on investment (ROI) 73, 76, 182,
    184, 185
Richardson 46–48
right strategy wrong problem 133
rocket 112, 139
Rudolf diesel 139

Schizophrenia 41
second order change 125, 128
second seven river crossing bridge 115
secondary stakeholders 10, 15
SERVQUAL model 53, 63
shared creation 172
shell directional policy matrix 24,
    25, 27
SME 31
solutions 3, 31, 53, 91, 94, 103, 107,
    126, 142, 143, 150, 153, 156,
    189, 191
sources of organizational change 124
splitting stakeholders 10
stakeholder 9, 10, 11, 12, 15, 78, 79, 110,
    164, 186
STEEP analysis 20, 24
stock market 108
strategic
  analysis 9, 40
  approach 2, 17, 50, 51
    marketing 17, 19
    market mix 50
  business
    development 7, 9
    issues 1
    units 3, 26
  choice 9, 164
  for success 46
  management process 9
  partnerships 163

strengths, weaknesses, opportunities and
    threats (SWOT) 2, 21, 23, 24, 26, 32,
    33, 42, 48, 54

teleological model 127
Theory 46, 47, 51, 72, 126–128, 131,
    133, 145
total installed cost (TIC) 181
total quality management (TQM) 3, 81,
    83, 84
transactions 10
trusting the team 168
types of change 128, 129, 131
    first order 125, 128
    second order 125, 128
    third order 125

UK construction
    business 57
    company 11, 46

industry 57, 60, 167–170, 177
    market 41, 170, 171
Unit of change 127, 128

Virtual organization 152, 153, 169
Vulnerability assessment 181–183, 185

Waterside development 108
Web-based
    extranet 171
    internet 141
    technology 171
Wilbur and Orville wright 139
winning
    bid 62, 148
    strategy 181
Win Plan 181–183, 185, 192

Y2K 2